# A Routledge Literary Sourcebook on

# Herman Melville's
## *Moby-Dick*

Since 1851, Herman Melville's *Moby-Dick; or The Whale* has inspired, challenged and delighted readers of all kinds. No book is more central to the study of nineteenth-century American literary history, or speaks as powerfully to readers today.

Through a combination of original documents and student-oriented annotation, this volume examines the literary context and critical response to Melville's work as well as the spirit of the age in which it was written. It brings together a contextual overview and relevant contextual documents including: letters written by Melville; a chronology of key events related to the novel and the period in which it was written; a survey of critical responses to *Moby-Dick* and extracts from important reviews and academic studies; clearly introduced key passages with full annotation and cross-references to documents reproduced earlier in the volume. The guide concludes with a useful list of further reading.

Offering a broad range of materials including lucid, insightful discussions of a novel every student should read, this Routledge Literary Sourcebook is the ideal resource for any reader new to *Moby-Dick*.

**Michael J. Davey** is Assistant Professor of Early American Literature at Valdosta State University in Valdosta, Georgia.

# Routledge Literary Sourcebooks

Series Editor: Duncan Wu, St Catherine's College, Oxford University

Also available are Routledge Literary Sourcebooks on:
William Shakespeare's *The Merchant of Venice* edited by S. P. Cerasano
E. M. Forster's *A Passage to India* edited by Peter Childs
Mary Wollstonecraft's *A Vindication of the Rights of Woman* edited by
  Adriana Craciun
Charles Dickens's *David Copperfield* edited by Richard J. Dunn
William Shakespeare's *Othello* edited by Andrew Hadfield
Henrik Ibsen's *Hedda Gabler* edited by Christopher Innes
William Shakespeare's *King Lear* edited by Grace Ioppolo
Mary Shelley's *Frankenstein* edited by Timothy Morton
The Poems of W. B. Yeats edited by Michael O'Neill
Harriet Beecher Stowe's *Uncle Tom's Cabin* edited by Debra J. Rosenthal
The Poems of John Keats edited by John Strachan

# A Routledge Literary Sourcebook on

# Herman Melville's
# *Moby-Dick*

*Edited by Michael J. Davey*

Routledge
Taylor & Francis Group

NEW YORK AND LONDON

First published 2004

Simultaneously published in the UK, USA and Canada
by Routledge
29 West 35th Street, New York, NY 10001

and Routledge
11 New Fetter Lane, London EC4P 4EE

*Routledge is an imprint of the Taylor & Francis Group*

Selection and editorial matter © 2004 Michael J. Davey

Typeset in Sabon and Gill Sans by RefineCatch Limited, Bungay, Suffolk
Printed and bound in Great Britain by
TJ International Ltd, Padstow, Cornwall

*Library of Congress Cataloging in Publication Data*
Davey, Michael, 1967–
A Routledge literary sourcebook on Herman Melville's *Moby-Dick* /
Michael J. Davey.
     p.   cm.—(Routledge literary sourcebooks)
Includes bibliographical references and index.
1. Melville, Herman, 1819–1891. Moby Dick.   2. Psychological fiction,
American—History and criticism.   3. Sea stories, American—History and
criticism.   4. Whaling in literature.   5. Whales in literature.   I. Title.
II. Series.
PS2384.M62D385   2003
813'.3—dc21                                           2003002141

*British Library Cataloguing in Publication Data*
A catalogue record for this book is available from the British Library

ISBN 0–415–24770–5 (hbk)
ISBN 0–415–24771–3 (pbk)

# Contents

# 2: Interpretations

# 3: Key Passages

# 4: Further Reading

# Series Editor's Preface

The Routledge Literary Sourcebook series has been designed to provide students with the materials required to begin serious study of individual literary works, all in a single volume. This includes an overview of the critical history of the work, including extracts from important critical debates of recent decades, and a selection of key passages from the text itself. Volume editors provide introductory commentaries and annotation for the reader's guidance. These handy books provide almost everything most students will need for the contextual and critical overview of literature expected in schools and universities today.

This aim is reflected in the structure of each Sourcebook. Section 1, 'Contexts', provides biographical data in the form of an author chronology and contemporary documents relating to the author and his or her work. In Section 2, 'Interpretations', the editor assembles extracts from the most influential and important criticism throughout the history of the work. In some cases this includes materials relating to performances or adaptations. The third section, 'Key Passages', gathers together the essential episodes from the literary text connected by editorial commentary and annotation so as to relate them to ideas raised earlier in the volume. The final section offers suggestions for further reading, including recommended editions and critical volumes.

Annotation is a key feature of this series. Both the original notes from the reprinted texts and new annotations by the editor appear at the bottom of the relevant page. The reprinted notes are prefaced with the author's name in square brackets, e.g. [Robinson's note.].

Routledge Literary Sourcebooks offer the ideal introduction to single literary works, combining primary and secondary materials, chosen by experts, in accessible form.

Duncan Wu

# Acknowledgments

I would like to thank John Carroll University and Valdosta State University for research and professional support while editing the current volume. I would especially like to thank my colleagues Debra Rosenthal and Jeanne Colleran, both of JCU, whose support of my teaching and research led to this project. Finally, I wish to acknowledge the assistance of my graduate assistants Eric Meljac and Paula Hennesey, whose help was indispensable to successful and timely completion of the manuscript.

Most importantly, I would like to thank my beloved wife Lois Moon for her unqualified loving support of my work and life.

The author would like to thank the publishers and copyright holders for permission to reprint extracts from the following works:

# Introduction

Herman Melville's *Moby-Dick; or The Whale* was first published in 1851 and
has alternately inspired, befuddled and delighted readers ever since. Heralded
in his day as the "man who lived among the cannibals," Melville struggled
deliberately to be more than a mere writer of travel narratives – a popular and
fairly lucrative genre for the period. His first books were commercially successful
and afforded him a unique sort of literary fame (as some have argued, he was the
first American literary sex symbol – a roguish sailor turned writer who had lived
with the promiscuous and exotic natives of the Marquesas Islands). However,
the books he "preferred" to write were generally ignored and at times attacked
by an unsympathetic public. The mid-nineteenth-century audience for fiction
was overwhelmingly composed of middle-class women, most of whom preferred
conventional stories about the world they knew best: the domestic sphere of
home and family, the purview of the so-called "Cult of True Womanhood" or
"Cult of Domesticity". Such novels were typically sentimental, at times melodramatic, always apolitical, and more often than not reinforced traditional
religious and moral values. Melville's tendency to explore grand philosophical
questions and to write in a style readers in his own era found verbose at best and
excessive at worst did not sit well with the majority of readers and professional
critics (see Early Critical Reception, **pp. 66–74**). Whereas his first books had
"merely" attacked such targets as religious missionaries and the practice of
flogging on US naval vessels, his more mature works explored and often ridiculed
the very foundations of conventional religious, sociopolitical and philosophical
thought. Melville described the ostensive moral of *Moby-Dick* in a letter to his
friend and mentor Nathaniel Hawthorne, writing "This is the book's motto (the
secret one),—*Ego non baptizo te in nomine*—but make out the rest yourself."[1]
The "rest" was the second half of Ahab's proclamation in Chapter 113 that the
harpoon he will use in his doomed attempt to kill Moby Dick is being baptized
"*in nomine diaboli!*" – in the name of the devil. That the book's secret motto

---

1   "Letter to Nathaniel Hawthorne," June 29, 1851, in Horth, 1993: 194–6 (see Further Reading).
    *Ego non baptize te in nominee*: "I baptize you not in the name of the Father, but in the name of
    the Devil!"

was perhaps not so secret and thus did not sit well with the majority of mid-nineteenth-century readers is perhaps not surprising. If critics weren't complaining about Melville's diction they were denouncing bitterly the apparent morals of his most ambitious works. That Melville did not anticipate the hostility his book would engender signals also how complex and conflicted a relationship he had with his audience and with the print culture of his era (see Melville and Antebellum America, **p. 26**). As he began drafting *Moby-Dick* he was struggling to earn a living in a highly competitive book market dominated by women writers and readers, most of whom preferred books less ambitious than those Melville was determined to write.[2] Further, the moralistic and conservative tastes of the majority of critics meant that any writer who violated accepted literary conventions or social mores risked more than just their livelihoods – their very personal reputations were at stake. Most importantly, Melville throughout his life experienced first hand the economic, cultural and political upheavals which characterized American life in the five decades before the Civil War, experiences which had a cumulative effect on both him and his art as he labored on *Moby-Dick* (see Melville's Career and the Writing of *Moby-Dick*, **p. 18**).

As a work of fictional narrative *Moby-Dick* is a formidable book. Its reputation generally precedes it and certainly no reader comes to the text without having at least heard about "that long book on whales." Becoming familiar with the conventions[3] of nineteenth-century fictional narrative, especially the penchant of American writers to eschew mimesis in favor of a more imaginative style (see **pp. 12** and **40–1**) will only take the reader so far. Melville assumed his audience would be familiar with the popular and serious fiction of his day and deliberately crafted a work that took established literary conventions and bent and hammered them in the fiery forge of his imagination to such an extent that even the mere "skimmer of pages" – Melville's derogatory term for the average reader – would recognize that here was a book written *beyond* convention. The two opening sections, "Etymology" and "Extracts," which seriocomically parody nineteenth-century use of the epigraph,[4] make this clear from the start. Most importantly, Melville's highly poetic narrative style was as unique in its own time as it is today. Based primarily on his deep and insightful reading of Shakespeare and the Bible, especially the Old Testament, Melville's prose is grandly metaphorical even at its most literal moments.

Furthermore, and perhaps most notably, the book's major characters are as unique as any in the Western canon. If, as some critics have argued, *Moby-Dick* is *sui generis*[5] then Ahab, Ishmael, Starbuck, Queequeg and several others are *sui naturis*.[6] Ishmael, the cosmopolitan and ironic narrator, is a precursor to all the ironic, unreliable and semi-reliable narrators to come since, including Huck Finn,

---

2 Melville has traditionally been cast as an isolated male genius at odds with a feminine print culture. This image, however, has recently been reexamined and shown to be problematic in important ways. See Critical History, **p. 64**.

3 For example, the epigraph in Shuffelton (see **pp. 98–100**).

4 See n. 3.

5 A genre unto itself; unique.

6 In this sense, characters unto themselves.

Nick Caraway, and Humbert Humbert[7] among others. Throughout the narrative Ishmael eruditely[8] draws on seemingly every discourse imaginable, from law to politics to ancient and contemporary philosophy, only to exhaust the potential of each to meaningfully recount the tale of the obsessive pursuit of Moby Dick by Ahab. Indeed, whether language itself can in fact convey meaning is one of the book's great themes. And Ahab, like other powerful and enigmatic characters from Western literature, evokes both fear and awe in Ishmael. Based on Shakespeare's Lear and presented as a modern Job (see Principal Biblical Allusions, p. 130), he defies everyone and everything in his rageful and dogged pursuit of Moby Dick. Ahab's need for revenge may be personal, but as Ishmael describes it in Chapter 41 (see pp. 153–5), Moby Dick represents more than just revenge to Ahab:

> The White Whale swam before him as the monomaniac[9] incarnation of all those malicious agencies which some deep men feel eating in them, till they are left living on with half a heart and half a lung . . . All that most maddens and torments; all that stirs up the lees[10] of things; all truth with malice in it; all that cracks the sinews and cakes the brain; all the subtle demonisms of life and thought; all evil, to crazy Ahab, were visibly personified, and made practically assailable in Moby Dick. He piled upon the whale's white hump the sum of all the general rage and hate felt by his whole race from Adam down; and then, as if his chest had been a mortar, he burst his hot heart's shell upon it.

Ahab's torments are the problems of existence all men face once the beliefs which have sustained civilization since human societies first formed begin to rot and fall away beneath them, leaving them to cling to whatever philosophical wreckage they happen to find floating nearby. Ahab can neither bring himself to believe nor rest in his unbelief – precisely how Hawthorne described Melville following one of their last meetings. And like an angry, orphaned child he rages at his seeming abandonment, choosing to break through the wall of appearances to the reality it hides even if "there's naught beyond." That Ahab meets annihilation on his own terms rather than those prescribed for him by society or conventional conceptions of the divine is what makes him the tragic hero he is for many readers.

The present volume is a collection of secondary source materials on *Moby-Dick*, Melville and his times. Section 1, Contexts, provides an overview of Melville's life and career, and especially of the difficult circumstances under which he labored to write *Moby-Dick*. It also presents an overview of the major historical trends of the decades preceding the publication of Melville's whale, and of how Melville's life in many ways reflects the forces that profoundly affected life in America

---

7 The first-person narrators of *Huckleberry Finn*, *The Great Gatsby*, and *Lolita* respectively.
8 Erudite: well learned.
9 Pathologically obsessive.
10 That which settles at the bottom, i.e., the dregs as in wine.

between roughly 1820 and the beginning of the Civil War in 1861. The remainder of the section is composed of excerpts from key source materials written by Melville and some of his important contemporaries. These include letters by Melville to Hawthorne, an excerpt from the tale upon which the plot of *Moby-Dick* is based, and essays by Hawthorne and Emerson that shed much light on the intellectual and literary life of Melville's era.

Section 2, Interpretations, includes an overview of the critical response to *Moby-Dick* from its original reception up to the current moment, and offers excerpts from articles by leading Melville scholars from the 1920s to the present, as well as excerpts from important contemporary reviews of *Moby-Dick* and of relevant earlier works.

The next section, Key Passages, includes annotated excerpts from those passages in *Moby-Dick* which have most often captured the interests and imaginations of readers and critics. The critical or interpretive significance of each passage is briefly introduced and full annotation facilitates close reading and discussion as does cross-referencing to contextual and critical documents.

Finally, Section 4, Further Reading, is a selected bibliography of recommended editions, key articles and books considered especially beneficial to those reading and studying *Moby-Dick* for the first time.

All the materials in this Sourcebook are included to enable a better under-standing of the historical context of Melville's work, especially those factors which most affected the production and reception of the primary text. It is hoped that the source materials will provide a concrete picture of what most influenced Melville as he wrote, what he may have hoped to accomplish, and why readers reacted as they did. Most importantly, the excerpts from important critical articles on *Moby-Dick* are included to make the student a better reader of *Moby-Dick* first and foremost and not simply a better one of the work's critical history. In each case, a particular essay or book chapter has been excerpted because it addresses an important interpretive or critical issue that in every case is tied directly to the challenge of reading and interpreting the narrative itself. The variety of materials included is meant to make the sourcebook useful to a wide range of student interests and questions.

Finally, it is important to reiterate that the selected criticism which follows this history, especially the selections in *Moby-Dick* Rising: Melville Criticism 1919–70, **pp. 82–98**, and *Moby-Dick* at the Millennium, **pp. 98–125**, do not attempt to represent comprehensively the vast range of opinions on the novel since the revival. Rather, they are meant to provide first-time readers with power-ful hermeneutic and interpretive tools to engage as fully as possible with Melville's fictional world *on their own*. Literary history unfolds one reader at a time and *Moby-Dick* was not written in a vacuum but deliberately crafted to shape an antebellum reader's response to its use of convention. As such, Melville's narra-tive is treated here as a historical literary artifact of sorts, one that is intimately interconnected with the material circumstances of its production and reception but also one that has a powerful *rhetorical* dimension as well. Accordingly, the governing premise of the selections is that the informed reader, made aware of the dominant political, literary and sociocultural issues of Melville's times, will be better able to render the rhetoric of Melville's fiction intelligible no matter what their approach or critical focus. In every case, an excerpt addresses an important interpretive or critical issue in such a way that the textual power of the reader as an inference-maker is enhanced rather than prematurely circumscribed by the voice of the critic. For example, rather than teaching the major critical arguments over what *Moby-Dick* may or may not *mean* (the so-called "teach the controversies approach"), the excerpts have been selected to better allow the reader to construct his or her own meanings based on experience of the primary text *as informed* by an understanding of the major issues of Melville's day. The student is never asked to take sides in a critical debate, but to learn something about the basic terms required to follow a particular conversation and only then to enter it on their own terms or those set by the instructor.

# 1

# Contexts

# Contextual Overview[1]

## Melville's Career and the Writing of *Moby-Dick*

Herman Melville was born in New York City on August 1, 1819. His father, Allan Melvill (the "e" was added later), was the grandson of a wealthy Scottish émigré to the US and the son of Major Thomas Melvill, a participant in the Boston Tea Party[27] and Revolutionary War veteran. Allan thus inherited a noble patrimony but little of his father's or his grandfather's knack for success. A middling businessman, in 1830 Allan was forced to flee New York City with his family for Albany[3] in order to avoid debtor's prison. The family of Herman's mother, Maria Gansevoort, was slightly more prestigious. The first Gansevoorts had immigrated to Albany from Holland in the mid-seventeenth century and had subsequently intermarried with many of the wealthiest Dutch families in the region, including the Van Rensselaers, one of the most powerful families in New York State. The flight to Albany thus marked a rather depressing turn of events for Melville's parents, both of whom had been raised to consider themselves above the fluctuations of mere economic cycles.

In 1832 Allan died, leaving the family debt-ridden, and Herman was forced to

---

1   Every scholar of Melville is greatly indebted to his principal modern biographers, Hershel Parker and Laurie Robertson-Lorant, and to the editors of the Northwestern–Newberry editions of Melville's collected works, which provide standard critical editions of all the fiction as well as his collected letters. This introduction draws heavily on that material as well as on the work of other scholars cited as appropriate and listed in Further Reading. See, among others, Hershel Parker, *Herman Melville: A Biography, Volume I 1819–1851* and *Volume II 1851–1891* (Baltimore, Md. and London: Johns Hopkins University Press, 1996 and 2002); Laurie Robertson-Lorant, *Herman Melville: A Biography* (New York, Clarkson Potter, 1996); "Historical Note," in Harrison Hayford, Hershel Parker, and G. Thomas Tanselle, eds, *Moby-Dick; or The Whale* (Evanston and Chicago, Ill.: Northwestern University Press and The Newberry Library, 1988).

2   In 1773 the British parliament repealed several taxes but retained a tax on tea as a symbol of its right to tax the colonies as well as to aid the financially strapped East India Company. On the night of December 16, 1773, a party of colonists disguised as Indians boarded several cargo ships in Boston harbor and threw the tea they carried into the sea to protest.

3   Albany, N.Y., a city on the Hudson river approximately 150 miles (241 km) north of New York City.

quit school to find work, becoming a clerk in his uncle's bank in Albany. He struggled to find work as an adolescent and young man, working as teacher and then in 1839 as a common seaman aboard the *St. Lawrence*, a merchant ship that took him on his first trip overseas to Liverpool. There is little evidence that Melville was bookish or that he would eventually become a creative writer. He would have read the popular literature of his day but it was not until he spent nearly three years at sea that his imagination and his deep interest in reading were fully kindled. Unable to find work in the winter of 1841–2 Herman signed as a "Green Hand" on the whaleship *Acushnet* bound for the South Pacific whaling grounds out of Fairhaven, Connecticut. Life on board a nineteenth-century whaler was anything but romantic.[4] The work was dangerous and required long, grueling days of hard, physical labor. As whale stocks depleted through-out the nineteenth century ships needed to stay at sea and "cruise" for whales for as long as four years in order to see a profit – something which was far from guaranteed. Crews were often cheated out of their small share of the ship's profits by unscrupulous agents on land as well as owners, both of whom typically charged exorbitant prices for the necessary equipment. Like 60–75 percent of all crews Melville deserted, jumping ship in 1842 at the Marquesas and choosing to risk living among the indigenous tribes on Nukuhiva – at least some of which were practicing cannibals – rather than to continue to suffer on board ship. After about a month Melville was taken up by an Australian whaler bound for Tahiti. By August he had arrived at Hawaii on yet another whale-ship and had apparently seen enough of the whale fishery and of the South Pacific, deciding to seek work on dry land and perhaps stay in the islands tem-porarily. The US Frigate *United States*, however, was looking for enlistees and presented the opportunity of a paid passage home. Melville quickly changed plans and signed on as a common sailor, outward bound for Boston with several ports of call in between.

In Chapter 24 of *Moby-Dick* Ishmael claims in a gently ironic tone that "a whaleship was my Yale College and my Harvard,"[5] and the available evidence suggests Melville's experiences in the South Pacific had a profound impact on his personal development (see Parker in Further Reading, **p. 182**). In a letter to fellow writer Nathaniel Hawthorne in 1851 he claimed that:

I am like one of those seeds taken out of the Egyptian Pyramids, which, after being three thousand years a seed and nothing but a seed, being planted in English soil, it developed itself, grew to greenness, and then fell to mould. So I. Until I was twenty-five, I had no development at all. From my twenty-fifth year I date my life. Three weeks have scarcely

---

4    See Briton Cooper Busch, *"Whaling Will Never Do for Me": The American Whaleman in the Nineteenth Century*, (Lexington, Ky.: The University Press of Kentucky, 1994).
5    112. All citations of the primary text are from Harrison Hayford, Hershel Parker, G. Thomas Tanselle, eds., *Moby-Dick; or The Whale* (Evanston and Chicago, Ill.: Northwestern University Press and The Newberry Library, 1988).

passed, at any time between then and now, that I have not unfolded within myself.[6]

Melville turned twenty-five in 1844, just days before he signed on the *United States*, and scholars now know he read voraciously while in the Pacific. Once back in the States he began to acquire books as fast as he possibly could. Indeed, many of the profits from the sales of his first successful works were eaten up by books he bought from his publishers on account.

Discharged at Boston in October 1844, by December Melville had begun drafting his first book, *Typee* (1846), a travel narrative based on his experiences in the Marquesas. Writing *Typee*, ostensibly a work of nonfiction, required factual accuracy and so Melville relied heavily on secondary sources to supplement his memory. This compositional method, drawing equally on experience, imagination, observation and research – if not outright theft – served Melville his whole career. Although he claimed at the time that both *Typee* and *Omoo* (1847) (the sequel to *Typee*) were the "unvarnished truth," close scrutiny of internal and external evidence has revealed that Melville depended heavily on research undertaken subsequent to his travels to supplement and enhance the narrative of his personal experience.

*Typee* and *Omoo* were successes both commercially and critically. Some critics, especially in England, found it dubious that a common seaman could have produced something as literate as *Typee*, and his attacks on Methodist missionaries drew heavy fire from religious officials and some critics in the US, but overall Melville had secured a rather ripe fame from his first two books. With his life and career on the upswing Melville soon married the daughter of Chief Justice Lemuel Shaw of the Massachusetts Supreme Court. The pleasing prospect of possibly recovering some financial stability and respectability for the houses of Melvill and Gansevoort must have played no small part in Melville's musings at this point.

His very next book, however, was a misstep. In a letter to John Murray, the English publisher of his first books, Melville discussed how his third book would mark a definite artistic shift from his earlier work:

> My object in now writing you—I should have done so ere this—is to inform you of a change in my determinations. To be blunt: the work I shall next publish will in downright earnest a 'Romance of Polynesian Adventure'—But why this? The truth is, Sir, that the reiterated imputation of being a romancer in disguise has at last pricked me into a resolution to show those who may take any interest in the matter, that a *real* romance of mine is no Typee or Omoo, & is made of different

---

6 "Letter to Nathaniel Hawthorne," [June 1?] 1851, in Horth, 1993: pp. 188–94. Melville was a notoriously poor speller as well as found of neologisms – words he made up to suit his purposes. In the present volume all idiosyncratic diction and spellings are retained in both the excerpts of the primary text and the letters.

stuff altogether . . . My *instinct* is to out with the Romance, & let me say that instincts are prophetic, & better than acquired wisdom . . .[7]

In the context of nineteenth-century narrative poetics, "Romance" meant first and foremost "fiction," but it also connoted a variety of other meanings depending on how a writer used it. Section 2, Interpretations, provides an excerpt from the preface to Hawthorne's *The Scarlet Letter* (1851) (see **pp. 40–1**), perhaps the clearest articulation of the term from the period and one with which Melville would have been familiar. There Hawthorne defines the provenance of the romancer as an imaginative space somewhere between the actual and the imaginary requiring a careful blending of fact and fiction, realism and romance, in any example of the genre. And although currently there is some debate about how best to understand nineteenth-century uses of the term,[8] in the context of Melville's career Hawthorne's letter strongly intimates that unlike his previous nonfiction works, *Mardi* (1849) would be a bona fide work of imaginative fiction. As such, and as in Hawthorne's popular works, Melville would take certain liberties with its degree of verisimilitude,[9] sacrificing the probable for the possible, the imaginary for the realistic. Melville also decided to draw on a wide variety of literary genres and nonfiction discursive forms in order to introduce and explore the grand philosophical issues he was intent on investigating in his fiction – a technique he would return to in *Moby-Dick*.

Unfortunately, instincts in this case were not prophetic of success as *Mardi*'s reception was poor. Editors and readers not used to the mixing of so many different genres in a single volume were generally puzzled by the book's epic combination of satire, sentiment, politics, and philosophy – to name only a few of the discourses Melville incorporated into the massive work. By June of 1849, just months after reaching a sort of professional peak, it had become clear that *Mardi* was a commercial and critical failure. As a result, the demands of a growing family on someone whose sole source of income was the pen began to weigh heavily on Melville. So much so that over the summer of 1849 he worked feverishly to produce and publish two full-length works – *Redburn* (1849) and *White Jacket* (1850) – both of which were intended to satisfy popular and critical taste. Writing to Richard Bentley, the English publisher of *Mardi*, Melville wrote:

> The critics on your side of the water seem to have fired quite a broadside into "Mardi"; but it was not altogether unexpected. In fact the book is of a nature to attract compliments of that sort from some quarters; and as you may be aware yourself, it is judged only as a work meant to entertain . . . the peculiar thoughts & fancies of a Yankee upon politics & other matters could hardly be presumed to delight that class of

---

7   "Letter to John Murray," March 25, 1848, in Horth, 1993: pp. 105–8.
8   See especially Joel Porte, Michael Davitt Bell, Emily Miller Budick, and Richard Chase in the Further Reading section.
9   Fidelity to actuality in representation, the degree to which elements of the fictional world are realistically portrayed.

gentleman who conduct your leading journals; while the metaphysical ingredients (for want of a better term) of the book, must of course repel some of those who read simply for amusement.[10]

His next work, he goes on to say, will be nothing of the kind – that is, "no metaphysics, no conic-sections, nothing but cakes & ale." This time Melville's instincts *were* prophetic and readers and critics were pleased that he had returned to subjects they liked best – semi-fictional narratives (today we might call them creative nonfiction) about the sea and shipboard life.

As Melville begins drafting the book that would become *Moby-Dick*, then, he is at the height of his critical and popular success as a writer but also at a crossroads professionally and artistically. Both *Redburn* and *White Jacket* would eventually sell fairly well, and both were well received by critics, yet Melville remained profoundly dissatisfied with his niche in his chosen profession. Writing to his father-in-law in the fall of 1849 he immediately distanced himself from his most recent books, dismissing them both out of hand:

> For Redburn I anticipate no particular reception of any kind. It may be deemed a book of tolerable entertainment;—& may be accounted dull.—As for the other book [*White Jacket*], it will be sure to be attacked in some quarters. But no reputation that is gratifying to me, can possibly be achieved by either of these books. They are two *jobs*, which I have done for money—being forced to it, as other men are to sawing wood . . . Being books, then, written in this way, my only desire for their "success" (as it is called) springs from my pocket, & not from my heart. So far as I am individually concerned, & independent of my pocket, it is my earnest desire to write those sort of books which are said to "fail."[11]

Ironically, and perhaps tragically, Melville's earnest desire would eventually be entirely satisfied. *Moby-Dick* would be the first of three ambitious novels in a row[12] that were just the sort of books Melville *preferred* to write, and all three were commercial if not artistic failures, driving their author out of the business of authorship entirely (but not from the practice of writing). After the third of these, *The Confidence Man* (1857), Melville wrote poetry almost exclusively, which he published privately up to his death. Although at the height of his critical and popular success and about to demonstrate by writing *Moby-Dick* that he was also at the peak of his imaginative powers, Melville felt sharply alienated from a print culture within which he could not thrive except by compromising his art in ways he found intolerable.[13]

---

10  "Letter to Richard Bentley," June 5, 1849, in Horth, 1993: pp. 130–3.
11  See Lawrence W. Levine, *Highbrow/Lowbrow: The Emergence of Cultural Hierarchy in America* (Boston, Mass.: Harvard University Press, 1988).
12  *Moby-Dick* (1851), *Pierre; or the Ambiguities* (1852), and *The Confidence Man* (1857). Melville published largely short stories between 1852 and 1857 (see Chronology, **p. 28**).
13  Although Melville has thus traditionally been cast as the consummate isolated and under-appreciated artist, this characterization has become increasingly tenuous (see **p. 64**).

Melville began conceiving and perhaps researching *Moby-Dick* on a return voyage from London in December 1849 where he had been presenting *White Jacket* to prospective publishers. In May 1850 he indicated in a letter to fellow American writer R. H. Dana Jr., whose *Two Years Before the Mast* (1840) Melville (like many Americans) had read and admired, that he was half-way finished with his next book. In a letter to Bentley in June 1850 he told his British publisher that the new manuscript would be ready by the fall:

> My Dear Sir,—In the latter part of the coming autumn I shall have ready a new work; and I write you now to propose its publication in England.
>    The book is a romance of adventure, founded upon certain wild legends in the Southern Sperm Whale Fisheries, and illustrated by the author's own personal experience, of two years & more, as a harpooneer.[14]

Although he had probably never served as a harpooneer, Melville did have enough experience on American whaleships to imaginatively transform those experiences into a sort of "*Mardi*-an" story about whaling. Stories of whales attacking whale boats were in wide circulation throughout the period, and in 1839 a story about the taking of Mocha Dick, a famous albino whale in the South Pacific fishery, appeared in the *Knickerbocker* magazine which Melville may have seen. In 1841, while on the *Acushnet*, he may also have met the son of Owen Chase, first mate of the whaleship *Essex* which had been destroyed by a whale and whose crew had then faced a harrowing 2,000-mile journey in small boats from the middle of the Pacific to the South American Coast (see Chase extract, **pp. 34–7**). Only two of the three boats survived and survivors in both had resorted to cannibalism. As he worked to finish *Moby-Dick* in 1851 Melville acquired his own copy of Chase's narrative from his father-in-law and most likely drew on it as he worked feverishly to bring his tale to its catastrophic close.[15] The basic plot of his next book was thus not original – at least until he radically reconceived the book's direction in August 1850.

That August Melville wrote a review of Hawthorne's *Mosses from an Old Manse* (see **pp. 38–40**) for his friend and editor Evert Duyckinck's *Literary World* magazine. Other than a few scant letters and the novels themselves this review is the fullest expression of Melville's burgeoning aesthetic that we have. As such it sheds much light on how Melville's conception of his art had evolved since the heady days of *Typee* and his initial fame as a literary sex symbol – the literate sailor who had lived among the dangerous and promiscuous cannibals of the South Pacific. Part review, part literary manifesto, part primary document of American literary nationalism, "Hawthorne and His Mosses" announces the arrival of the American Shakespeare (Hawthorne) whose oblique representations of the

14  "Letter to Richard Bentley," June 27, 1850, in Horth, 1993: pp. 162–5.
15  See James Barbour, "'All My Books Are Botches': Melville's Struggle with The Whale," in James Barbour and Tom Quirk, eds, *Writing the American Classics* (Chapel Hill, N.C. and London: The University of North Carolina Press, 1990), pp. 25–52.

dark truths most writers tremble to tell give his writings a power of blackness "ten times black." According to Melville, the great literary artist is he who eschews the delicate sensibilities of the mere skimmer-of-pages (in Melville's terms – the common reader who reads a book merely for entertainment; see Charvat extract, **pp. 82–3**) and tackles those truths of the human condition that get at the very "axis of reality." Doing so requires that the writer disguise much of what he is doing lest he offend the greater part of his audience: "For in this world of lies, Truth is forced to fly like a scared white doe in the woodlands; and only by cunning glimpses will she reveal herself, as in Shakespeare and other masters of the great Art of Telling the Truth . . . covertly, and by snatches."[16] To the mere skimmer, then, Hawthorne's tales appear to be all sunlight and goodness yet:

> spite of all the Indian-summer sunlight on the hither side of Haw-
> thorne's soul, the other side—like the dark half of the physical sphere—
> is shrouded in a blackness, ten times black . . . You may be witched by
> his sunlight,—transported by the bright gildings in the skies he builds
> over you;—but there is the blackness of darkness beyond; and even his
> bright gildings but fringe, and play upon the edges of thunder-clouds.[17]

Critics argue over how much of Melville's aesthetic is actually applicable to Hawthorne and how much is really only Melville describing his own ideal. Clearly,
however, Melville's ideas about the Great Art of Telling the Truth are applicable
to the book he was fully immersed in at the time he wrote "Mosses" – *Moby-
Dick*.

By the end of the summer of 1850 then, Melville had decided to transform
*Moby-Dick* into the sort of book that would meet his now fully crystallized
poetics – to write a book full of the blackness ten times black he so admired in the
work of his kindred spirit Hawthorne. Melville had already demonstrated a
penchant for interrogating the Truth – what he called "metaphysics" – in *Mardi*.
*White Jacket* and *Redburn* had been two "jobs" done to tide him over until the
real work began on a mighty book that would meet the criteria he no doubt had
conceived of prior to writing "Mosses," but which he had not worked out most
fully until the review itself. *Moby-Dick*, then, would mark the full flowering
of Melville's unfolding within himself begun in his twenty-fifth year. It would be
a mighty book on a mighty theme, with a plot that focused on the whale fishery
and on the legends in somewhat wide circulation about a white whale that was
known to attack whaleboats with a seemingly malicious volition. This surface
plot, however, would be but a pretence for exploring the very "axis of reality"
with which Melville, like his fictional captain Ahab (whom Melville would
portray as an American Lear), was obsessed. In effect, he would answer his own

16 Melville, "Hawthorne and His Mosses: By a Virginian Spending July in Vermont," in Harrison
   Hayford, Alma A. MacDougall, and G. Thomas Tanselle *et al.*, eds, *The Piazza Tales and Other
   Prose Pieces: 1839–1860*, (Evanston and Chicago, Ill.: Northwestern University Press and The
   Newberry Library, 1987), p. 244.
17 Ibid., 243.

call in "Mosses" for an American Shakespeare, but one who would write a great American novel. Deeply influenced at this point by Hawthorne, Carlyle's *Sartor Resartus*,[18] and drawing heavily on numerous secondary works on whaling – Melville followed his usual compositional method but this time exhaustively combed as many sources on whaling as he could find – Melville transformed the hunt for whales and for the great white whale in particular into a dense, fictional world within which he could explore the deepest profundities of the universe and the human soul, all of which were embodied symbolically in Moby Dick himself.

Melville, however, did not resume writing *Moby-Dick* in earnest until December 1850. By January he was in deep debt in a house filled with a wife, young son, and two sisters (Helen and Augusta), and his only hope for providing for that house was dependent on the success of his next book. He saw few royalties from his early works because he was usually in debt to both his American and British publishers. Sales of his works seldom outstripped his advances and the cost of manufacturing and distributing a book needed to be met before the author would see any profit. Some years after his death his wife, affectionately known as Lizzie, recalled that *Moby-Dick* was written under "unfavorable circumstances." Throughout the winter Melville would rise very early to get the chores out of the way and then would write all day, stopping only late in the afternoon when the light began to fail. He would then head to the village before returning to listen to Lizzie or one of his sisters read. Lizzie and his sisters would also proofread the manuscript, providing fair copies of what he had written in the preceding week or so sans punctuation which Melville would then go over, adding punctuation as he went. In a letter to Duyckinck Melville described his daily routine at *Arrowhead* in minute detail:

> Do you want to know how I pass my time?—I rise at eight—there-abouts—& go to my barn—say good-morning to the horse, & give him his breakfast ... Then, pay a visit to my cow—cut up a pumpkin or two for her, & stand by to see her eat it—for it's a pleasant sight to see a cow move her jaws—she does it so mildly & with such a sanctity.— My own breakfast over, I go to my workroom & light my fire—then spread my M.S.S on the table—take one business squint at it, & fall to with a will. At 2 1/2 P.M. I hear a preconcerted knock at my door, which (by request) continues till I rise & go to the door, which serves to wean me effectively from my writing, however interested I may be.[19]

The afternoons and evenings were spent getting the papers and mail in town, handling chores on the farm, and listening to Lizzie or one of his sisters read

18  Thomas Carlyle was a widely read writer and essayist who in *Sartor Resartus* used German philosophy to satirize conventional wisdom on a wide variety of subjects. Carlyle's influence on Melville can be most closely traced in each man's attitude towards conventional modes of thought as well as a tongue-in-cheek sense of irony and absurdity. See extract from Howard, **pp. 88–90**.
19  "Letter to Evert Duyckinck," December 13, 1850, in Horth, 1993: pp. 172–5.

aloud – Melville's eyes were weak and he could not stand the strain of reading in dim light, and certainly not by candlelight after dark. Although the letter to Duyckinck suggests that perhaps in the late fall or first part of December working conditions were almost bucolic, by the start of the New Year, in a house full of women and children (Lizzie would soon be pregnant with their second child), Melville was feeling the pressures of domesticity and of financial need profoundly.

In a letter to Hawthorne written in June 1851 Melville revealed just how frustrating things had become by the following summer:

> In a week or so, I go to New York, to bury myself in a third-story room, and work and slave on my "Whale" while it is driving through the press. *That* is the only way I can finish it now,—I am so pulled hither and thither by circumstances. The calm, the coolness, the silent grass-growing mood in which a man *ought* always to compose,—that, I fear, can seldom be mine. Dollars damn me; and the malicious Devil is forever grinning in upon me, holding the door ajar . . . What I feel most moved to write, that is banned,—it will not pay. Yet, altogether, write the *other* way I cannot. So the product is a final hash, and all my books are botches.[20]

Melville's greatest fear, born of his conviction that he would not be able to successfully negotiate between the demands of his art and the demands of the book-buying public – a schism he first encountered in the critical and popular response to *Mardi* – was that *Moby-Dick* would drop stillborn from the press, a botched book that failed to satisfy either Melville or his readers. "Truth is the silliest thing under the sun. Try to get a living by the Truth—and go to the Soup Societies." As he had first articulated in "Mosses," and as his struggles with his whale had now convinced him, there was a *necessary* conflict between the demands placed on a writer by his duty to dive for great Truths on the one hand and the everyday reader's expectations on the other. This sharply conflicted relation to his audience would come to a head in the critical reception to what he considered to be his greatest book, yet, in spite of his confession to Hawthorne that he feared otherwise.

In April of 1851 Melville had borrowed money from a friend to pay for part of the original purchase price of *Arrowhead* and its remodeling costs, but also to pay for the manufacture of the stereotype plates of his next book. Stereotype plates were metal plates cast from the raised type used for printing print media. Once the plates were cast it was relatively easy to transport them and to print additional editions of any single book. Having *Moby-Dick* printed at his own expense would allow him to sell the plates to the highest bidder and would make the book more desirable to a publisher who would not have to risk the cost of the plates as part of the initial publication cost. This was a sensible move on

---

20  "Letter to Nathaniel Hawthorne," [June 1? 1851], in Horth, 1993: pp. 188–94.

Melville's part, but one of the effects of it was that he was forced to finish drafting the book even as the first half or more was being set for manufacture of the plates. In many ways this was a fitting end to the writing of a book that had been conceived amidst the untamed seas of the North Atlantic in winter and forged in a crucible of acute artistic, financial, and domestic pressure. That summer he worked in both New York and Pittsfield to get the plates made and find a publisher. In spite of all the distractions the work was finished by the fall and published by Bentley in London in October and by the Harpers in New York in November. Astonishingly, Melville was already at work on his next book, *Pierre; or the Ambiguities* (1852), by the end of the year.

As a result of such a complicated compositional history and of the subsequent dash to publication throughout the summer of 1851, the final product *was* in certain respects botched. And critics have long been aware that there are substantial textual differences between the British and American first editions.[21] Schematically, the stereotyped plates can be considered to represent the fair copy of the manuscript proofread by Melville before he handed it to the compositor for manufacture of the plates. The compositor may have made small changes as well as mistakes which escaped Melville's proofreading, but at the end of the day the American edition was typeset with no interference by the publisher or any of his employees. Most importantly, because Melville was finishing the book as earlier chapters were being typeset, any inconsistencies between early chapters and the last sections of the manuscript would be impossible to remedy. Bulkington, for example, a character who appears early on in Chapter 3, and who is clearly meant to be a principal character, is abruptly killed off in Chapter 23 (see "The Lee Shore," **pp. 144–5**). Further, the proofs for the British edition were made from the stereotypes, but Melville had them for nearly two months before sending them on to England, during which time, textual scholars have concluded, he made additional changes. Finally, once Bentley received the proofs from Melville he and/or his editors made additional substantial revisions, both to correct punctuation and grammar but also to tone down what Bentley considered to be the work's more blasphemous sections. This meant removing any sexual or religious allusions that could be deemed offensive, especially passages that could be interpreted (rightly or wrongly) as sacrilegious. Queequeg's comment that, "de god wat made shark must be one dam Ingin" was removed. And even the most harmless passages were often cut out by sensitive or zealous editors. Ishmael's recollection that "I lay there dismally calculating that sixteen entire hours must elapse before I could hope for resurrection" became "before I could hope to get out of bed again." All told the three-volume British edition, entitled *The Whale*, was over 2,000 words shorter than the one-volume American *Moby-Dick*, with several hundred substantive variants between the two. Most noticeably perhaps, the English edition

---

21 See "Historical Note," in Harrison Hayford, Hershel Parker, and G. Thomas Tanselle, eds, *Moby-Dick; or The Whale* (Evanston and Chicago, Ill.: Northwestern University Press and The Newberry Library, 1988).

had no epilogue, leaving British readers to wonder just what had happened to Ishmael.

Given the differences between the English and American versions it is not surprising that readers and critics on different sides of the Atlantic reacted differently. As one critic has noted:

> The English reaction, generally positive, was based on a three-volume, beautifully bound book physically designed for the circulating libraries, and toned down in its potential blasphemies and references to sex and bodily parts to make it acceptable in those quarters. The implications of the work, however, did not escape sophisticated English readers. The English edition was never popular, though that may have had to do with its price and its general inappropriateness for the usual circulating library readership – it didn't have a love story.[22]

The American reaction was – with a few notable exceptions including Hawthorne's – generally poor. Most critics found the book's philosophical musings in the cetological chapters (the chapters in which Melville used detailed descriptions of the craft of hunting whales to explore various philosophical issues), as well as its wildly romantic treatment of the pursuit of Moby Dick, bewildering. A reviewer in the *Boston Post* noted, "We have read nearly one half of this book, and are satisfied that the London *Athenæum* is right in calling it 'an ill compounded mixture of romance and matter of fact.' It is a crazy sort of affair, stuffed with conceits and oddities of all kinds, put in artificially, deliberately and affectedly . . ."[23] It is important to note that there were contemporary readers who were excited by the book's powerful use of language and imagery (see *New York Evangelist* review on **pp. 69–70**), and for these few, and certainly for many, many twentieth-century readers, Melville's book was an epic fusion of metaphysics, fact, and poetic prose – as scarred and imposing as the head of Moby Dick himself but a startlingly imaginative and *successful* departure from the stylistic and thematic conventions of the period.

Melville, however, saw few if any of the positive reviews from England, and the poor reception and poor sales of *Moby-Dick* in the US were a great disappointment. From 1851 to 1887, the date of the Harpers' last statement to Melville, a period of nearly thirty-six years, *Moby-Dick* sold a mere 3,215 copies, 2,300 of which sold in the first year-and-a-half after publication (see Charvat extract on **pp. 82–3**). Melville's total earnings from *Moby-Dick* over his lifetime were $556.37,[24] less than for any of his earlier works. Bentley had advanced Melville £150 (about $700)[25] prior to publication and never recovered the cost

22  Peter Shillingsburg, "The Three *Moby-Dick*s," *American Literary History* 2 (1990), p. 121.
23  Review of *Moby-Dick*, *Boston Post*, Nov. 20, 1851, in Brian Higgins and Hershel Parker, eds, *Herman Melville: The Contemporary Reviews* (New York: Cambridge University Press, 1995), p. 378.
24  About $11,600 or £7,358 in 2002 values.
25  The figures are from 1851; about $16,000 or £10,149 in 2002.

of the advance plus the cost of publication. The reception of *Pierre* and *The Confidence Man* were each worse in succession, and by the end of the decade Melville was no longer writing with the intent of publishing. Starting around the Civil War (1861), and then for the rest of his life, he wrote and privately published several collections of poetry, including a long epic poem, *Clarel* (1876). By the time Melville died in 1891, leaving several poems as well as the short story *Billy Budd* (1924) in manuscript, he was an anonymous figure on the American cultural landscape. His death warranted only a few obituary notices. *Moby-Dick* was all but forgotten.

## Melville and Antebellum America

*Moby-Dick* was published during a period in which the United States was coming of age politically and economically, and was experiencing tumultuous and often violent growing pains as a result. Political struggles among various emerging interest groups – farmers versus emerging industry, workers versus owners, and immigrants versus an Anglo-Protestant majority to name a few – were coming to a head. The Civil War was not quite a foregone conclusion in 1851, but a majority of Americans realized that in a country with strong regional differences and interests (for example, slavery), the economic and political instability brought about by rapid economic and geographic growth might not be easily settled. Additionally, the pressures faced by the growing nation began to tear at its cultural and political fabric *in spite of* a massive territorial expansion that only added to existing tensions with each new state or territory. The Mexican–American War (1846–8), a conflict historians now see as a war of aggression initiated by the US with little justification, destroyed the illusions many Americans had harbored that the US as it matured would avoid the empire building and conflict that continued to plague the Old World. And many critics of Melville now see *Moby-Dick* as more than obliquely concerned with such contemporary issues as empire, liberty and American individualism, the latter what Ralph Waldo Emerson, one of the leading thinkers and literary figures of the era, would refer to as "self-reliance" (see **p. 44**).

Throughout the antebellum period more and more Americans moved to the cities, presaging the rapid urban growth of the post-Civil War era. And Americans also settled further and further west, exacerbating the displacement and effective genocide of the indigenous peoples of North America. Most importantly, westward expansion drove the country steadily and irreversibly towards civil war. As new states were added to the Union, political struggles over which would be slave and which would be free were fierce. In the decades preceding the calamity of 1861–5, the US congress enacted a series of legislative compromises designed to stave off the disintegration of the Union (see Chronology, **p. 28**). Yet most of these failed to satisfy citizens in either the North or South and instead drove each side closer toward open conflict. In these and other ways the very landscape[1] and character of the United States were changing at a pace the average American found disturbing. In the midst of this period of uncertainty Americans as a whole were struggling culturally and politically to define what it meant to be an "American," and especially to determine how the American experiment in democracy would turn out.

At the outset of the nineteenth century, American print culture and the American artistic scene were as young and raw as the country itself. But by the 1850s both the publishing industry and American *belles-lettres*[2] were maturing rapidly, resulting in the decade that noted American critic F. O. Matthiessen, in his highly influential book *American Renaissance: Art and Expression in the Age of Emerson and Whitman* (1941), first called the "American Renaissance." Matthiessen argued that because several mature works by Hawthorne, Melville, Whitman, Emerson and Thoreau all appeared between 1850 and 1855[3] this constituted the first full flowering of high literary art in the US. Matthiessen's book was also instrumental in furthering the study of American literature in the US which prior to the Second World War had only recently emerged as a field of serious study. As a result, the idea of the American Renaissance held sway over the study of American literature for several decades, dominating the discourse on nineteenth-century American literature until very recently (see **pp. 63–4**). And to be sure, the emergence throughout the 1850s of important works by now classic American writers, including the five studied by Matthiessen as well as such figures as Poe, Stowe and Frederick Douglass,[4] would seem to confirm Matthiessen's view.

Yet a majority of literary historians now agree that Matthiessen's analysis – although important and powerful in many ways – was myopic at best, and certainly an inaccurate assessment of nineteenth-century American literary history. Foremost among the problems now associated with Matthiessen's analysis is the fact that a majority of readers in the period were largely unfamiliar with the writers he identified as constituting the first bonafide eruption of literary genius on American soil. Left out were the hundreds of women writers whose fictional documentation of the domestic sphere overwhelmingly dominated book sales in the period. Equally significant is the fact that the poetics of the writers discussed

---

1    In 1800, the US was composed of only that land east of the Mississippi River, and not all of this was organized into federated states. Instead, much of it remained mere "territories." The Louisiana Purchase (1803) expanded this to include virtually all land east of the Rocky Mountains. Following the Mexican–American War (1846–8; see **p. 30** in Chronology) US territories and states encompassed virtually the entire area that now makes up the so-called "lower forty-eight."
2    Literature, typically highbrow, regarded for its aesthetic merit rather than for its didactic or informative content.
3    Hawthorne, *The Scarlet Letter* (1850) and *The House of Seven Gables* (1851); Melville, *Moby-Dick* (1851) and *Pierre* (1852); Whitman, *Leaves of Grass* (1855); Emerson, *Representative Men* (1850); and Thoreau, *Walden* (1854).
4    Edgar Allan Poe (1809–49), American critic, short-story writer and poet; Harriet Beecher Stowe (1811–96), American novelist and author of *Uncle Tom's Cabin* (1851); Frederick Douglass (1817–95), African-American writer and ex-slave who wrote the autobiographical *Narrative of the Life of Frederic Douglass, an American Slave* (1845).

by Matthiessen in his work (a poetics Matthiessen identified vaguely as a "commitment to the potential of democracy") was rivaled in its own period both by the aesthetic of the domestic sphere and by a competing vision equally ambitious as that of the writers of Matthiessen's renaissance – but one that had little to do with democracy and instead looked to England for its artistic models. Matthiessen and others, however, were under the sway of a thinly veiled American literary and cultural nationalism – a by-product of the crisis of the Second World War. What they chose thus to emphasize was often at odds with a more historically accurate understanding of Melville and his whale (see **pp. 62–4** in Critical History).

In a review of Hawthorne's *Mosses from an Old Manse*, written by Melville as he worked on *Moby-Dick*, he had said:

> Let America . . . prize and cherish her writers; yea, let her glorify them. They are not so many in number, as to exhaust her good-will. And while she has good kith and kin of her own, to take to her bosom, let her not lavish her embraces upon the household of an alien. For believe it or not England, after all, is, in many things, an alien to us. China has more bowels of real love for us than she.[5]

Melville's comments were part of an ongoing call by writers centered in New York City and closely allied and associated with the Democratic Party to promote an indigenous fiction that, unlike the works of writers praised and supported by the American Whigs,[6] no longer looked to England for its literary inspiration. The debates between the two were contentious and often heated – although largely bloodless. On the one side were writers like Melville associated with the so-called "Young America" movement led by his friend and editor Evert Duyckinck, who promoted the development of an indigenous and uniquely American imaginative literature. On the other were writers who took their cue from Washington Irving and were more urbane and cosmopolitan in their literary orientations and more conservative in their politics.

---

5    Melville, "Hawthorne and His Mosses" (1851), a review of Nathaniel Hawthorne's collection of short stories, *Mosses from an Old Manse* (1846).
6    The modern Democratic Party first emerged and came to power during Andrew Jackson's presidency (1829–37). Following Jackson's lead the Party trumpeted the values of the "common man," and Jackson himself oversaw a massive expansion of real democratic power, resulting by the end of his presidency in universal white male suffrage. Although Jackson himself was a sort of royal personage, wielding presidential power like no president before him, establishing (for example) the veto as an acceptable expression of the power of the Presidency, he and his party were profoundly hostile to the upper class, strong central government, and especially the banks. Although Jackson is usually credited with the expansion of democratic power, he is also "credited" with a series of disastrous policy decisions which wreaked havoc on the US economic system, resulting in the Panic of 1837 among other problems. The American Whig Party arose as an opposition party to the Democrats, and generally favored a strong central government that protected the upper class as well as merchants and commerce. As tensions between slave and non-slave states intensified in the 1850s, many Whigs defected to the newly formed Republican Party whose major goal was to isolate the slave-holding South. By 1856 the Whig Party was defunct, and the two-party system in the US firmly established.

The literary "wars" of the 1840s are perhaps more understandable once we consider the long slow development of American literature and literary production following the War of 1812. Like any post-colonial nation the US struggled initially to shrug off the political and cultural legacy of its mother country. Although by the end of the War of 1812 the US had defeated England in two wars it had yet to develop a secure and homogeneous national identity which the average American felt was safe from either external or *internal* counterrevolution. Following the Treaty of Ghent[7] Americans began to believe that the fruits of the Revolution were safe, but the process of developing a uniquely American and – what was more important – *non-English* national identity – was slow in maturing. Until the massive influx of German and Irish immigrants, most of whom were Catholic, in the 1840s, the US remained overwhelmingly Anglo and Protestant. As well, although early writers and critics began to advocate an indigenous national fiction as early as the first decades of the century, in its youth the US was inherently regional in character. A truly national culture only began to coalesce following such advances as the opening of the Erie Canal and, most importantly, the advent of the railroad and the telegraph. The Erie Canal connected New York City to the western frontier via the Great Lakes and greatly expanded trade between the East Coast and the Ohio and Upper Mississippi valleys. The railroad allowed citizens all over the US greater access to manufactured goods and especially allowed the widespread distribution of Eastern newspapers and magazines. The increased availability of media targeted at the entire nation and no longer simply at local or regional interests quickened the growth of a national culture exponentially. The call for and emergence of a national fiction thus began to gather steam once a nonsectarian national culture began to emerge, but the country's cultural relation to its European, and especially its English, roots remained deeply conflicted. Literate Americans greatly admired English writers and so could not simply reject or ignore their country's profound linguistic and historical ties to England. And Washington Irving had drawn unabashedly on English rhetorical and fictional models to become the first successful professional American writer, helped in no small measure by the support of Sir Walter Scott.[8] Yet the literary "wars" centered in New York reveal just how much disagreement there was on how best to accomplish the shared goal of fostering a uniquely American literary tradition, or even on what such a thing might look like. Finally, but equally significantly, as late as the mid-century American novelists had to compete not only with the cultural legacy represented by British contemporaries like Dickens (who was incredibly popular on both sides of the Atlantic) but also with the economic realities of a fairly primitive book trade. Due to lack of copyright agreement between England and the US pirated copies of British novels in the US sold for a fraction of the price of books by American authors and British presses demanded American writers publish in England first in order to secure copyright

---

7  The treaty negotiated to end the War of 1812.
8  Sir Walter Scott (1771–1832). British poet, novelist, editor and critic, his Waverley novels, some of the first historical fiction, were extremely popular in the US and Britain, constituting a major influence on early American writers such as Washington Irving and James Fenimore Cooper.

there (see Charvat extract, **pp. 82–3**). As a result, by the 1850s economic competition between English and American writers and publishers was fierce.[9]

In short, there may in fact have been a literary renaissance in the US in the 1850s. But it was as much material and economic as it was aesthetic. Certainly the book trade had matured to the point where the 5,000 copies sold of James Fenimore Cooper's *Last of the Mohicans* in 1826 could be eclipsed by the over 100,000 copies sold of Harriet Beecher Stowe's *Uncle Tom's Cabin* in 1851. But the American literary scene was far from homogeneous, and most critics now agree that to limit one's definition of a "renaissance" to a small group of writers who for the most part were obscure in their own lifetimes and who remain unrepresentative of the diversity of literary production in the period is problematic.

Politically as well, the antebellum US can be difficult to understand, especially from the standpoint of current US politics. And the relative alignments among artists, the emerging middle and working classes, and the established economic elite vis-à-vis the major political parties in the era were complicated at best, resulting in at times conflicting and overlapping interests among various socio-economic groups. Perhaps no event brings this fact into relief more than the Astor Place Riot of May 1849, an event Melville participated in only peripherally but which reveals much about the man and his times.

The riot at the Astor Place Theatre was the culmination of a heated rivalry between two famous Shakespearean actors, one British and one American, each of whom came to represent in the popular mind two competing visions of America. Shakespeare was extremely popular in the nineteenth-century US among all social classes, and Edwin Forrest was one of the first Americans to gain fame in both the US and Europe as a professional actor. By all accounts his style catered to the groundlings of his day – it was physical, grandiose, and far from subtle. One critic described him as "a vast animal bewildered by a grain of genius." William C. Macready was the most celebrated British actor of his day and one of the first to elevate stagecraft to something like the respectable art form we know it as today. His style was refined and understated, and yet – although admired by his fellow actors – he was not well liked. Even his English peers considered him a snob. Forrest, contrastingly, was a stalwart democrat and self-proclaimed American "patriot," beloved by working men and especially the "Bowery B'hoys"[10] in New York City. In the crude logic of the times among the working class, elitism was anti-egalitarian, and anything anti-egalitarian was anti-democratic and therefore anti-American. Forrest was a walking masculine embodiment of democracy, but also perhaps the first "ugly American" and certainly the first well-known example. Vain, jingoistic, and ill-mannered by even

9  See Robert Weisbuch, *Atlantic Double-Cross: American Literature and British Influence in the Age of Emerson* (Chicago, Ill.: University of Chicago Press, 1986).
10 These were young working-class men who dressed like the upper class but in an exaggerated way. Essentially they were boisterous mimics of aristocratic manners, going to Shakespeare and the opera and frequently disrupting the performances and harassing anyone they perceived as being a real aristocrat – in short, a sort of dandified, working-class hooligan.

American standards, Forrest once hissed and booed Macready during a public performance in Edinburgh, outraging the English press. Even the great champion of the working man Walt Whitman found the overt catering to the mob in his performances distasteful. By 1849, the rivalry between Macready and Forrest was intense and widely reported.

All of this would be a mere footnote in the history of nineteenth-century American theatre were it not for the events of May 7 and 10, 1849. Both men were performing in competing productions of *Macbeth* in New York, Macready at the Astor Place Opera House and Forrest at the Broadway Theater. The Astor was the preferred theatre of New York's elite and symbolized for New York's working class everything the Revolution had been fought to purge from American soil: effeminacy, snobbery, aristocracy, decadence, and anti-Yankeeism. On the evening of May 7 working-class supporters of Forrest packed the Astor where Macready was performing, disrupting his performance with catcalls before chasing him from the stage with hurled fruit and a chair or two from the balcony. New York's literary and art community, most of whom were democrats and so in some measure sympathetic with the working class, at least politically, were outraged. Melville, along with other New York literati, including Duyckinck and Washington Irving, signed an open letter published in local papers expressing their dismay, urging Macready not to leave New York and to continue his run at the Astor. Bolstered, Macready agreed and flyers appeared announcing a performance on May 10. Flyers also appeared throughout the Bowery district, however, calling for a protest of all working men at the "English ARISTO-CRATIC Opera House." Promoters at the Astor asked for and received police protection and some 200 unarmed officers were assigned to keep the peace. Forrest supporters once again gained entrance and disrupted the performance, while between 10,000 and 15,000 gawkers, troublemakers and legitimate supporters of Forrest gathered outside the hall. A small portion of the mob, roughly 200–500 mostly young men, began pelting the police with bricks from a nearby construction site and attempted to rush the theatre. The police summoned local National Guard units and two regiments arrived to keep the crowd at bay. The mob rushed the militia and in the ensuing confrontation the troops fired three volleys, dispersing the crowd but killing twenty-three people and wounding thirty.

The Astor Place riot and its relevance to Melville studies has only recently emerged as a significant area of study. Certainly Melville's role was small at best, but the tensions which came to a head that night reveal the interdependence among many different threads of antebellum social, political, and artistic life. The Jacksonian era (1820–40) transformed American politics from a system controlled almost entirely by a landed elite to a system run by professional politicians. In order to gain and hold power these proto-modern politicians had to garner support from a body politic growing increasingly diverse economically and culturally. Certainly one of the principal tensions at the heart of the Astor riot was whether any sort of elitism – artistic, political or otherwise – was consistent with "democracy" and with fundamental "American values." The place of high art in an ostensive meritocracy was often acrimoniously debated among newspaper editors, politicians and writers. Melville's claim that Hawthorne was an "American Shakespeare" was part of this discourse and represented Young America's belief that high art should not come at the expense of "literary flunkeyism" toward aristocratic England. Whig literati contrastingly believed only literature based on English models deserved recognition. Meanwhile, the working class increasingly wanted nothing to do with either, preferring sensational fiction and bawdy drama that reflected their own life-experiences to anything offered to them by an elite they held in contempt and whom they saw as politically threatening. Add to all this the fact that distinctions between what could rightly be considered highbrow and what low were highly fluid and at times impossible to identify – especially over 150 years removed from actual events[11] – and all we can say with certainty is that the result of such a dynamic and rapidly evolving political, economic and cultural milieu was a highly fluid and complex system of shifting and often conflicting alliances among the various literary, social and political constituencies.

Not surprisingly, Melville's relation to all this was complex. The grandson of a Revolutionary war hero and connected through the Gansevoorts on his mother's side to some of the wealthiest Dutch families in New York State (see **p. 9**), Melville was born into a quasi-American gentry and yet the economic misfortunes he experienced as a result of his father's failures as a businessman and of his own frustrated experiences with the book market revealed to him just how tenuous social hierarchy and the cultural and political forms associated with it became once they were subject to the whims of a dynamic and unstable market. His family was descended from a type of quasi-American gentry, but most were staunch Democrats. His brother made a short career giving speeches for the party and in 1847 Melville himself wrote a series of scathing attacks on the Whigs, including their popular presidential candidate Zachary Taylor, the hero of the Mexican–American War (see **p. 30** in Chronology). Having served "before the mast" as a common seaman Melville was not unfamiliar with manual labor, yet his own ambitions were to join the growing class of nonmanual white-collar workers, and his intellectual orientation was decidedly highbrow. In a sense, Melville embodied many of the most glaring and quintessentially American contradictions of the period – that between medium social rank and high culture; between manners and social mores modeled on an upper class the majority of Americans aspired to but whom they often criticized, attacking them for their elitism; and between a deep ideological commitment to democracy and an abhorrence of a working-class democratic culture growing increasingly vulgar and reactionary toward anything it perceived as remotely anti-egalitarian. Indeed, almost as soon as Jacksonian democracy was successful in legitimizing the common man's place in the political order, middle-class democrats often found themselves aligned against the working class on cultural and political issues. In Melville's case, the Astor Place Riot brought into relief his own conflicted relation to democracy as an ideal and democracy as a reality, especially the leveling effect it threatened to have on the development of serious art. The upper class in the US

11  See Lawrence W. Levine, *Highbrow/Lowbrow: The Emergence of Cultural Hierarchy in America* (Boston, Mass.: Harvard University Press, 1988).

had traditionally been the arbiters of literary taste, controlling the major literary magazines and attacking literary works and authors which challenged conventional wisdom and traditional social mores. Melville thus found himself on the outside looking in at a print culture that necessarily excluded any writer who refused to write for either popular tastes – something Melville had done only reluctantly when economic circumstances required it[12] – or for the conservative tastes of the traditional elite.

This is not to say, however, that Melville was neither engaged with nor unaware of important issues in the period. There is a strong thread in early and mid-twentieth-century Melville criticism representing him as a desperate, iconoclastic figure marginalized and defiantly at odds with his times, choosing to "fail" rather than succumb to conventionality (see **pp. 59–61**). And certainly *how* Melville chose to engage with his times – obliquely through serious and challenging fictional narrative – suggests he was at least in some measure a type of Isolato[13] – an artist who strove to remain above the fray of antebellum social and political strife. However, as many of the selections in Section 2 show, this image has been replaced of late by that of a writer deeply engaged with many of the dominant issues of his time, albeit in uniquely Melvillean ways. Although at least marginally associated with Young America, for example, he never fully embraced its basic premises and was too enamored of British and German Romanticism (see **pp. 42–4** in Transcendentalism) not to draw on them in his own work. Melville's experiences in the Marquesas and the Pacific had exposed him to the great cultural diversity of the world and so he abhorred racial prejudice. As one critic has described it, once he returned from the Pacific "never again did Melville take for granted either the superiority of white Christian civilization or the benefit of imposing it on others. Never again did he judge nonwhite peoples by ethnocentric standards. On the contrary, he began to reexamine his own society through the eyes of 'savages'."[14] Yet there is no record of him reacting strongly to the Compromise of 1850 nor to the Fugitive Slave Act (see **p. 31** in Chronology), which most Americans did (he was of course immersed in writing *Moby-Dick* at the time). Nor do we know how he reacted to his father-in-law's ruling on a celebrated case involving an escaped slave freed briefly by an abolitionist mob. Melville was, in short, no abolitionist, and his direct interest in contemporary politics prior to the Civil War seems to have been limited to broadly exploring ideological and political issues in his literary works – flogging in *Redburn* and missionary work in *Typee* are two examples.

12  For example, the publication of *Redburn* and *White Jacket*.
13  In Chapter 27 Ishmael describes the crew of the *Pequod* collectively as follows, "They were nearly all Islanders in the Pequod, *Isolatoes* too, I call such, not acknowledging the common continent of men, but each *Isolato* living on a separate continent of his own. Yet now, federated along one keel, what a set these Isolatoes were!"
14  See Carolyn L. Karcher, *Shadow over the Promised Land: Slavery, Race and Violence in Melville's America* (Baton Rouge, La.: Louisiana State University Press, 1980), p. 2.

# Chronology

- Indicates events in author's life and career
* Indicates contextual events

1819
- August 1, Herman Melville born in New York City to Allan and Maria Gansevoort Melvill

1820
* Second Great Awakening begins; this was the rise of evangelical Protestantism across the US, but especially in upstate New York, resulting in the formation of dozens of sects, all of which shared a belief in deeply personal and emotional expressions of religious conversion and faith; the Missouri Compromise establishes 36°30′ as the dividing line for slavery. Any new state admitted to the Union south of this line could allow slavery

1820–50
* One direct result of the Second Great Awakening is the widespread rise of female reform groups, including temperance and abolition; the overwhelming majority of women, especially in the middle and upper classes, participated in these societies in some form (see Reynolds extract on **pp. 105–7**)

1825–30
- Herman Melville attends New York Male High School and Columbia Grammar School

1825
* Erie Canal completed allowing easier trade with western states and the frontier; publishing industry begins to grow exponentially as a result

1830
- Melville's father's business fails and family flees New York City in October, moving to Albany to escape creditors

1830–4
• October 1830 to late 1831, Herman Melville enrolled at Albany Academy; January 1832, Allan Melvill dies debt ridden; Herman, pulled from the Albany Academy in December 1831, becomes clerk at the New York State Bank in Albany where he remains until 1834
* August 1831, slaves, led by the evangelical and self-proclaimed prophet Nat Turner, kill fifty-five whites in a revolt in Virginia; following suppression of the revolt, whites kill over two hundred blacks in retaliation; Virginia briefly considers repealing slavery but the effort fails, resulting in policies of increased suppression of blacks in the state

1834–7
• May 6, 1834, Gansevoort's factory destroyed by fire; Herman Melville is pulled from bank to work for Gansevoort

1836
* Texas declares its independence from Mexico; Mexico sends its army to suppress the revolt; the Texans' victory at the battle of San Jacinto forces the Mexican army to withdraw; the New Republic of Texas is seen by the Mexican government as a rebellious province that eventually will be retaken

1837–8
• April 15, 1837 Gansevoort files for bankruptcy, another victim of the Panic of 1837; this was the first widespread economic collapse suffered in the US, resulting in the complete failure of the banking system and the financial ruin of thousands; in June 1837 Herman Melville goes to work on Uncle Thomas Melvill's farm in Pittsfield, Massachusetts; by the fall he has taken a job as schoolmaster in nearby Sikes District School where he remains through the fall term (early 1838)

1838–9
• Melville returns to Albany in January 1838; May 4 and 18, 1839, he publishes two short pieces in the *Democratic Press and Lansingburgh Advertiser*, collectively known as "Fragments from a Writing Desk"; although immature juvenilia these were Melville's first publications; June 5, 1839, unable to find work, Herman Melville sails as a common seaman aboard the *St. Lawrence*, arriving in Liverpool on July 4; he arrives back in New York City on September 30

1841–2
• Unable to land any promising position, Herman Melville signs papers as a "Green Hand" aboard the whaleship *Acushnet*, bound for the whaling grounds in the South Pacific; on July 9, 1842 Herman Melville and his friend Richard Tobias Greene are granted shore leave at Nukuhiva Bay, Marquesas, and decide to desert; Melville spends approximately one month on Nukuhiva before embarking on August 9 on the Australian whaler *Lucy Ann*; September 20, 1842, the *Lucy Ann* arrives at Tahiti and Herman

Melville is put ashore along with ten crew members accused of mutiny; by the end of October Melville has grown tired of his rather benign captivity and is able to arrange passage on yet another whaleship, the *Charles and Henry*

**1843–4**

- On April 27, 1843 the *Charles and Henry* arrives at Lahaina on the island of Maui; Herman Melville remains in Hawaii on first Maui and then Oahu. He works various odd jobs until August when he signs on as an ordinary sailor on the US frigate *United States*; the ship arrives at Boston on October 3, 1844; Melville is discharged on October 14 and after visiting with relatives in Boston, and most likely spending time with his future wife, Elizabeth Shaw, daughter of Chief Justice Lemuel Shaw of the Massachusetts Supreme Court, he returns to Lansingburgh after an absence of over three years

**1844–5**

- By December 1844 Herman Melville is living in New York City and has begun drafting a book based on his experiences in the South Pacific

**1846**

- February 26, Melville's first book is published by Murray in London as *Narrative of a Four Months' Residence among the Natives of a Valley of the Marquesas Islands*, and as *Typee* by Wiley and Putnam in New York in March as part of their Library of American Books series under the supervision of Evert Duyckinck; by August Melville is already at work on *Omoo*, the sequel to *Typee*; in the fall of this year, Melville becomes engaged to Elizabeth Shaw

**1846–8**

* US Congress votes to annex Texas and sends troops to guard the disputed border with Mexico; skirmishes between US and Mexican forces result in the US declaring war on Mexico in 1846; Mexico is defeated in a series of battles resulting in the fall of Mexico City in 1847; the Treaty of Guadalupe Hidalgo is signed in 1848 wherein Mexico agrees to cede 55 percent of its territory in exchange for 15 million dollars in compensation for war-related damage to Mexican property

**1847**

- *Omoo* is published by Murray in London in March and by the Harpers in New York in May; that summer Melville publishes in Duyckinck's *Yankee Doodle* a series of satirical attacks on the Mexican–American War, General Zachary Taylor, the Whigs, and jingoistic American expansionism; Melville and Elizabeth are married in Boston on August 4; the couple then settles in New York City

1847–8
• Herman Melville begins drafting *Mardi* by the end of 1847

1849
• A son, Malcolm, is born on February 16; *Mardi* is published by Richard Bentley in London in March and by the Harpers in New York in April; in May Melville signs the petition that precipitates the Astor Place Riot in NYC (see **pp. 22–7**); *Redburn* is published by Bentley in London in October and by the Harpers in New York in November; Melville signs a contract with the Harpers for *White Jacket* in September, and in October departs New York for London to shop *White Jacket* there

1850
• On the return voyage from England, Melville begins to plan and most likely research *Moby-Dick*; he arrives back at New York on January 31 and by the end of February has begun drafting his whale; *White Jacket* is published by Bentley in London in January and by the Harpers in New York in March; in September Melville borrows money from his father-in-law against his wife's inheritance and purchases a farm near Pittsfield which he christens *Arrowhead*; the family moves there in October
* Passage of the Compromise of 1850 and the Fugitive Slave Act by the US Congress staves off open conflict between free and slave states but only temporarily; both measures fail to please either side and tensions increase (see Melville and Antebellum America, **p. 20**)

1851
• During the winter and spring Melville continues to work on *Moby-Dick* under less than optimal circumstances; torn between his devotion to his book and the needs of his family and farm, *Moby-Dick* is finished under far from ideal circumstances (see Melville's Career and the Writing of *Moby-Dick*, **p. 9**); Melville's sixth and perhaps greatest novel is published by Bentley in London in October as *The Whale* and as *Moby-Dick* by the Harpers in New York in November; Melville's second son, Stanwix, is born October 22; by the end of the year he is planning or already at work on *Pierre*; Melville's father-in-law, Chief Justice of the Massachusetts Supreme Court Lemuel Shaw, is involved in a famous and controversial case involving a runaway slave and the Fugitive Slave Act; Shaw upholds the law, angering abolitionists throughout the North and especially in New England

1852
• The reviews of *Moby-Dick* are generally poor, if not scathing, and sales of the book are small; *Pierre* is published by the Harpers in New York in August and by Sampson Low in London in November, but it is even less of a commercial success than *Moby-Dick*

**1853**

- During the winter of 1853 Melville's family attempts unsuccessfully to secure him a US consulship; Melville's and Elizabeth's first daughter, Elizabeth, is born May 22

**1853–6**

- By the summer of 1853 Melville is writing short pieces for *Harper's New Monthly Magazine* and *Putnam's Magazine* which begin to appear in December 1853; these pieces include "Bartleby the Scrivener: A Story of Wall Street" (November and December 1853), among others; he continues to publish short pieces through 1856 when Dix and Edwards publish *The Piazza Tales*, a collection of five of the pieces written for *Putnam's*, as well as one newly written piece

**1854**

* Kansas–Nebraska Act, allowing citizens in both states to decide whether to allow slavery, effectively repeals the Missouri Compromise, infuriating Northerners already upset by the passage of the Fugitive Slave Act

**1855**

- *Israel Potter* is published by G. P. Putnam in New York after having been serialized in *Putnam's Monthly Magazine* July 1854 through March 1855, and without Melville's permission by George Routledge in London in May; a daughter, Frances, is born March 2

**1856–7**

- October 1856 to May 1857, Melville takes a trip overseas, financed by his father-in-law, to benefit his health

**1857**

- *The Confidence Man* is published by Dix and Edwards in New York in April and by Longman, Brown, Green, Longmans, and Roberts in London in early April; its commercial and critical failure results in Melville abandoning professional authorship
* Dred Scott case: in a complicated case and ruling, the US Supreme Court led by justices from Southern states rules that the Missouri Compromise is unconstitutional and that any black "whose ancestors were sold as slaves" was not entitled to the rights of a federal citizen; the court's verdict further inflamed tensions between North and South, especially outraging Northerners

**1857–60**

- Melville tries the lecture circuit for three years with no success

**1860**

* Abraham Lincoln's election to the Presidency from the free state of Illinois precipitates Southern secession; South Carolina secedes in December

1861

* April 12, Federal Fort Sumter in Charleston, South Carolina harbor is shelled by Confederates: US Civil War begins

1863

• Melville trades *Arrowhead* for his brother Allen's house in New York

1866

• Publishes several poems on the Civil War in *Harper's*; a collection of his Civil War poetry is subsequently published by the Harpers in August as *Battle-Pieces and Aspects of the War*; obtains position as customs inspector for the port of New York in December, which he retains until 1885

1876

• *Clarel*, an epic poem, is published at his Uncle Peter's expense by Putnam in June

1888

• *John Marr and Other Sailors*, a collection of poems, is printed privately as an edition of only twenty-five copies

1891

• *Timoleon* published privately through Caxton Press, a total of twenty-eight copies printed; on September 28, 1891, Melville dies and is buried in New York City, leaving a number of poems as well as *Billy Budd, Sailor*, a novella, in manuscript

# Contemporary Documents

The following excerpts from selected source materials and from Melville's letters are all related to either Melville's poetics and his struggle to write *Moby-Dick* or to the intellectual and historical trends which together are intended to represent the context within which *Moby-Dick* was written and received by nineteenth-century readers. It is hoped that the selected readings will provide the student of *Moby-Dick* with useful insight into Melville's relation to his times and to nineteenth-century print culture as a whole, and into his vision of and struggle with his whale. Except where noted, original footnotes have not been retained.

## From **Owen Chase, *The Wreck of the Whaleship Essex*** (1821), Iola Haverstick and Betty Shepard, eds, San Diego, New York, and London: Harcourt Brace & Co. (1993), 9–16

Owen Chase's narrative was widely read in the period and is the primary source for the plot of *Moby-Dick*, although what Melville does with the basic story of a whale attacking a whaleship goes far beyond the non-fiction narrative written by Chase. Most importantly perhaps, Chase's factual description of the disastrous sinking of the *Essex* reveals both just how dangerous whaling in fact was, and just how realistically Melville portrays the intricacies of such hunts throughout *Moby-Dick*. As well it represents one of Melville's principal techniques – borrowing heavily from secondary sources. For example, compare Chase's description of the attack on his ship by the whale to the dramatic action of Chapter 135 (see **pp. 173–6**).

[. .] On the 20th of November (cruising in latitude 0°40′ south, longitude 119° 0′ west), a shoal[1] of whales was discovered off the lee bow. The weather at this time was extremely fine and clear; it was about eight o'clock in the morning that

---

1   A school of fish or other marine animals.

the man at the masthead gave the usual cry of "There she blows." The ship was immediately put away, and we ran down in the direction for them. When we had got within half a mile of the place where they were observed, all our boats[2] were lowered down, manned, and we started in pursuit of the shoal. The ship, in the meantime, was brought to the wind and the main topsail hove aback to wait for us.[3] I had the harpoon in the second boat; the captain preceded me in the first.

When I arrived at the spot where we calculated they were, nothing was at first to be seen. We lay on our oars in anxious expectation of discovering them come up somewhere near us.[4] Presently one rose and spouted a short distance ahead of my boat. I made all speed towards him, came up with him, and struck him. Feeling the harpoon, he threw himself in an agony over towards the boat (which at that time was up alongside of him), and giving a severe blow with his tail, struck the boat near the edge of the water, amidships, and stove[5] a hole in her. I immediately took up the boat hatchet and cut the line from the harpoon to disengage the boat from the whale, which by this time was running off with great velocity. I succeeded in getting clear of him, with the loss of the harpoon and line, and finding the water to pour fast in the boat, I hastily stuffed three or four of our jackets in the hole, ordered one man to keep constantly bailing and the rest to pull immediately for the ship. We succeeded in keeping the boat free and shortly gained the ship. The captain and the second mate, in the other two boats, kept up the pursuit and soon struck another whale. They being at this time a considerable distance to leeward,[6] I went forward, braced around the main yard, and put the ship off in a direction for them.

The boat which had been stove was immediately hoisted in, and after examining the hole, I found that I could, by nailing a piece of canvas over it, get her ready to join in a fresh pursuit sooner than by lowering down the other remaining boat which belonged to the ship. I accordingly turned her over upon the quarter and was in the act of nailing on the canvas when I observed a very large spermaceti whale, as well as I could judge about eighty-five feet in length. He broke water about twenty rods[7] off our weather bow and was lying quietly, with his head in a direction for the ship. He spouted two or three times and then disappeared. In less than two or three seconds, he came up again, about the length of the ship off, and made directly for us at the rate of about three knots.[8] The ship was then

---

2   In proper nautical terms a "ship" is a large vessel and a "boat" is a small one, such as a rowboat or lifeboat. A true sailor never refers to a ship as a boat or vice versa.
3   Turned into the wind and the main sail dropped so the ship would cease moving.
4   When whalers approached a shoal of whales, once the whales became startled they would frequently dive. Whalers would then wait for the whales to resurface, often keeping time so as to be prepared when they did in fact rise. Coordination among the boats and the ship allowed them to position themselves so they could attempt to take a whale soon after the shoal emerged from its dive.
5   Stove: to break or smash in.
6   Down wind, making pursuit easier for the ship.
7   A rod is 5.5 yards or 5.03 meters.
8   A knot is one nautical mile and as a unit of speed is equivalent to about 1.15 miles per hour or 1.85 kilometers per hour. Here, 3.45 mph and 5.55 kph respectively – in short, rather fast for a whale.

going with about the same velocity. His appearance and attitude gave us at first no alarm, but while I stood watching his movements and observing him, but a ship's length off, coming down for us with great celerity,[9] I involuntarily ordered the boy at the helm to put it hard up, intending to sheer off and avoid him.

The words were scarcely out of my mouth before he came down upon us with full speed and struck the ship with his head, just forward of the fore-chains.[10] He gave us such an appalling and tremendous jar as nearly threw us all on our faces. The ship brought up as suddenly and violently as if she had struck a rock and trembled for a few seconds like a leaf.

We looked at each other with perfect amazement, deprived almost of the power of speech. Many minutes elapsed before we were able to realize the dreadful accident. During this time the whale passed under the ship, grazing her keel as he went along. He came up alongside of her to leeward and lay on the top of the water, apparently stunned with the violence of the blow, for the space of a minute. He then suddenly started off in a direction to leeward.

After a few moments' reflection and recovering, in some measure, from the sudden consternation that had seized us, I of course concluded that he had stove a hole in the ship and that it would be necessary to set the pumps going. Accordingly, they were rigged but had not been in operation more than one minute before I perceived the head of the ship to be gradually settling down in the water. I then ordered the signal to be set for the other boats, which scarcely had I dispatched before I again discovered the whale, apparently in convulsions, on the top of the water about one hundred rods to leeward. He was enveloped in the foam of the sea that his continual and violent thrashing about in the water had created around him, and I could distinctly see him smite his jaws together, as if distracted with rage and fury. He remained a short time in this situation and then started off with great velocity across the bow of the ship to windward.

By this time the ship had settled down a considerable distance in the water, and I gave her up as lost. I, however, ordered the pumps to be kept constantly going and endeavoured to collect my thoughts for the occasion. I turned to the boats, two of which we then had with the ship, with an intention of clearing them away and getting all things ready to embark in them if there should be no other resource left. While my attention was thus engaged for a moment, I was aroused with the cry of a man at the hatchway: "Here he is—he is making for us again."

I turned around and saw him, about one hundred rods directly ahead of us, coming down apparently with twice his ordinary speed and, it appeared to me at that moment, with tenfold fury and vengeance in his aspect. The surf flew in all directions about him, and his course towards us was marked by white foam a rod in width, which he made with the continual violent thrashing of his tail. His head was about half out of water, and in that way he came upon and again struck the ship.

I was in hopes, when I descried him making for us, that, by a dexterous[11]

---

9  Speed.
10  The chains on the bow of the ship used for hauling in the forward anchor.
11  Skillful or deft.

movement of putting the ship away immediately, I should be able to cross the line of his approach before he could get up to us and thus avoid what I knew, if he should strike us again, would prove our inevitable destruction. I bawled out to the helmsman, "Hard up!" But she had not fallen off more than a point[12] before we took the second shock. I should judge the speed of the ship to have been at this time about three knots and that of the whale about six. He struck her to windward, directly under the cathead,[13] and completely stove in her bow. He passed under the ship again, went off to leeward, and we saw no more of him.

Our situation at this juncture can be more readily imagined than described. The shock to our feelings was such as I am sure none can have an adequate conception of that were not there. The misfortune befell us at a moment when we least dreamt of any accident. From the pleasing anticipations we had formed of realizing the certain profits of our labour, we were dejected by a sudden, most mysterious, and overwhelming calamity [. . .]

We lay at this time in our boat—about two ship lengths off from the wreck—in perfect silence, calmly contemplating her situation and absorbed in our own melancholy reflections, when the other boats were discovered rowing up to us. They had but shortly before discovered that some accident had befallen us, but of the nature of it they were entirely ignorant. The sudden and mysterious disappearance of the ship was first discovered by the boat-steerer in the captain's boat. With a horror-struck countenance[14] and voice, he suddenly exclaimed: "Oh, my God! Where is the ship?"

Upon this, their operations were instantly suspended, and a general cry of horror and despair burst from the lips of every man, as their looks were directed for the ship, in vain, over every part of the ocean.

They immediately made all haste towards us. The captain's boat was the first that reached us. He stopped about a boat's length off but had no power to utter a single syllable. He was so completely overpowered with the spectacle before him that he sat down in his boat, pale and speechless. He appeared to be so much altered, awed, and overcome with the oppression of his feelings and the dreadful reality that lay before him that I could scarcely recognize his countenance. He was in a short time, however, enabled to address an inquiry to me. "My God, Mr. Chase, what is the matter?"

I answered: "We have been stove by a whale." [. . .]

12 That is, turned a point (one degree of 360) off her original course.
13 A beam projecting out from the bow or front of the ship used to support and lift the anchor.
14 The look on one's face.

From **Herman Melville, "Hawthorne and His Mosses"** (1850),
Harrison Hayford, Alma A. MacDougall, G. Thomas Tanselle et al. eds, in
*The Piazza Tales, and other Prose Pieces, 1839–1860*, Evanston and Chicago, Ill.:
Northwestern University Press and The Newberry Library, 1987

> "Hawthorne and His Mosses" not only explains Melville's rapidly coalescing
> aesthetic in detail (see Melville's Career and the Writing of *Moby-Dick*, **p. 9**), it
> is also one of the most important primary documents of American Literary
> Nationalism. Melville's close friend Evert Duyckinck was a founding member of
> the Young America movement, a group of New York writers, publishers and
> critics committed to the development of a native literature (see also Melville
> and Antebellum America, **p. 22**). Most importantly, however, "Mosses" cap-
> tures a glimpse of Melville's views on the craft and purpose of fiction writing –
> what he calls the great art of telling the truth – precisely as he was drafting his
> most ambitious work to date.

[. . .] Where Hawthorne is known, he seems to be deemed a pleasant writer, with a
pleasant style,—a sequestered, harmless man, from whom any deep and weighty
thing would hardly be anticipated:—a man who means no meanings. But there
is no man, in whom humor and love, like mountain peaks, soar to such a rapt
height, as to receive the irradiations of the upper skies;—there is no man in whom
humor and love are developed in that high form called genius; no such man can
exist without also possessing, as the indispensable complement of these, a great,
deep intellect, which drops down into the universe like a plummet.[1]
    [. . .] "The Christmas Banquet," and "The Bosom Serpent"[2] would be fine
subjects for a curious and elaborate analysis, touching the conjectural parts of
the mind that produced them. For spite of all the Indian-summer sunlight on the
hither side of Hawthorne's soul, the other side—like the dark half of the physical
sphere—is shrouded in a blackness, ten times black. But this darkness but
gives more effect to the evermoving dawn, that forever advances through it,
and circumnavigates his world. Whether Hawthorne has simply availed himself
of this mystical blackness as a means to the wondrous effects he makes it to
produce in his lights and shades; or whether there really lurks in him, perhaps
unknown to himself, a touch of Puritanic[3] gloom,—this, I cannot altogether tell.
Certain it is, however, that this great power of blackness in him derives its force
from its appeals to that Calvinistic[4] sense of Innate Depravity and Original Sin,

1  A heavy lead weight attached to the end of a line, used to measure depth.
2  Two stories by Hawthorne in his book *Mosses from an Old Manse* (1846).
3  For American readers, the Puritans conjure up images of superstition, witch burnings, and repressed
   (by even nineteenth-century standards) social mores. And as Melville goes on to explain, the
   "gloom" here also refers to their bleak Calvinistic view of human nature and fate. See n. 4 below.
4  Calvinism is a Protestant denomination established by reformer John Calvin in the sixteenth
   century. Its distinguishing tenets include election or predestination, the total depravity of man,
   complete sovereignty of God, limited atonement, and the irresistibility of grace. Melville was
   baptized in but eventually came to reject the Reformed Dutch Calvinism of his mother's family,
   the Gansevoorts (see also Transcendentalism, **pp. 41–4**).

from whose visitations, in some shape or other, no deeply thinking mind is always and wholly free. For, in certain moods, no man can weigh this world, without throwing in something, somehow like Original Sin, to strike the uneven balance. At all events, perhaps no writer has ever wielded this terrific thought with greater terror than this same harmless Hawthorne. Still more: this black conceit pervades him, through and through. You may be witched by his sunlight,—transported by the bright gildings in the skies he builds over you;—but there is the blackness of darkness beyond; and even his bright gildings but fringe, and play upon the edges of thunder-clouds.—In one word, the world is mistaken in this Nathaniel Hawthorne. He himself must often have smiled at its absurd misconception of him. He is immeasurably deeper than the plummet of the mere critic. For it is not the brain that can test such a man; it is only the heart. You cannot come to know greatness by inspecting it; there is no glimpse to be caught of it, except by intuition; you need not ring it, you but touch it, and you find it is gold.

Now it is that blackness in Hawthorne, of which I have spoken, that so fixes and fascinates me. It may be, nevertheless, that it is too largely developed in him. Perhaps he does not give us a ray of his light for every shade of his dark. But however this may be, this blackness it is that furnishes the infinite obscure of his background,—that background, against which Shakespeare plays his grandest conceits,[5] the things that have made for Shakespeare his loftiest, but most circum-scribed renown, as the profoundest of thinkers. For by philosophers Shakespeare is not adored as the great man of tragedy and comedy.—"Off with his head! so much for Buckingham!"[6] this sort of rant, interlined by another hand, brings down the house,—those mistaken souls, who dream of Shakespeare as a mere man of Richard-the-Third humps, and Macbeth daggers.[7] But it is those deep faraway things in him; those occasional flashings-forth of the intuitive Truth in him; those short, quick probings at the very axis of reality:—these are the things that make Shakespeare, Shakespeare. Through the mouths of the dark characters of Hamlet, Timon, Lear, and Iago,[8] he craftily says, or sometimes insinuates the things, which we feel to be so terrifically true, that it were all but madness for any good man, in his own proper character, to utter, or even hint of them. Tormented into desperation, Lear the frantic King tears off the mask, and speaks the sane madness of vital truth. [. . .] And if I magnify Shakespeare, it is not so much for what he did do, as for what he did not do, or refrained from doing. For in this world of lies, Truth is forced to fly like a scared white doe in the woodlands; and only by cunning glimpses will she reveal herself, as in Shakespeare and other masters of the great Art of Telling the Truth,—even though it be covertly, and by snatches. [. . .]

Let America then prize and cherish her writers; yea, let her glorify them. They

---

5   Here, an ingenious or witty idea.
6   A character in several of Shakespeare's plays; here the reference is most likely to *Richard III.*
7   Two tragedies by Shakespeare: the character King Richard III is distinguished by a humped
    back and Macbeth is haunted by visions of the daggers he has used to murder his political rivals.
    Melville's point is that such things are meant to entertain the masses (or in Shakespeare's case, the
    groundlings) but the real meaning of each play goes far beyond such dramatic embellishments.
8   Characters from *Hamlet, Timon of Athens, King Lear,* and *Othello,* respectively.

are not so many in number, as to exhaust her good-will. And while she has good kith and kin of her own, to take to her bosom, let her not lavish her embraces upon the household of an alien. For believe it or not England, after all, is, in many things, an alien to us. China has more bowels of real love for us than she. But even were there no Hawthorne, no Emerson, no Whittier, no Irving, no Bryant, no Dana, no Cooper, no Willis[9] (not the author of the "Darter," but the author of the "Belfry Pigeon")—were there none of these, and others of like calibre, nevertheless, let America first praise mediocrity even, in her own children, before she praises (for everywhere, merit demands acknowledgment from every one) the best excellence in the children of any other land. Let her own authors, I say, have the priority of appreciation. I was much pleased with a hot-headed Carolina cousin of mine, who once said,—"If there were no other American to stand by, in Literature,—why, then, I would stand by Pop Emmons and his 'Fredoniad',[10] and till a better epic came along, swear it was not very far behind the 'Iliad'."[11] Take away the words, and in spirit he was sound. [. . .]

## From **Nathaniel Hawthorne, "The Custom-House Sketch"** (1850), Preface to *The Scarlet Letter*, Columbus, Ohio: Ohio State University Press, 1962

> The excerpt from Hawthorne's "The Custom-House Sketch" is an important source for understanding the development of the form of the American novel, and especially what Melville meant when he told his publisher that *Mardi* would be a "romance." Hawthorne's description of the craft of the romancer was one with which Melville was familiar, and one which influenced him to at least some extent as he labored to transform the facts of whaling into something vastly different from his earlier travel narratives. It is also especially useful for following critical discussions of *Moby-Dick*'s genre and structure, as for several decades critics used the Romance theory of the American novel as a tool for explaining why *Moby-Dick*'s composite form violated so many established rules associated with the nineteenth-century realistic novel. (See especially **pp. 11–12** in Melville's Career and the Writing of *Moby-Dick*, and **pp. 60–1** in Critical History.)

[. . .] Moonlight, in a familiar room, falling so white upon the carpet, and showing all its figures so distinctly,—making every object so minutely visible,

---

9  Nathaniel Hawthorne (1804–64); Ralph Waldo Emerson (1803–82); John Greenleaf Whittier (1807–92), American critic and poet; Washington Irving (1783–1859); William Cullen Bryant (1794–1878), poet and editor; Richard H. Dana, Jr. (1815–82), novelist; James Fenimore Cooper (1789–1851); Nathaniel Parker Willis (1806–57), journalist, poet and friend of Melville.

10 Richard Emmons (b. 1788) wrote the *Fredoniad; or Independence Preserved—an Epic Poem of the War of 1812*, a forgettable work of jingoistic American Nationalism. Melville is here poking fun at the fervor of the nativism he is espousing.

11 Homer's *Iliad* (*c.* 700 BCE), an epic Greek poem that recounts events set during the Trojan War (*c.* 1200 BCE).

yet so unlike a morning or noontide visibility,—is a medium the most suitable for a romance-writer to get acquainted with his illusive guests. There is the little domestic scenery of the well-known apartment; the chairs, with each its separate individuality; the centre-table, sustaining a work-basket, a volume or two, and an extinguished lamp; the sofa; the book-case; the picture on the wall;—all these details, so completely seen, are so spiritualized by the unusual light, that they seem to lose their actual substance, and become things of intellect. Nothing is too small or too trifling to undergo this change, and acquire dignity thereby. A child's shoe; the doll, seated in her little wicker carriage; the hobby-horse;—whatever, in a word, has been used or played with, during the day, is now invested with a quality of strangeness and remoteness, though still almost as vividly present as by daylight. Thus, therefore, the floor of our familiar room has become a neutral territory, somewhere between the real world and fairyland, where the Actual and the Imaginary may meet, and each imbue itself with the nature of the other. Ghosts might enter here, without affrighting us. It would be too much in keeping with the scene to excite surprise, were we to look about us and discover a form, beloved, but gone hence, now sitting quietly in a streak of this magic moonshine, with an aspect that would make us doubt whether it had returned from afar, or had never once stirred from our fireside.

The somewhat dim coal-fire has an essential influence in producing the effect which I would describe. It throws its unobtrusive[1] tinge throughout the room, with a faint ruddiness upon the walls and ceiling, and a reflected gleam from the polish of the furniture. This warmer light mingles itself with the cold spirituality of the moonbeams, and communicates, as it were, a heart and sensibilities of human tenderness to the forms which fancy summons up. It converts them from snow-images into men and women. Glancing at the looking-glass, we behold— deep within its haunted verge—the smouldering glow of the half-extinguished anthracite,[2] the white moonbeams on the floor, and a repetition of all the gleam and shadow of the picture, with one remove farther from the actual, and nearer to the imaginative. Then, at such an hour, and with this scene before him, if a man, sitting all alone, cannot dream strange things, and make them look like truth, he need never try to write romances. [. . .]

## Transcendentalism

Transcendentalism can best be understood as an intellectual movement centered in New England whose most important historical contexts were the general impact of science and secularization on orthodox religious belief in Europe and the US, especially as this intensified throughout the eighteenth and nineteenth centuries, and the influx of European Romanticism, especially German philosophy and literature, to the US throughout the first decades of the nineteenth century.

---

1 Here, mild, nonglaring, soft light.
2 Coal.

The term "Transcendental" was the semi-official name of an informal club formed in 1836 by Ralph Waldo Emerson and several other like-minded young men. The term itself came from German philosopher Immanuel Kant's *Critique of Practical Reason* (1788), wherein Kant had stated, "I call all knowledge transcendental which is concerned, not with objects, but with our mode of knowing objects so far as this is possible *a priori*." Emerson's group decided to meet regularly to discuss and nurture the development of a nascent movement among Unitarian clergy to broaden Unitarian theology to include European philosophical and literary ideas. Historically, orthodox Unitarianism had emerged as the result of a split in the Congregationalist Church (the direct descendant of the Puritan Church in the US) concerning the Calvinist belief in innate depravity. Prior to the maturation of American Protestantism during the Second Great Awakening (roughly 1820–50; see Chronology, **p. 28**) Calvinist doctrine dominated Protestant sects in the US, especially in the New England region. Schematically, it held that all of humanity was innately depraved due to original sin. The vast majority of humankind was thus predestined to eternal damnation and only a select few would ever receive divine grace and thus salvation from an eternity of suffering. As well, even the few elected through God's grace were undeserving of such salvation regardless of their works on earth, nor could any mere mortal ever hope to come to an understanding of either God or His divine will.

Increasingly, liberal Unitarian ministers under the influence of the Enlightenment, especially as it was filtered through the discourse of the American Revolution, found such a belief to be both morbid and superstitious. Some even argued it was inconsistent if not dangerous in a Republic founded on classical liberalism and respect for individual rights. The influential Unitarian minister William Ellery Channing (1780–1842) had gone so far as to argue in an 1820 essay that as for Calvinism, "It is plain that a doctrine which contradicts our best ideas of goodness and justice, cannot come from the just and good God, or be a true representation of his character." Unitarianism thus emerged as an example of what religious historian Gerald Bray has termed the "rational orthodoxy," religious sects that "sought to harmonize basic Christian doctrine with the findings of natural science" rather than reject either science or religion entirely. As part of this general class of reactions among the devout to advances in the sciences, Unitarians believed that religious truths could be arrived at by empirical study and rational inference making. Young Unitarian ministers like Emerson were thus extremely receptive to such advances as historical-critical analysis of scripture, the so-called German "High Criticism" method of exegesis which attempted to interpret scripture from a concrete understanding of its historical context. Moses, for example, was treated by such critics as a real historical figure (albeit inspired by God) who could not but have drawn on established Hebrew practices and laws as he drafted the Pentateuch – the first five books of the Old Testament traditionally believed to have been written by the Jewish patriarch.

Equally important for understanding Transcendentalism, by the first few decades of the nineteenth century young Unitarian clergy were coming under the influence of the European Romanticism of such writers as Coleridge, Carlyle,

Goethe and Kant – especially Carlyle and his translations of and critical essays on various German philosophers, poets, and novelists (see Howard extract, pp. 88–90). Orthodox Unitarians saw themselves as enlightened Christians espousing a rational orthodoxy that attempted to reconcile basic Christian doctrines with advances in the natural sciences, including archeology and geology. Contrastingly, Transcendentalists saw themselves as the vanguard of European thought in America and as capable of bringing about a final revolution in American theology, one that elicited a complete break with the Unitarian Church's ties to its gloomy Puritanical past and to what they saw as orthodox Unitarianism's failed attempt to rationalize the belief in the divine.

In place of the rational empiricism of Locke which dominated orthodox Unitarian doctrine, the Transcendentalists combined the philosophical idealism of Kant and the Neoplatonists with the Romantic celebration of the sanctity of the individual, especially the latter's belief that nature was itself a link to and symbol of the divine. Like many spiritual movements throughout the Second Great Awakening, Transcendentalists believed that man could have direct experience of the holy. And although Transcendental writers like Emerson at times could sound as if they were talking about the very sort of "revival" of man's close, personal relationship to the divine and of conversion being celebrated with great fervor by the emergent evangelical sects, their own intellectual traditions, as well as their enthusiasm for the English and German Romantics, gave Transcendentalism a set of intellectual teeth unlike any other religious sect or community. The bewildering array of low-church Protestant sects mushrooming across the US were for the most part inherently and dogmatically anti-intellectual, treating scripture as literal truth. Emerson and other Transcendentalists, contrastingly, were trained in a rich tradition both oral and literary and saw such figures as Carlyle and Goethe as ideal models of their own religious, cultural and intellectual practices. Carlyle's philosophy in particular, in actuality a set of loosely related but rigorously interrogated opinions on everything from politics to philosophy, was just the sort of intellectual cultivation of the self that was a central tenet of Unitarian belief. Unitarians traditionally believed that all humankind should strive for self-improvement, cultivating the divine essence that existed in all men and which connected them to nature. Following the Neoplatonists, nature was seen as a universal sign or symbol of the spiritual universe, part of what Emerson would eventually call the Oversoul. Most importantly, it was not through rational observation and reflection that one could come in contact with the godhead but through direct experience of the divine in moments of apperception that transcended rational states of consciousness (see extract from Emerson's *Nature*, p. 45). The individual was thus the spiritual center of the universe and duplicated the structure of the universe internally.

Melville read and admired Carlyle, Coleridge and the German idealists, and as the letter following the excerpts by Emerson below makes clear, once saw Emerson speak and admired him greatly. And as Merton M. Sealts Jr. notes in his essay "Melville and Emerson's Rainbow," excerpted in the present volume (see pp. 85–8):

However much or little of Emerson Melville had read by 1850 and 1851, he obviously knew other Transcendental scripture, and it seems safe to say that his reading of one book in particular—Carlyle's *Sartor Resartus*, with its central idea of "all visible things" as "emblems" of the invisible, and of Nature itself as *"the living visible Garment of God"*— had at least as much to do with the symbolism of *Moby-Dick* as anything in the "Language" chapter of Emerson's *Nature*.

In other words, Emerson's correspondence theory of language – the idea that words and the things they represent have a necessary relation – as well as his idealist philosophy espousing close correspondences among self, nature, and Spirit or the ideal are just two of the many ideas Melville explores in *Moby-Dick*. And if the Emersonian self-reliant hero is original in all respects, someone who almost compulsively breaks with convention, then Ahab is the self-reliant man unleashed on democratic society and Melville himself the consummate self-reliant artist (see extracts from Niemeyer, **pp. 100–3** and Alvis, **pp. 103–4**). Ahab's utterances often read like the manic sermons of an American frontier preacher intoxicated by the ideas of leading German philosophers such as Kant and Hegel, both of whom influenced Emerson's Transcendental philosophy.

The excerpts from two of Emerson's most famous works, "Self-Reliance" and *Nature*, as well as Melville's letter to Duyckinck describing his reaction to seeing Emerson lecture (see **p. 48**), provide insight into Melville's attitude toward Transcendentalism, one of the leading American intellectual movements of the day and the version of German Idealism with which Melville was perhaps most familiar. Notice also Melville's reiteration of his commitment to the idea of Art as a search for Truth in the letter to Duyckinck about Emerson. (See especially Chapter 70, "The Sphinx" on **pp. 159–60**, and extract from Sealts, **pp. 85–8**.)

## From **Ralph Waldo Emerson, "Self-Reliance"** (1841), The Norton Anthology of American Literature, 5th edition, Nina Baym ed., New York: Norton, 1999

I read the other day some verses written by an eminent painter which were original and not conventional. Always the soul hears an admonition[1] in such lines, let the subject be what it may. The sentiment they instil is of more value than any thought they may contain. To believe your own thought, to believe that what is true for you in your private heart, is true for all men,—that is genius. Speak your latent conviction and it shall be the universal sense; for always the inmost becomes the outmost,—and our first thought is rendered back to us by

1   Mild rebuke or warning.

the trumpets of the Last Judgment. Familiar as the voice of the mind is to each, the highest merit we ascribe to Moses, Plato, and Milton,[2] is that they set at naught books and traditions, and spoke not what men wrote but what they thought. A man should learn to detect and watch that gleam of light which flashes across his mind from within, more than the lustre of the firmament of bards and sages. Yet he dismisses without notice his thought, because it is his. In every work of genius we recognize our own rejected thoughts: they come back to us with a certain alienated majesty. Great works of art have no more affecting lesson for us than this. They teach us to abide by our spontaneous impression with good humored inflexibility when the whole cry of voices is on the other side. [. . .]

There is a time in every man's education when he arrives at the conviction that envy is ignorance; that imitation is suicide; that he must take himself for better, for worse, as his portion; that though the wide universe is full of good, no kernel of nourishing corn can come to him but through his toil bestowed on that plot of ground which is given to him to till. [. . .]

[. . .] Society everywhere is in conspiracy against the manhood[3] of every one of its members. Society is a joint-stock company[4] in which the members agree for the better securing of his bread to each shareholder, to surrender the liberty and culture of the eater. The virtue in most request is conformity. Self-reliance is its aversion. It loves not realities and creators, but names and customs.

[. . .] What I must do, is all that concerns me, not what the people think. This rule, equally arduous[5] in actual and in intellectual life, may serve for the whole distinction between greatness and meanness.[6] It is the harder, because you will always find those who think they know what is your duty better than you know it. It is easy in the world to live after the world's opinion; it is easy in solitude to live after our own; but the great man is he who in the midst of the crowd keeps with perfect sweetness the independence of solitude. [. . .]

From **Ralph Waldo Emerson, *Nature*** (1836), The Norton Anthology of American Literature, 5th edition, Nina Baym ed., New York: Norton, 1999

[. . .] Philosophically considered, the universe is composed of Nature and the Soul. Strictly speaking, therefore, all that is separate from us, all which Philosophy distinguishes as the NOT ME,[1] that is, both nature and art, all other men and my

---

2   Moses: Jewish patriarch who in Judeo-Christian tradition led the Israelites out of bondage in Egypt
    *c.* thirteenth century BCE; Plato (*c.* 427–347 BCE) Greek philosopher; John Milton (1608–74)),
    English poet whose best-known work is the epic poem *Paradise Lost* (1667).
3   Here, individuality.
4   A business whose shares are held equally by several owners.
5   Here, difficult to follow or live by.
6   Meanness: here, what is common, low.

---

1   Emerson takes "not me" from Thomas Carlyle's *Sartor Resartus* (1833–4), where it appears as a
    translation of the recent German philosophical term for everything but the self.

own body, must be ranked under this name, NATURE. In enumerating the values of nature and casting up their sum, I shall use the word in both senses;—in its common and in its philosophical import. In inquiries so general as our present one, the inaccuracy is not material; no confusion of thought will occur. *Nature*, in the common sense, refers to essences unchanged by man; space, the air, the river, the leaf. *Art*[2] is applied to the mixture of his will with the same things, as in a house, a canal, a statue, a picture. But his operations taken together are so insignificant, a little chipping, baking, patching, and washing, that in an impression so grand as that of the world on the human mind, they do not vary the result. [. . .]

When we speak of nature in this manner, we have a distinct but most poetical sense in the mind. We mean the integrity of impression made by manifold natural objects. It is this which distinguishes the stick of timber of the wood-cutter, from the tree of the poet. [. . .]

[. . .] In the woods, we return to reason and faith. There I feel that nothing can befal me in life,—no disgrace, no calamity, (leaving me my eyes,) which nature cannot repair. Standing on the bare ground,—my head bathed by the blithe air, and uplifted into infinite space,—all mean egotism[3] vanishes. I become a transparent eye-ball. I am nothing. I see all. The currents of the Universal Being circulate through me; I am part or particle of God. The name of the nearest friend sounds then foreign and accidental. To be brothers, to be acquaintances,—master or servant, is then a trifle and a disturbance. I am the lover of uncontained and immortal beauty. In the wilderness, I find something more dear and connate than in streets or villages. In the tranquil landscape, and especially in the distant line of the horizon, man beholds somewhat as beautiful as his own nature. [. . .]

## From **Ralph Waldo Emerson,** *Nature*: **"Chapter IV. Language"**
(1836), The Norton Anthology of American Literature, 5th edition, Nina Baym ed., New York: Norton, 1999

A third use which Nature subserves to man is that of Language. Nature is the vehicle of thought, and in a simple, double, and threefold degree.

1. Words are Signs of natural facts.
2. Particular natural facts are symbols of particular spiritual facts.
3. Nature is the symbol of spirit.

  1. Words are signs of natural facts. The use of natural history is to give us aid in supernatural history.[1] The use of the outer creation is to give us language for

2   Art, here more akin to craft or skill than imaginative expression.
3   Here, subjectivity or solipsism.

1   Here, the world of Spirit, or in Emerson's terms, the Oversoul.

the beings and changes of the inward creation. Every word which is used to express a moral or intellectual fact, if traced to its root, is found to be borrowed from some material appearance. *Right* originally means *straight; wrong* means *twisted. Spirit* primarily means *wind; transgression*, the crossing of a *line; supercilious*, the *raising of the eye-brow*. We say the *heart* to express emotion, the *head* to denote thought; and *thought* and *emotion* are, in their turn, words borrowed from sensible things, and now appropriated to spiritual nature. Most of the process by which this transformation is made, is hidden from us in the remote time when language was framed; but the same tendency may be daily observed in children. Children and savages[2] use only nouns or names of things, which they continually convert into verbs, and apply to analogous mental acts.

2.   But this origin of all words that convey a spiritual import,—so conspicuous a fact in the history of language,—is our least debt to nature. It is not words only that are emblematic; it is things which are emblematic. Every natural fact is a symbol of some spiritual fact. Every appearance in nature Corresponds to some state of the mind, and that state of the mind can only be described by presenting that natural appearance as its picture. An enraged man is a lion, a cunning man is a fox, a firm man is a rock, a learned man is a torch. A lamb is innocence; a snake is subtle spite; flowers express to us the delicate affections. Light and darkness are our familiar expression for knowledge and ignorance; and heat for love. Visible distance behind and before us, is respectively our image of memory and hope.

Who looks upon a river in a meditative hour, and is not reminded of the flux of all things? Throw a stone into the stream, and the circles that propagate themselves are the beautiful type of all influence. Man is conscious of a universal soul within or behind his individual life, wherein, as in a firmament, the natures of Justice, Truth, Love, Freedom, arise and shine. This universal soul, he calls Reason: it is not mine or thine or his, but we are its; we are its property and men. And the blue sky in which the private earth is buried, the sky with its eternal calm, and full of everlasting orbs, is the type of Reason. That which, intellectually considered, we call Reason, considered in relation to nature, we call Spirit. Spirit is the Creator. Spirit hath life in itself. And man in all ages and countries, embodies it in his language, as the FATHER. [. . .][3]

Because of this radical correspondence between visible things and human thoughts, savages, who have only what is necessary, converse in figures. As we go back in history, language becomes more picturesque, until its infancy, when it is all poetry; or, all spiritual facts are represented by natural symbols. The same symbols are found to make the original elements of all languages. It has moreover been observed, that the idioms of all languages approach each other in passages of the greatest eloquence and power. And as this is the first language, so is it the last. This immediate dependence of language upon nature, this conversion of an outward phenomenon into a type of somewhat in human life, never loses its

2    Mildly pejorative term for primitive peoples.
3    One of many expressions of Emerson's philosophical idealism as derived from his reading of German Romanticism and philosophy. Schematically, idealism is the view that mind or spirit constitutes the fundamental reality as opposed to the empirical world of the senses.

power to affect us. It is this which gives that piquancy[4] to the conversation of a strong natured farmer or back-woodsman, which all men relish.

[. . .] Hundreds of writers may be found in every long-civilized nation, who for a short time believe, and make others believe, that they see and utter truths, who do not of themselves clothe one thought in its natural garment, but who feed unconsciously upon the language created by the primary writers of the country, those, namely, who hold primarily on nature.

But wise men pierce this rotten diction and fasten words again to visible things; so that picturesque language is at once a commanding certificate that he who employs it, is a man in alliance with truth and God. The moment our discourse rises above the ground line of familiar facts, and is inflamed with passion or exalted by thought, it clothes itself in images. A man conversing in earnest, if he watch his intellectual processes, will find that always a material image, more or less luminous, arises in his mind, contemporaneous with every thought, which furnishes the vestment of the thought. Hence, good writing and brilliant discourse are perpetual allegories.[5] This imagery is spontaneous. It is the blending of experience with the present action of the mind. It is proper creation. It is the working of the Original Cause through the instruments he has already made. [. . .]

# Selected Letters[1]

## From **Melville to Evert A. Duyckinck**, March 3, 1848

Nay, I do not oscillate in Emerson's rainbow, but prefer rather to hang myself in mine own halter than swing in any other man's swing.[2] Yet I think Emerson is more than a brilliant fellow.[3] Be his stuff begged, borrowed, or stolen, or of his own domestic manufacture he is an uncommon man. Swear he is a humbug[4]—then is he no common humbug. Lay it down that had not Sir Thomas Browne[5] lived, Emerson would not have mystified—I will answer, that had not Old Zack's

---

4    Spiciness or pungency. Here, colorful use of colloquial expressions bordering on the risqué.
5    Emerson's point here is that because there is a necessary relation between signifier and signified, between words and the objects they represent, language is allegorical and not ambiguously figurative. Also, as he outlines presently, the original cause (Spirit, God) is manifest in its effects, in this case language as an expression of thought, which is always also an expression of truth or Spirit.

---

1    Melville was a notoriously poor speller as well as found of neologisms – words he made up to suit his own purposes. Idiosyncratic diction and spellings have been retained in the letters.
2    Melville's point is that he's no transcendentalist, and certainly no follower of Emerson. Yet as he goes on to explain, he greatly admires "all men who dive"; that is, all men who search for the truth.
3    See Letter, Melville to Nathaniel Hawthorne, April 16, 1851 on **pp. 49–51**.
4    A charlatan or fake.
5    Sir Thomas Browne, an English essayist who wrote on death, the divine and ethics in an extremely personal and idiosyncratic style. Melville read both Browne and his French counterpart Montaigne, and shared with both men a deep interest in philosophical questions as well as an almost breezy and whimsical (one could say "Ishmaelian") style of investigating such questions.

father begot him, Old Zack[6] would never have been the hero of Palo Alto.[7] The truth is that we are all sons, grandsons, or nephews or great-nephews of those who go before us. No one is his own sire.—I was very agreeably disappointed in M[r] Emerson. I had heard of him as full of transcendentalisms, myths & oracular gibberish; I had only glanced at a book[8] of his once in Putnam's store—that was all I knew of him, till I heard him lecture.—To my surprise, I found him quite intelligible, tho' to say truth, they told me that that night he was unusually plain.

——Now, there is a something about every man elevated above mediocrity, which is, for the most part, instinctively perceptible. This I see in M[r] Emerson. And, frankly, for the sake of the argument, let us call him a fool;—then had I rather be a fool than a wise man.—I love all men who *dive*.[9] Any fish can swim near the surface, but it takes a great whale to go down stairs five miles or more; & if he dont attain the bottom, why, all the lead in Galena[10] can't fashion the plummet that will. I'm not talking of M[r] Emerson now—but of the whole corps of thought-divers, that have been diving & coming up again with blood-shot eyes since the world began. [. . .]

—I would to God Shakspeare had lived later, & promenaded in Broadway.[11] Not that I might have had the pleasure of leaving my card for him at the Astor,[12] or made merry with him over a bowl of the fine Duyckinck punch; but that the muzzle which all men wore on their souls in the Elizebethan day, might not have intercepted Shakspere's full articulations.[13] For I hold it a verity,[14] that even Shakspeare, was not a frank man to the uttermost. And, indeed, who in this intolerant Universe is, or can be? But the Declaration of Independence makes a difference.—There, I have driven my horse so hard that I have made my inn before sundown. I was going to say something more—It was this.—You complain that Emerson tho' a denizen of the land of gingerbread, is above munching a plain cake in company of jolly fellows, & swiging off his ale like you & me. Ah, my dear sir, that's his misfortune, not his fault. His belly, sir, is in his chest, & his brains descend down into his neck, & offer an obstacle to a draught of ale or a mouthful of cake. But here I am. Good bye.

## From **Melville to Nathaniel Hawthorne**, April 16, 1851

The letters to Hawthorne offer a window into Melville's psyche as he unfolded within himself as a writer of imaginative fiction, providing important insight into his developing poetics. Melville and Hawthorne were close friends

---

6  Zachary Taylor, "hero" of the Mexican–American War and eventual US President. Melville, along with most American intellectuals, was opposed to the first major US war of colonial expansion.
7  Battle in the Mexican–American War (1846–8). See **p. 20** in Melville and Antebellum America.
8  See extract from Sealts (**pp. 85–8**) for a discussion of Melville's reading of Emerson.
9  See also **p. 153** for a discussion of Melville and the search for truth vis-à-vis *Moby-Dick*.
10  Galena, Illinois, a major area of lead mining in the US.
11  Major street in New York, center of fashionable public life.
12  Major hotel in New York City.
13  That is, not everyone in Shakespeare's day would have fully understood the meanings of his plays.
14  A truth.

(although some critics question the extent to which Hawthorne returned Melville's admiration), and *Moby-Dick* is dedicated fondly to Melville's mentor. Notice, for example, how *Moby-Dick* and its narrator compare to the poetic and philosophic principles espoused in the letters, especially Melville's claim that what he most admires in Hawthorne is his tendency to say "NO! in thunder" – to, in effect, defy conventional wisdom.

[. . .] There is a certain tragic phase of humanity which, in our opinion, was never more powerfully embodied than by Hawthorne. We mean the tragicalness of human thought in its own unbiased, native, and profounder workings. We think that into no recorded mind has the intense feeling of the visable truth ever entered more deeply than into this man's. By visable truth, we mean the apprehension of the absolute condition of present things as they strike the eye of the man who fears them not, though they do their worst to him,—the man who, like Russia or the British Empire, declares himself a sovereign nature (in himself) amid the powers of heaven, hell, and earth.[1] He may perish; but so long as he exists he insists upon treating with all Powers upon an equal basis. If any of those other Powers choose to withhold certain secrets, let them; that does not impair my sovereignty in myself; that does not make me tributary. And perhaps, after all, there is *no* secret. We incline to think that the Problem of the Universe is like the Freemason's mighty secret, so terrible to all children. It turns out, at last, to consist in a triangle, a mallet, and an apron,—nothing more! We incline to think that God cannot explain His own secrets, and that He would like a little information upon certain points Himself. We mortals astonish Him as much as He us. But it is this *Being* of the matter; there lies the knot with which we choke ourselves. As soon as you say *Me*, a *God*, a *Nature*, so soon you jump off from your stool and hang from the beam. Yes, that word is the hangman. Take God out of the dictionary, and you would have Him in the street.

There is the grand truth about Nathaniel Hawthorne. He says NO! in thunder; but the Devil himself cannot make him say *yes*. For all men who say *yes*, lie; and all men who say *no*,—why, they are in the happy condition of judicious, unincumbered travellers in Europe; they cross the frontiers into Eternity with nothing but a carpet-bag,[2]—that is to say, the Ego. Whereas those *yes*-gentry, they travel with heaps of baggage, and, damn them! they will never get through the Custom House. What's the reason, Mr. Hawthorne, that in the last stages of metaphysics a fellow always falls to *swearing* so? I could rip an hour. You see, I

---

1   For a useful discussion of Melville and empire see Wai Chee Dimock, *Empire for Liberty: Melville and the Poetics of Individualism* (Princeton, N.J.: Princeton University Press, 1989).
2   Small satchel or duffel bag. Presumably, because those who say "NO!" do not lie, they do not blaspheme. Because they do not blaspheme, they go to heaven without being washed down by the baggage of sin. However, the whole passage is deeply ironic and in fact blasphemous by nineteenth-century standards because to say "No" is to refute conventional religious and ethical thinking.

began with a little criticism extracted for your benefit from the "Pittsfield Secret Review," and here I have landed in Africa [. . .][3]

## From **Melville to Nathaniel Hawthorne**, [June 1?], 1851

[. . .] It is but nature to be shy of a mortal who boldly declares that a thief in jail is as honorable a personage as Gen. George Washington.[1] This is ludicrous. But Truth is the silliest thing under the sun. Try to get a living by the Truth—and go to the Soup Societies. Heavens! Let any clergyman try to preach the Truth from its very stronghold, the pulpit, and they would ride him out of his church on his own pulpit bannister. It can hardly be doubted that all Reformers are bottomed upon the truth, more or less; and to the world at large are not reformers almost universally laughing-stocks? Why so? Truth is ridiculous to men [. . .]

[. . .] In a week or so, I go to New York, to bury myself in a third-story room, and work and slave on my "Whale" while it is driving through the press. *That* is the only way I can finish it now,—I am so pulled hither and thither by circumstances. The calm, the coolness, the silent grass-growing mood in which a man *ought* always to compose,—that, I fear, can seldom be mine. Dollars damn me; and the malicious Devil is forever grinning in upon me, holding the door ajar. My dear Sir, a presentiment[2] is on me,—I shall at last be worn out and perish, like an old nutmeg-grater, grated to pieces by the constant attrition of the wood, that is, the nutmeg. What I feel most moved to write, that is banned,—it will not pay. Yet, altogether, write the *other* way I cannot. So the product is a final hash, and all my books are botches. I'm rather sore, perhaps, in this letter; but see my hand!— four blisters on this palm, made by hoes and hammers within the last few days. It is a rainy morning; so I am indoors, and all work suspended. I feel cheerfully disposed, and therefore I write a little bluely. Would the Gin[3] were here! If ever, my dear Hawthorne, in the eternal times that are to come, you and I shall sit down in Paradise, in some little shady corner by ourselves; and if we shall by any means be able to smuggle a basket of champagne there (I won't believe in a Temperance Heaven[4]), and if we shall then cross our celestial legs in the celestial grass that is forever tropical, and strike our glasses and our heads together, till both musically ring in concert,—then, O my dear fellow-mortal, how shall we pleasantly discourse of all the things manifold which now so distress us,—when all the earth shall be but a reminiscence, yea, its final dissolution an antiquity. Then shall songs be composed as when wars are over; humorous, comic songs,—"Oh, when I lived

---

3  In other words, started out discussing one topic and ended up discussing a completely different one.

---

1  American Revolutionary General and hero; first President of the United States.
2  Premonition.
3  That is, would we had a bottle of gin here to share between us. Both Hawthorne and Melville enjoyed their liquor.
4  An oblique reference to the temperance movements sweeping the country. See p. 28 in Chronology.

in that queer little hole called the world," or, "Oh, when I toiled and sweated below," or, "Oh, when I knocked and was knocked in the fight"—yes, let us look forward to such things. Let us swear that, though now we sweat, yet it is because of the dry heat which is indispensable to the nourishment of the vine which is to bear the grapes that are to give us the champagne hereafter. [. . .]

## From **Melville to Nathaniel Hawthorne**, November 1851

[. . .] Your letter[1] was handed me last night on the road going to Mr. Morewood's, and I read it there. Had I been at home, I would have sat down at once and answered it. In me divine magnanimities[2] are spontaneous and instantaneous — catch them while you can. The world goes round, and the other side comes up. So now I can't write what I felt. But I felt pantheistic[3] then—your heart beat in my ribs and mine in yours, and both in God's. A sense of unspeakable security is in me this moment, on account of your having understood the book.[4] I have written a wicked book, and feel spotless as the lamb. Ineffable socialities are in me. I would sit down and dine with you and all the gods in old Rome's Pantheon.[5] It is a strange feeling—no hopefulness is in it, no despair. Content—that is it; and irresponsibility; but without licentious inclination. I speak now of my profoundest sense of being, not of an incidental feeling.

Whence come you, Hawthorne? By what right do you drink from my flagon[6] of life? And when I put it to my lips—lo, they are yours and not mine. I feel that the Godhead[7] is broken up like the bread at the Supper, and that we are the pieces.[8] Hence this infinite fraternity of feeling. Now, sympathizing with the paper, my angel turns over another page. You did not care a penny for the book. But, now and then as you read, you understood the pervading thought that impelled the book—and that you praised. Was it not so? You were archangel enough to despise the imperfect body, and embrace the soul. Once you hugged the ugly Socrates[9] because you saw the flame in the mouth, and heard the rushing of the demon,—the familiar,—and recognized the sound; for you have heard it in your own solitudes.

My dear Hawthorne, the atmospheric skepticisms steal into me now, and make me doubtful of my sanity in writing you thus. But, believe me, I am not mad, most

1    A lost letter from Hawthorne to Melville expressing admiration for *Moby-Dick*.
2    Magnanimity: extremely liberal generosity of spirit. Melville's use is idiosyncratic.
3    A belief in and/or worship of all gods.
4    *Moby-Dick*; the letter from Hawthorne to which Melville is responding is lost.
5    Melville had not visited Rome at the writing of this letter. He would first visit Italy on a trip 1856–7. See **p. 32** in Chronology.
6    A large vessel, usually for wine or liquor, with a handle and a spout.
7    The essence or spirit of God.
8    An allusion to the Last Supper but also to the Catholic mass where the bread of the Eucharist (called the "host") is broken up by the priest and placed on the tongue of each member of the congregation. According to Catholic doctrine, the wine and bread are transformed at this moment into the body and blood of Jesus.
9    Socrates (469–399 BCE), famous Greek philosopher who was notoriously unattractive.

noble Festus![10] But truth is ever incoherent, and when the big hearts strike together, the concussion is a little stunning. Farewell. Don't write a word about the book. That would be robbing me of my miserly delight. I am heartily sorry I ever wrote anything about you—it was paltry. Lord, when shall we be done growing? As long as we have anything more to do, we have done nothing. So, now, let us add Moby Dick to our blessing, and step from that. Leviathan is not the biggest fish;—I have heard of Krakens.[11] [. . .]

## From **Melville to Sarah Huyler Morewood**, September 1851[1]

The letter to Sarah Morewood, a close friend of both Melville and Hawthorne, provides primary evidence for discussions of *Moby-Dick* and gender. Middle-class women formed the largest audience for fiction in the period, and Melville here seems to be claiming that his book will by no means be well received by this readership. Yet the traditional image of Melville as a "masculine" writer in conflict with female readers and female writers is no longer as tenable as it may have once been. Indeed, his very next book, *Pierre*, would be targeted for precisely this audience. (See especially extracts from Schultz, "The Sentimental Subtext of *Moby-Dick*: Melville's Response to the 'World of Woe'" on **pp. 109–12**, and from Person, "Melville's Cassock: Putting on Masculinity in *Moby-Dick*" on **pp. 113–15**.)

If to receive some thoughtful kindness from one, upon whom self-delusion whispers we have some claims,—if this be so agreeable to us; then how far more delightful, to be the recipient of amiable offices from one who has claims upon ourselves, not we upon them. This indeed is to sow the true seed of Christianity among all the asperities[2] of mankind; this converts infidels, & gives misanthropy no foot to stand on.[3] [. . .]

Concerning my own forthcoming book—it is off my hands, but must cross the sea before publication here. Dont you buy it—dont you read it, when it does come

---

10 Porcius Festus was the Roman procurator or civil administrator of Judea (AD 60–2). In Acts, Festus finds Paul in prison and gives him a fair hearing before sending him to Rome where tradition holds he was martyred. Here Melville is asking Hawthorne to hear him out and not judge him prematurely.

11 The reference here is to *Pierre; or The Ambiguities*, the book Melville was already at work on as reviews of *Moby-Dick* began to appear in the press. A Kraken is a huge sea monster according to Scandinavian legend. Critics interpret this reference as an indication that Melville believed his next book, *Pierre*, would be even more ambitious than *Moby-Dick*.

---

1  Morewood was a friend of both Hawthorne and Melville who lived near Arrowhead and with whom either or both men may have been romantically involved.

2  Harsh or ill-tempered aspects of humanity, especially ill-tempered people.

3  Kindness converts unbelievers and allows no excuse for hating mankind.

out, because it is by no means the sort of book for you. It is not a peice of fine feminine Spitalfields silk[4]—but is of the horrible texture of a fabric that should be woven of ships' cables & hausers.[5] A Polar wind blows through it, & birds of prey hover over it. Warn all gentle fastidious people from so much as peeping into the book—on risk of a lumbago & sciatics.[6] [. . .]

4   Fine silk manufactured in Spitalfields, England, the center of silk weaving in Britain from about 1700 to 1860 when trade wars with France decimated English weavers.
5   Hawsers: large ropes used for towing.
6   Lumbago, pain in the lower back; sciatics, pain down the leg as a result of irritation of the sciatic nerve.

# 2

# Interpretations

# Critical History

The challenges *Moby-Dick* presents to professional critics and scholars are as daunting as those faced by first-time readers of Melville's great work – only of a different order. *Moby-Dick* is a dense, highly wrought, highly allusive and fractured narrative, with a highly complicated publication history as described in Section 1. And as is made clear throughout the novel, including Chapter 99, "The Doubloon" (see **pp. 165–9**), the limits of human knowledge and of language as an effective tool for making sense of the empirical world are two of the novel's major themes. As Flask notes while observing several crew members interpreting the doubloon nailed to the ship's mast, "There's another rendering now; but still one text. All sorts of men in one kind of world, you see . . . Here's the ship's navel, this doubloon here, and they are all on fire to unscrew it. But, unscrew your navel,[1] and what's the consequence?" (see **p. 168**). Applying Flask's logic to *Moby-Dick*, the reader is faced with the following conundrum, "How does one interpret a book that questions the very feasibility of interpretation itself?" This question hangs over the book and over any interpretive analysis of it, and is one reason the novel has defied comprehensive analysis by any single critical approach. As a result, it is especially difficult to identify any major trends per se in *Moby-Dick* criticism over the last eighty years without representing as relatively homogeneous that which is inherently diverse – and often contentious. Although interpretive issues vis-à-vis the novel's ideational content abound, the first generation of Melville scholars devoted most of their collective energy to the biographical, historical, and textual issues discussed in Contexts, much of it undertaken to learn as much as possible about a figure who had been largely forgotten. Typically this work also attempted to recast *Moby-Dick* as a unified and coherent literary work as opposed to the "botch" it had been seen as in Melville's own time. Predictably, as more and more information about Melville and his immediate family and literary circles was uncovered, more work began to appear addressing the novel's interpretive issues proper, with the result that thematic criticism on *Moby-Dick* began to snowball.

---

1   See **n. 15, p. 168**.

Yet as editors of critical anthologies on *Moby-Dick* have noted consistently since the 1960s, criticism on *Moby-Dick* at any given moment has been characterized more by difference than by consensus. Certain issues draw regular attention – *Moby-Dick* and philosophy, *Moby-Dick* and political discourse, *Moby-Dick* and language, *Moby-Dick* and race, *Moby-Dick* and religion – but the range and diversity of critical approaches and opinions on these and many other issues is extremely broad – and perhaps uniquely so to *Moby-Dick*. As well, the sheer volume of work on Melville and his whale can be overwhelming for the reader approaching the secondary material for the first time. Compounding matters is the fact that literary studies in the US over the last two decades have become increasingly splintered, resulting in almost as many different methodologies and critical foci as there are critics. Dominant "schools" (certainly the term is a misnomer) include deconstruction, feminism, New Historicism and psychoanalysis, but even within these subgroups competing readings and competing methodologies abound. This can be especially frustrating for students trying to decide to which conversations on *Moby-Dick* they should pay most attention.

It is not possible to construct a narrative history of *Moby-Dick* criticism without leaving out some approach, some essay, or some book that at least one scholar or community of scholars considers vital to understanding Melville and his leviathan. The following account is by no means exhaustive. Rather, the reader is referred to Further Reading (**pp. 181–6**), which in conjunction with the following summary provides an overview of the breadth and depth of work on *Moby-Dick* since the Melville Revival. The latter was the critical and popular resurrection of *Moby-Dick* around 1919 which brought Melville out of obscurity. Yet, although any critical history on *Moby-Dick* must begin with the revival, how the historian proceeds and which taxonomy he or she uses to organize such an account is to some degree arbitrary. In the history that follows, the focus is on broad issues related to the novel's general structure and especially on the predominant images of "Melville" and "*Moby-Dick*" constructed by critics over the last several decades. The methodology is deliberately descriptive and anecdotal and only minimally analytical – and never normative. It is not so much a forensic attempt to trace in detail the different ways in which *Moby-Dick* has been interpreted – and certainly not to evaluate the relative merit of any single school or approach – but to provide a general sense of how dominant versions of both "Melville" and "*Moby-Dick*" came to the fore in the first decades following their rise from mutual obscurity.

As outlined in Section 1, *Moby-Dick* was not well received, falling virtually stillborn from the press. Among critics there is much debate over the characterization of Melville as a "failure," and yet there can be little doubt his professional career was sub-par by even the most sympathetic of standards. Although critics in England reacted more favorably than in the US, sales of *Moby-Dick* were poor on both sides of the Atlantic with the predictable result that terms for his subsequent books were far from favorable to their author – something Melville deeply resented. Between his death and the First World War Melville was known only as an obscure writer of travel narratives and romantic sea novels, traditions that were widely read but given little merit by serious readers and scholars. *Moby-Dick* itself was largely forgotten. There were a few articles written praising Melville and calling for a reassessment of *Moby-Dick* prior to 1919, but these were generally ignored. Still, the book was passed among a select and soon-to-be influential group of admirers in the US and especially in England, where the author of *The Whale* was considered a classic American writer.

In 1919 a revival of interest in Melville and in *Moby-Dick* erupted on both sides of the Atlantic securing the sort of fame for Melville and his novel that would have seemed impossible at the time of his death. Dozens of articles were published (many of them as part of celebrations marking the centenary of his birth) which transformed Melville from an obscure figure to an American master replete with the sort of cultural status previously afforded only to such writers as Hawthorne, Whitman and Henry James. Maligned and then ignored in his own time Melville had been transformed into the consummate unappreciated artist. Ostensibly light-years ahead of its time his greatest work had at last found an audience fully capable of appreciating its merits. Reports of the revival made it into popular magazines and newspapers and the public at large began to learn about this long-forgotten "genius." D. H. Lawrence, E. M. Forster, and Virginia Woolf, among other well-known British writers of the period, wrote articles praising *Moby-Dick*. And influential American and British critics published widely read reviews of Melville's whale, including reviews of a new Oxford World Classics edition which appeared in 1920. H. M. Tomlinson, one of the most important figures in the Melville Revival in England, put it this way in 1921:

> I do not know whether Americans are aware of the position of their Melville as a writer, but I find it difficult to write of his great book within measure, for I have no doubt "Moby Dick" goes into that small company of big, extravagant, generative books which have made other writers fertile in all ages—I mean the books we cannot classify, but which must be read by every man who writes—"Gargantua and Pantagruel," "Don Quixote," "Gulliver's Travels," "Tristram Shandy," and the "Pickwick Papers."[2] That is where "Moby Dick" is, and it is therefore as important a creative effort as America has made in her

---

2   Tomlinson's point is that like these sprawling, comic, satiric, and experimental novels, *Moby-Dick* is as important and compelling as it is challenging to classify and to read. *Gargantua and Pantagruel* by François Rabelais (1483–1553), published from 1532 to 1562, is an epic comic satire; *Don Quixote* by Cervantes (1547–1616), published in two parts in 1605 and 1615, is a comic satire of the chivalric Romance; *Gulliver's Travels* by Jonathan Swift (1667–1745) was published in 1726 and is a comic satire of human nature and society; *Tristram Shandy* by Laurence Sterne (1713–68) was published 1760–7 and is a comic, metafictional exploration of literary convention; *The Pickwick Papers* by Charles Dickens (1812–70) was published serially from 1836–7 and is a comic account of the travels of the fictional Pickwick Club.

history. I will sing "The Star-Spangled Banner,"[3] if that is the right hymn, with fervor and the deepest sense of debt and gratitude, at any patriotic thanksgiving service for "Moby Dick."[4]

By the 1930s *Moby-Dick* was being taught in university classrooms in the US with the predictable effect that scholarship on Melville began to flourish. American literature was rarely taught in England prior to the last decades of the twentieth century, and, although Melville enthusiasts in England had kept Melville's reputation alive and had been instrumental in initiating and sustaining the revival, few scholarly works on *Moby-Dick* emerged in England prior to the 1980s.

During the revival critics focused on learning as much as possible about Melville and his whale, and on communicating to others that *Moby-Dick* was worth reexamining. In the decades that followed critics also began to address the novel's complex thematics, and, as witnessed by the range of often contrasting readings from the first fifty or so years, it at times appears as though there are as many *Moby-Dick*s as there are critics.[5] Indeed, because Melville packed as much into the narrative as he could, and the novel is a fragmented and unorthodox blending of so many different discursive forms, tracing any single ideational thread to a definitive conclusion is difficult. One result of this has been that post-revival critics of Melville often found themselves struggling to show the method in the madness of *Moby-Dick*'s convoluted form regardless of any other concerns. For example, in the extracts in the current volume Bezanson's work (**pp. 83–5**) is that of a textual critic, Sealts's piece (**pp. 85–8**) is an example of intellectual historiography, and Murray's approach (**pp. 90–2**), is psychoanalytical, yet each excerpt argues for the structural and thematic coherence of *Moby-Dick*. Although not uniformly formalist, and often in fact taking very different approaches from each other, such first-generation Melvilleans were under the sway of New Criticism's devotion to the text as object-in-itself[6] and so tried to identify and 'solve' the work's major thematic and structural challenges. Chief among these, and perhaps one of the broadest interpretive problems, was the relation of the cetological chapters to the story of the *Pequod* and its crew.

Although differences of opinion have flourished there has been a strong consensus from the revival on that the novel's fragmentation is not in fact a

---

3    The US National Anthem written during the War of 1812. Ironically, the words were set by its writer, Francis Scott Key (1780–1843), to an old English drinking song.
4    Quoted in Brian Higgins and Hershel Parker, eds, *Critical Essays on Herman Melville's Moby-Dick* (New York: Macmillan, 1992), pp. 172–3.
5    See Robert S. Levine, ed., *The Cambridge Companion to Herman Melville* (Cambridge: Cambridge University Press, 1998), for an excellent bibliographical overview.
6    The New Criticism which dominated literary studies between roughly the First World War and the 1950s and 1960s was really more a loose collection of attitudes toward literature and toward the value of literature for society than it was a single, coherent methodological approach. Yet we can also say that work from the height of the New Criticism was consistent in its focus on literary form (on the work of art as an object in itself) and on a hostile reaction to the biographical and historical criticism that preceded it.

"botch." Rather, it intentionally mirrors both the indeterminable and malignant universe and the limited power of language and of philosophy to render it intelligible. Although the blending of fact and fiction befuddled Melville's contemporaries, critics in the first decades following the revival treated the novel's structural complexity as Melville's greatest achievement. Indeed, the book's sprawling and formidable use of a wide variety of discourses and conventions from both fiction and nonfiction (what critics of the novel now call *heteroglossia*) is what made it so attractive to scholars in the newly emerged fields of American literature and American studies. Weaned on the high modernism of James Joyce, Virginia Woolf, T. S. Eliot[7] and others, *Moby-Dick*'s highly wrought structure and grand poetic prose were just the things critics in the 1920s, 1930s and 1940s tended to admire. Certainly there was much debate over whether *Moby-Dick* was ultimately Idealist, antinominian, Emersonian or Platonist, as well as a vast array of conflicting opinions on myriad other issues,[8] but critics generally agreed that the work was a profound exploration of fundamental philosophical issues whose structure embodied the very profundities which Melville was most interested in exploring.

It was in this period too that the dominant image of "Melville" emerged, one that has only recently begun to be reexamined. Depicted by some as an only-barely self-controlled, brawling intellectual outcast – the very sort of nonconformist genius described by Emerson in the "American Scholar" and "Self-Reliance" – Melville's initial image was as the consummate marginalized *artiste*, deeply alienated from his culture and deeply critical of conventional wisdom on the vast range of issues his narrator takes up in the dogged attempt to recount Ahab's hunt for the white whale. Among even those critics who disagreed most deeply about *Moby-Dick*'s thematics, Melville was almost universally characterized as an "Isolato."[9] Matthiessen's discussion of Melville in *American Renaissance* merely set in stone what had by 1941 become the consensus among two generations of scholars of Melville and *Moby-Dick*.

The dominant construction of "Melville," however, changed steadily throughout the 1970s, 1980s, and 1990s, due in large part to the ways in which literary studies were changing over the same period. For example, the shift in focus in the US to issues of race, class, and gender began to result in fundamental revisions of much conventional wisdom on *Moby-Dick* and Melville. And as more information became available about Melville's life, and about the compositional history of *Moby-Dick*, the efforts by critics to argue that the work's apparent inconsistencies were actually deliberate narrative strategies became less and less plausible. It eventually became clear that any efforts to suture the different parts of *Moby-Dick* together without taking the work's full compositional history

---

7   James Joyce (1882–1941); Virginia Woolf (1881–1941); T. S. Eliot (1888–1965).
8   See Robert S. Levine, ed., *The Cambridge Companion to Herman Melville* (Cambridge: Cambridge University Press, 1998).
9   In Chapter 27 Ishmael describes the crew of the *Pequod* collectively as follows, "They were nearly all Islanders in the Pequod, *Isolatoes* too, I call such, not acknowledging the common continent of men, but each *Isolato* living on a separate continent of his own. Yet now, federated along one keel, what a set these Isolatoes were!"

under consideration were misguided efforts to make whole that which was both intentionally and *unintentionally* fractured. As outlined in Section 1, *Moby-Dick was* botched, and the challenge of reconciling the cetological chapters with the other parts of the narrative eventually resulted in the so-called theory of the "Two *Moby-Dicks*" that emerged in the 1950s. George R. Stewart (1954) and James Barbour (1988) were the first critics to tease out the full implications of the compositional history of the book outlined in Section 1. Much of the work of the first and second waves of Melville scholarship had focused on coming up with different ways of accounting for the novel's complexity, but doing so in a manner that preserved the notion that it had a sort of grand organic unity.[10] Unlike these and other critics who tried to explain away the book's fragmented structure by discovering some overarching theme or themes that brought the different parts of the narrative together, Stewart and Barbour argued that the complex circumstances of its composition meant that *Moby-Dick* was really two novels in one. Accordingly, the work Melville had undertaken in the winter and spring of 1851 to reconcile the two halves of his book was now seen as having been only partially successful (see **pp. 17–19**).

By the mid-1990s, critics were also beginning to reexamine the discourse of the revival itself, as well as the impact history and ideology might have had on the reemergence of Melville and his whale. Following the lead of Paul Lauter's "Melville Climbs the Canon," published in 1994, critics began to focus on the cultural upheavals that had characterized American life in the first ten years or so after the First World War, and especially on the reaction of academics to a perceived crisis in the fabric of American national identity in this period. The year 1919 was an especially tumultuous one in American history. The First World War was over but American and British forces were fighting Russian Bolsheviks in Russia. Anti-socialist and anti-communist sentiment in the US was especially strong, resulting in the deportation and persecution of thousands of labor organizers and suspected communist sympathizers. Labor strife was widespread and race riots in many major American cities turned African-American neighborhoods and business districts into war zones. Massive immigration to the US during this period of uncertainty exacerbated racial tensions and energized anti-immigrant movements, including militant racist groups such as the Ku Klux Klan.

The Melville Revival erupted during these social and political uncertainties and scholars now believe the tensions outlined above fueled the reevaluation of Melville and of *Moby-Dick*, resulting in an image of both the writer and his book that was more modern than it was antebellum. Driven by concern among academics that without a homogeneous, unifying national culture American political and cultural unity was threatened, early twentieth-century academics projected their own interests and fears back on to a "Melville" cast summarily as a masculine artist-hero holding up the beacon of a triumphant high culture against an

10 See, for example, Howard Vincent, *The Trying Out of Moby-Dick* (Kent, Ohio: Kent State University Press, 1980).

antebellum society dominated by conservative, gentile and conventional writers on the one hand (most of them women), and a vulgar, democratic mass culture on the other.[11] Under the sway of modernist aesthetics and driven by their own anxieties about the dangers of a consumer culture dominated by the masses (whom they typically characterized as philistine), academics and early Melvilleans thus saw *Moby-Dick* as just the cultural artifact needed to provide a standard by which all things "Great" and "American" (especially literature) could be measured. By the time of the ascendancy of the New Criticism, a school of literary criticism devoted to close study of literary form rather than of biographical or historical context, *Moby-Dick*'s structural and interpretive complexities allowed it to become the benchmark American novel and Melville the consummate underappreciated artist.

Lauter's was the first critical analysis of the Melville Revival to address these issues and one of the first to argue persuasively that ideology played no small part in the reevaluation of Melville and his work. His broadest claim was simply that the standards used to reevaluate Melville and *Moby-Dick* following the initial explosion of interest at the outset of the revival were cultural and ideological mainly, and certainly not solely or even principally aesthetic – except in so far as a particular aesthetic could function ideologically for critics in the period. His analysis of the primary material of the revival included the work of such important figures as Raymond Weaver, (see **pp. 78–9**), Carl Van Doren (see **pp. 79–80**) and F. O. Matthiessen (see **pp. 21–2**) and his conclusion was that the Melville of the revival:

> was constructed in the 1920s as part of an ideological conflict which linked advocates of modernism and of traditional high cultural values— often connected to the academy—against a social and cultural "other," generally, if ambiguously, portrayed as feminine, genteel, exotic, dark, foreign, and numerous. In this contest a distinctively masculine, Anglo-Saxon image of Melville was deployed as a lone and powerful artistic beacon against the dangers presented by the masses . . .

Lauter's article appeared in a special issue of the journal *American Literature* devoted to *Moby-Dick* and was just one of several articles calling for a revaluation of *Moby-Dick*. It is now apparent that the appearance of Lauter's work and the work of others in that issue and elsewhere marked a shift in Melville studies toward scholarship and criticism that challenged the conventional wisdom on both Melville and *Moby-Dick* on its head, challenging the dominant images of Melville and *Moby-Dick* established in the decades following the revival. And no one was immune from reconsideration. Matthiessen's *American Renaissance* 1941), so central to any account of the history of the institutional study of American literature (see **pp. 21–2** in Melville and Antebellum America), was now seen as being as ideological an interpretation of Melville and of *Moby-Dick* as any espoused by critics during or after the revival. Matthiessen had been one of

---

11  See Paul Lauter, "Melville Climbs the Canon," *American Literature* 66.1 (1994).

the most important critics to have depicted Melville as a radical, marginalized critic of antebellum conventionality, as a writer who dared to say "No!" when every other writer was rushing to say "Yes". And until the 1980s, Matthiessen's reading pitting the democrat/worker Ishmael vs. the tyrant/capitalist Ahab dominated criticism on *Moby-Dick*. Throughout the 1990s however, critics began to show how Matthiessen had problematically cast Melville and Ishmael in particular as defiantly democratic and anti-authoritarian at the expense of other possibilities. Matthiessen's reading may have been precisely the sort of championing of democracy called for as fascism threatened Europe *(American Renaissance* was published in 1941), but it was one that distorted both Melville and his text.

In contrast to the unappreciated and marginalized genius of the revival and the first few decades that followed, the strongest trend in criticism on *Moby-Dick* in the last fifteen years has been the close study of the different ways Melville was in fact *deeply* immersed in the major political, literary, and philosophical issues of his time. Far from the Isolato of the first decades of Melville scholarship, "Melville" is now seen by a majority of critics as a struggling professional writer who in his mature works labored with varying degrees of success to reconcile the demands of his art with the demands of the print culture of his times. Most importantly, Melville is now seen as being very much a *part* of his times and not as having transcended them. It was not that a majority of critics now agreed that the old order was uniformly outdated, but that a growing consensus acknowledged that old texts subjected to new methods and critical foci inevitably resulted in very different versions of Melville and of *Moby-Dick* than had been given serious consideration previously. A whole slew of readings – feminist, queer, and otherwise – began to emerge in this period, some of which elicited hostile reactions from established critics. For example, accusations that Melville may have abused his wife, a fact early scholars were accused of covering up, caused deep divisions within Melville circles. Although still seen as inherently critical of conventional wisdom, critics including Michael Paul Rogin, David Reynolds, Donald Pease and Wai Chee Dimock (see **pp. 184–5**) among others, successfully changed the dominant image of Melville to that of a man deeply engaged with the dominant issues of his times. Pease, for example, has shown how the discourse of the Cold War affected dominant threads in *Moby-Dick* criticism after the Second World War, especially in regard to the development of the canon in American universities. And Dimock's book is one of many such efforts to recover a more proper (perhaps) historical understanding of the political discourse of Melville's life and times, resulting in powerful new insights into Melville's engagement with the discourse of liberty, empire, and westward expansion. In short, far from remaining outside the culture of his times looking in, both Melville and *Moby-Dick* are now seen as having directly engaged with many important issues affecting antebellum life, including many of the issues outlined in Melville and Antebellum America (**pp. 20–7**).

Still, if past generations of critics can be faulted for ascribing an anachronistic set of intentions and values to Melville and his work, they were correct in seeing Melville, like Carlyle and Brown among his other myriad influences as inherently critical of conventional belief systems. The latest generation of critics have simply tried to show how he did so very much from within the intellectual and professional currents of his era. And Melville's relevancy to the study of nineteenth-century American literature has never been seriously questioned. As received wisdom about what is worth while to teach has been reexamined, and as previously overlooked authors have been added to course syllabi, the study of Melville remains at the center of the study of nineteenth-century American fiction. As the editor of a recent collection of critical essays on Melville noted, no writer is perhaps more canonical or more representative of an elite, white, masculinist literary tradition than Melville, and yet "Melville has been as interesting and compelling a writer for New Historicists, Feminists, Deconstructionists, and African-Americanists as has any other American writer . . ."[11] Although many of the latest generation of Melvilleans take it for granted – rightly or not – that there are no transcendent texts and certainly no transcendent writers, Melville and *Moby-Dick* are still seen as vitally important for understanding the literary history of the pre-Civil War period. Strong differences of opinion and methodology remain between earlier generations of scholars and the most recent work, but the majority of critics and teachers agree on the unique importance and merit of Melville's mighty book. Critics now generally hold that books remain canonical not because they embody lasting transcendent values but because they still speak or are still useful to the current generation of readers – in other words that, for whatever reason, a work continues to prove fruitful to a variety of critical approaches. If this is the case, then *Moby-Dick* clearly continues to speak to a wide and diverse community of readers both inside and outside of the modern university.

12 Myra Jehlen, "Introduction," in Myra Jehlen, ed., *Herman Melville: A Collection of Critical Essays* (Englewood Cliffs, N.J.: Prentice-Hall, 1994), p. 2.

# Early Critical Reception

## Introduction

The reviews excerpted here start with the critical response to Melville's earliest works in order to provide a sense of just what readers expected from fiction in the period and from Melville in particular, as well as what they found distasteful. Realistic depictions of life on the sea, the crude manners of common sailors, as well as high adventure were all acceptable. *Moby-Dick*'s brash and larger-than-life characters, especially Ahab, were a bit too exaggerated for most readers, and Ishmael's philosophizing deemed boring as well as blasphemous. In these selections it is possible to trace the arc of Melville's professional career first hand and to discover just how keenly his own artistic sensibility clashed with that of the average reader (see Section 1, especially "Hawthorne and his Mosses," **pp. 38–40**, and the letters to Hawthorne, **pp. 49–53**. Except where noted, original footnotes in the extracts have not been retained.

### From **review of Typee**, *United States Nautical Magazine*, 3 (March 1846): 119

This is a lively and entertaining book of adventure ashore and afloat. Besides his notes of a four months' residence at the Marquesas, and the various perils incident to a life on board a Pacific whaleship,[1] the author furnishes some interesting statements regarding the French occupation of Tahiti, and the provisional cession of the Sandwich Islands to the English commander, Lord George Paulet.[2]

---

1 See Melville's Career and the Writing of *Moby-Dick*, **pp. 9–19**.
2 Known in the nineteenth century as the Sandwich Islands, Hawaii was an independent monarchy but was threatened with annexation by both the British and the French in spite of certain pro-US leanings among at least some of its rulers. On February 13, 1843 Lord George Paulet of HMS *Carysfort* attempted to annex the islands for alleged insults and abuses against British subjects – this in spite of the presence of a US warship, the USS *Boston*. Before the matter could become an international incident however, the actions of Lord Paulet were disavowed by the British government.

We have room for but one extract from these volumes, which is too good to pass unquoted. This is a specimen of what the author terms "nautical oratory;" a speech that fell from the lips of a master of a whaler while lying at the Marquesas. At the commencement of the sixth chapter the writer says:

"Early the next morning the starboard watch were mustered upon the quarter-deck, and our worthy captain, standing in the cabin gangway, harangued us as follows:

'Now, men, as we are just off a six months' cruise, and have got through most all our work in port here, I suppose you want to go ashore . . . At two bells the boat will be manned to take you off, and the Lord have mercy on you!'" [paras. 1–2]

The criticisms of the sailors which our author describes as following the above remarks from their worthy chief, are very characteristic of that race of beings; but, as we have before said, our limits will not admit of farther extracts. Those of our readers who would like to peruse an amusing work, should obtain these volumes.

## From **review of Typee**, Critic [London], 3 (March 7, 1846): 219–22

This is a most entertaining and refreshing book. It details the experiences of an American sailor, who, disgusted with the tedium of a long whaling voyage, and the arbitrary conduct of the captain, availed himself of the vessel's visit to Nukuheva for provisions, to run away and take his chance among the savages of that island.

The picture he has drawn of Polynesian life and scenery is incomparably the most vivid and forcible that has ever been laid before the public. The incidents, no doubt, are sometimes exaggerated, and the colouring is often overcharged, yet in the narrative generally there is *vraisemblance*[1] that cannot be feigned; for the minuteness, and novelty of the details, could only have been given by one who had before him nature for his model.

The writer of this narrative, though filling the post of a common sailor, is certainly no common man. His clear, lively, and pointed style, the skilful management of his descriptive, the philosophical reflections and sentimental apostrophes[2] scattered plentifully through the work, at first induced us to suppose it the joint production of an American sailor and a man of letters, of whom the one furnished the raw materials and the other gave them shape, order, and consistency, so as to tell with more effect upon the public. We have since learned, on good authority, that this was not the case; that, in fact, the narrative is the *bona fide* production

---

1 Fidelity to actuality in representation; realism.
2 Digressions.

of a brother to one of the gentlemen officially attached to the American Legation[3] in this country, and his alone. [. . .][4]

## From **review of Redburn**, Bentley's Miscellany [London], 26 (November 1849): 528–30

Indebted less for its interest to the regions of the fantastical and the ideal, than to the more intelligible domain of the actual and real, we are disposed to place a higher value upon this work than upon any of Mr. Melville's former productions. Perhaps it is that we understand it better, and the fault is not in Mr. Melville, but in ourselves, that we appreciate more satisfactorily the merits of a story of living experience than the dreams of fancy and the excursions of a vivid imagination.[1] There are occasional snatches even in this story of the same wild and visionary spirit which attracted so much curiosity in its predecessors, and they come in with excellent effect to relieve and heighten its literal delineations; but the general character is that of a narrative of palpable life, related with broad simplicity, and depending for its final influence over the sympathies of the reader upon closeness and truthfulness of portraiture. In the Dutch fidelity[2] and accumulation of the incidents, it is a sort of Robinson Crusoe[3] on ship-board.

[. . .] The action of the narrative embraces a voyage to Liverpool, a few adventures on shore, in the course of which Redburn is carried up to London, and a voyage back to New York. Slight as this framework is, it is filled with bustle, and the excitement never flags to the close. The charm lies in the vitality of the descriptions, in the minuteness with which every articulation of the sailorcraft is depicted, and in the natural development of the feelings of the boy throughout the startling ordeal of his first cruise. The ship, as in the masterly novels of Cooper and Marryat,[4] acquires a living interest; and the most elaborate pictures of land experiences could not more effectually fascinate the attention and stimulate curiosity, than the daily incidents of the most trivial kind which fill up the routine or mark the vicissitudes[5] of life on board this merchant-vessel. Nor is the canvas

---

3   The American diplomatic corps stationed in London. Melville's brother Gansevoort was a member.
4   There was much debate among critics whether a common sailor could have written something as literate as *Typee*. As a result, Melville was forced to defend himself against claims that he had never served as a common sailor and had made up all the incidents in his first book. In 1846, however, Richard Tobias Greene, the companion of Melville during his experiences in the Marquesas, known as Toby in *Typee*, appeared in Buffalo, N.Y., vouching for the book's authenticity in a letter published in the Buffalo *Commercial Advertiser*.

---

1   The reference here is to *Mardi*.
2   The reference here is to the Dutch genre painting of Vermeer and other artists whose paintings were noted for their extremely realistic portrayals of everyday life.
3   *Robinson Crusoe* (1719) by Daniel Defoe (1660–1731), a well-known novel based on the true story of a fugitive sailor who went to sea only to be willfully marooned on a deserted island in the South Pacific.
4   James Fenimore Cooper (1789–1851), American author of historical fiction including *Last of the Mohicans* and *The Deerslayer* and noted writer of sea fiction; Frederick Marryat (1792–1848), noted English writer of sea fiction who served twenty-four years in the English navy.
5   Alterations or changes in fortune, i.e., bad or good luck as the case may be.

deficient in variety of character. The sailors are individuals to a man, and one of them in especial is drawn with great force and originality. The captain, too, so bland and agreeable in his relations with the world ashore, and so despotic and inaccessible out at sea, and the queer little cabin-passenger, and the mysterious young lady with whom the captain parades the quarter-deck so royally, supply abundant materials to sustain a dramatic variety that never suffers the narrative to droop. [. . .]

From **review of Redburn**, New York Sunday Times and Noah's Weekly Messenger (November 18, 1849)

Mr. Melville's new book is fresh on the shelves of the Broadway stores, and the ink is scarcely dry on the show-bills. As the author took out the proof-sheets with him to England, it was, of course, published simultaneously on both sides of the Atlantic. This is an advantage which American authors have over their European brethren, as an offset for their many disadvantages. They can secure a copy-right at home, at the same time they sell one abroad; but the foreign author can only secure a copy-right to an American publisher by becoming an American citizen, or at least declaring his intention to become one. In this way the late Capt. Maryat sold a copy-right to a Philadelphia publishing house. He took the oath in due form; but if he had really any intention, beyond that of selling his book, he must have changed his mind afterwards.

Melville's first book, "Typee," was a wonderful success. It had a freshness and originality about it that took everybody by surprise. The leaders of English criticism awarded it unqualified and enthusiastic praise. "Omoo," a sequel to "Typee," met with an equally gratifying reception. Then came "Mardi;" but with it came a change. It was time the critics had something to carp at, and they got it. Mardi was a riddle that few took pains to solve. It found here and there enthusiastic admirers. It is the book on which the author would probably choose to rest his fame—a work of great thought and wonderful power; but it was not what any body expected from the author of "Typee" and "Omoo."

The third book [sic] is in the old vein. It is written for the million, and the million will doubtless be delighted with its racy descriptions of the life of a young sailor. The critics, having worked off their proverbial ill-nature on the unintelligible "Mardi," will be full of the praises of "Redburn," and our young American author will make the tour of Europe on the topmost wave of a trans-atlantic celebrity, whose reflux will land him here, high and dry, in an enviable position. [. . .]

From **review of Moby-Dick**, New York Evangelist (November 20, 1851)

Mr. Melville grows wilder and more untameable with every adventure. In Typee and Omoo, he began with the semblance of life and reality, though it was often but the faintest kind of semblance. As he advanced, he threw off the pretense of probability, and wandered from the verisimilitude of fiction into the mist and vagueness of poetry and fantasy, and now in this last venture, has reached the very limbo of eccentricity. From first to last, oddity is the governing characteristic. The extraordinary descriptive powers which Typee disclosed, are here in full strength. More graphic and terrible portraitures of hairbreadth scapes we never read. The delineation of character, too, is exquisitely humorous, sharp, individual and never-to-be forgotten. The description of Father Mapple's sermon[1] is a powerful piece of sailor-oratory; and passages of great eloquence, and artistic beauty and force, are to be found everywhere. It will add to Mr. Melville's repute as a writer, undoubtedly, and furnishes, incidentally, a most striking picture of sea life and adventures.

## From **review of Moby-Dick**, Boston Post (November 20, 1851)

We have read nearly one half of this book, and are satisfied that the London Athenæum[1] is right in calling it "an ill-compounded mixture of romance and matter-of-fact." It is a crazy sort of affair, stuffed with conceits and oddities of all kinds, put in artificially, deliberately and affectedly, by the side of strong, terse and brilliant passages of incident and description. The Athenæum's notice throughout seems to us a fair one, and we copy the greater portion for the sake of economy and good taste:

> "The style of his tale is in places disfigured by mad (rather than bad) English . . . Our author must be henceforth numbered in the company of the incorrigibles[2] who occasionally tantalize us with indications of genius, while they constantly summon us to endure monstrosities, carelessness, and other such harassing manifestations of bad taste as daring or disordered ingenuity can devise."

After giving an interesting and powerfully written extract, the Athenæum resumes:

> "The dark-complexioned harpooner turned out to be a cannibal, one Queequeg . . . Mr Melville has to thank himself only if his horrors and his heroics are flung aside by the general reader, as so much trash belonging to the worst school of Bedlam[3] literature—since he seems not so much unable to learn as disdainful of learning the craft of an artist."

The production under notice is now issued by the Harpers in a handsome bound volume for *one dollar and fifty cents*–no mean sum,[4] in these days. It seems

1    See Chapter 9, "The Sermon," on **pp. 137–9**.

1    British literary periodical.
2    Those who are incorrigible, or incapable of being corrected or reformed.
3    The word Bedlam is derived from Bethlehem Royal Hospital, the oldest institution dedicated to the treatment of the mentally ill in England and one of the oldest in Europe. Bedlam is thus used to describe any place or scene of wild confusion or disorder.
4    In 1851 $1.50 was equal to approximately $34 or £21 today.

to us that our publishers have gone from one extreme to the other, and that instead of publishing good books in too cheap a form, they are issuing poor books, in far too costly apparel. "The Whale" is not worth the money asked for it, either as a literary work or as a mass of printed paper. Few people would read it more than once, and yet it is issued at the usual cost of a standard volume. Published at *twenty five cents*, it might do to buy, but at any higher price, we think it a poor speculation.

## From **review of Moby-Dick**, Albion [New York], 10 (November 22, 1851): 561

This mere announcement of the book's and the author's name will prepare you in a measure for what follows; for you know just as well as we do that Herman Melville is a practical and practised sea-novelist, and that what comes from his pen will be worth the reading. And so indeed is "Moby-Dick," and not lacking much of being a great work. How it falls short of this, we shall presently endeavour to show [. . .]

Not only is there an immense amount of reliable information here before us; the *dramatis personæ*, mates, harpooners, carpenters, and cooks, are all vivid sketches done in the author's best style. What they do, and how they look, is brought to one's perception with wondrous elaborateness of detail; and yet this minuteness does not spoil the broad outline of each. It is only when Mr. Melville puts words into the mouths of these living and moving beings, that his cunning fails him, and the illusion passes away. From the Captain to the Cabin-boy, not a soul amongst them talks pure seaman's lingo; and as this is a grave charge, we feel bound to substantiate it—not by an ill-natured selection of isolated bits, but by such samples as may be considered an average [. . .]

But there is no pleasure in making these extracts; still less would there be in quoting anything of the stuff and nonsense spouted forth by the crazy Captain; for so indeed must nine-tenths of his dialogue be considered, even though one bears in mind that it has been compounded in a maniac's brain from the queer mixture of New England conventicle phraseology[1] with the devilish profanity too common on board South-Sea Whalers. The rarely-imagined character has been grievously spoiled, nay altogether ruined, by a vile overdaubing with a coat of book-learning and mysticism; there is no method in his madness; and we must needs pronounce the chief feature of the volume a perfect failure, and the work itself inartistic. There is nevertheless in it, as we have already hinted, abundant choice reading for these who can skip a page now and then, judiciously; and perhaps, when one's mind is made up to disregard the continuous interest, the separate portions may be better relished. [. . .]

Mr. Melville has crowded together in a few prefatory pages a large collection of brief and pithy extracts from authors innumerable, such as one might

---

1  A conventicle is a secret or illegal religious meeting, used here to allude to the Salem witch trials in seventeenth-century Massachusetts.

expect as headings for chapters. We do not like the innovation. It is having oil, mustard, vinegar, and pepper served up as a dish, in place of being scientifically administered saucewise.

## From **Evert A. Duyckinck, review of Moby-Dick**, Literary World, [New York], 250 (November 22, 1851): 381–3

A difficulty in the estimate of this, in common with one or two other of Mr. Melville's books, occurs from the double character under which they present themselves. In one light they are romantic fictions, in another statements of absolute fact.[1] When to this is added that the romance is made a vehicle of opinion and satire through a more or less opaque allegorical veil, as particularly in the latter half of Mardi, and to some extent in this present volume, the critical difficulty is considerably thickened. It becomes quite impossible to submit such books to a distinct classification as fact, fiction, or essay. Something of a parallel may be found in Jean Paul's German tales, with an admixture of Southey's Doctor.[2] Under these combined influences of personal observation, actual fidelity to local truthfulness in description, a taste for reading and sentiment, a fondness for fanciful analogies, near and remote, a rash daring in speculation, reckless at times of taste and propriety, again refined and eloquent, this volume of Moby Dick may be pronounced a most remarkable sea-dish—an intellectual chowder of romance, philosophy, natural history, fine writing, good feeling, bad sayings—but over which, in spite of all uncertainties, and in spite of the author himself, predominates his keen perceptive faculties, exhibited in vivid narration.

There are evidently two if not three books in Moby Dick rolled into one. Book No. I. we could describe as a thorough exhaustive account admirably given of the great Sperm Whale. The information is minute, brilliantly illustrated, as it should be—the whale himself so generously illuminating the midnight page on which his memoirs are written—has its level passages, its humorous touches, its quaint suggestion, its incident usually picturesque and occasionally sublime. All this is given in the most delightful manner in "The Whale." Book No. 2 is the romance of Captain Ahab, Queequeg, Tashtego, Pip & Co., who are more or less spiritual personages talking and acting differently from the general business run of the conversation on the decks of whalers. They are for the most part very serious people, and seem to be concerned a great deal about the problem of the universe. They are striking characters withal, of the romantic spiritual cast of the German drama; realities of some kinds at bottom, but veiled in all sorts of poetical incidents and expressions. As a bit of German melodrama, with

---

1   See for comparison the excerpt from "The Custom-House Sketch," **pp. 40–1.**
2   Jean Paul Richter (1763–1825), German Romantic whose works incorporated dream-like elements and mysticism; Robert Southey (1774–1843), British Romantic and poet laureate, friend of Coleridge, his *The Doctor*, a collection of anecdotes, quotations and comment, appeared 1834–7. See **pp. 42–4** for an overview of the impact of European Romanticism on American literary and intellectual life vis-à-vis Moby-Dick.

Captain Ahab for the Faust of the quarter-deck, and Queequeg with the crew, for Walpurgis night[3] revellers in the forecastle, it has its strong points, though here the limits as to space and treatment of the stage would improve it. Moby Dick in this view becomes a sort of fishy moralist, a leviathan metaphysician, a folio Doctor Dubitantium,[4] in fact, in the fresh water illustration of Mrs. Malaprop,[5] "an allegory on the banks of the Nile." After pursuing him in this melancholic company over a few hundred squares of latitude and longitude, we begin to have some faint idea of the association of whaling and lamentation, and why blubber is popularly synonymous with tears.

The intense Captain Ahab is too long drawn out; something more of *him* might, we think, be left to the reader's imagination. The value of this kind of writing can only be through the personal consciousness of the reader, what he brings to the book; and all this is sufficiently evoked by a dramatic trait or suggestion. If we had as much of Hamlet or Macbeth as Mr. Melville gives us of Ahab, we should be tired even of their sublime company. Yet Captain Ahab is a striking conception, firmly planted on the wild deck of the Pequod—a dark disturbed soul arraying itself with every ingenuity of material resources for a conflict at once natural and supernatural in his eye, with the most dangerous extant physical monster of the earth, embodying, in strongly drawn lines of mental association, the vaster moral evil of the world. The pursuit of the White Whale thus interweaves with the literal perils of the fishery—a problem of fate and destiny—to the tragic solution of which Ahab hurries on, amidst the wild stage scenery of the ocean. To this end the motley crew, the air, the sky, the sea, its inhabitants are idealized throughout. It is a noble and praiseworthy conception; and though our sympathies may not always accord with the train of thought, we would caution the reader against a light or hasty condemnation of this part of the work.

[. . .] With this we make an end of what we have been reluctantly compelled to object to this volume. With far greater pleasure, we acknowledge the acuteness of observation, the freshness of perception, with which the author brings home to us from the deep, "things unattempted yet in prose or rhyme," the weird influences of his ocean scenes, the salient imagination which connects them with the past and distant, the world of books and the life of experience—certain prevalent traits of manly sentiment. These are strong powers with which Mr. Melville wrestles in this book. It would be a great glory to subdue them to the highest uses of fiction. It is still a great honor, among the crowd of successful mediocrities which throng our publishers' counters, and know nothing of divine impulses, to be in the company of these nobler spirits on any terms.

3   According to German legend, Walpurgis Night, the eve of May Day, is a witches' Sabbath.
4   A book of religious allegory by Jeremy Taylor (1613–67). Dubitantium, from dubitative or dubita-
    tion, literally, "doubt," hence "Dr. Doubt," i.e., a skeptic.
5   Mrs. Malaprop is a character from the first play by Richard Sheridan (1751–1816), *The Rivals*
    (1775). A malapropism is a humorous misuse of a word, most often as a result of confusion with a
    word that sounds similar.

From **review of *Moby-Dick***, *Literary Gazette* [London], 1820
(December 6, 1851): 841–2

[. . .] This is an odd book, professing to be a novel; wantonly eccentric; outrageously bombastic; in places charmingly and vividly descriptive. The author has
read up laboriously to make a show of cetalogical learning. He has turned over
the articles Whale, Porpoise, Cachalot, Spermaceti, Baleen, and their relatives,
in every Encyclopædia within his reach. Thence he has resorted to the original
authorities—a difficult and tedious task, as every one who has sought out the
sources of statements set forth without reference in Cyclopædias knows too well.
For our own part, we believe that there must have been some old original
Cyclopædia, long since lost or destroyed, out of which all the others have been
compiled. For when one is compared with another, it becomes too plain that one
or other is a barefaced pillage and extract from a secondhand source. Herman
Melville is wise in this sort of wisdom. He uses it as stuffing to fill out his skeleton
story. Bad stuffing it makes, serving only to try the patience of his readers, and to
tempt them to wish both him and his whales at the bottom of an unfathomable
sea. If a man will light his lamp with whale oil, when gas and camphine[1] are at
hand, he must be content with a dull illumination.

[. . .] Mr. Herman Melville has earned a deservedly high reputation for his performances in descriptive fiction. He has gathered his own materials, and travelled
along fresh and untrodden literary paths, exhibiting powers of no common order,
and great originality. The more careful, therefore, should he be to maintain the
fame he so rapidly acquired, and not waste his strength on such purposeless and
unequal doings as these rambling volumes about spermaceti whales.

1    Camphene, a colorless crystalline compound used in the manufacture of camphor and insecticides.
     Camphor was used to manufacture a variety of goods, including explosives.

# Modern Criticism

## The Melville Revival

The Melville Revival largely originated in Great Britain and as English critics and writers such as H. M. Tomlinson and D. H. Lawrence began to write about Melville and about *Moby-Dick* in particular, American critics and scholars took note. Following the centenary of Melville's birth in 1919 articles began to appear calling for a reevaluation of this lost artist and of *Moby-Dick* especially. It was as if Melville's ideal audience had finally appeared, eager to follow his sprawling philosophical treatise to wherever it might lead them. The differences among the contemporary reviews and the selections from the Melville Revival are quite stark. Virtually everything his contemporary critics found problematic early twentieth-century readers found enthralling.

From **E. L. Grant Watson, review of Melville's *Moby-Dick*,** *London Mercury* 3 (1920): 180–6. Reprinted in Kevin J. Hayes, ed., *The Critical Response to Herman Melville's* Moby-Dick (1994), Westport, Conn.: Greenwood Press, 35–43

> Watson wrote this review of the Oxford *Moby-Dick* for J. C. Squire's conservative English literary magazine the *London Mercury* in 1920. The excerpt below examines the powerful attraction Ahab had for modern readers and is in stark contrast to reviews from Melville's own time which found the book's combination of so many different discursive forms bewildering, and Ahab and many of the other main characters exaggerated if not indecipherable. (See, for example, extracts from the review of *Moby-Dick*, *Boston Post*, November 20, 1851 on **pp. 70–1** and from the review of *Moby-Dick* by Evert A. Duyckinck, *Literary World* [New York], November 22, 1851 on **pp. 72–3**.)

[...] In *Moby Dick or the White Whale*, which is Melville's greatest and best-known work, there is a richness of material that might well puzzle the casual reader. He plunges, in the first pages, into schoolboy adventures with cannibal chiefs, to be followed quickly by rhetoric, by sermons, the magic of embarkation, the magic of voyages, of the sea and of ships. There is natural history, textbooks of cetology, wayside philosophisings, realistic descriptions of whale hunts, pictures of the sea and of the sea's dread and beauty such as no other man has penned, and, winding through the whole, giving cohesion and intensity, is the story of the author's own fiercely vivid life-consciousness, which, like the vindictive *Pequod*, journeys upon the most adventurous of all quests, drawn always onward by the beauty and terror of that symbol of madness, the white whale. This inner history is well hidden amongst high adventures. The lives of real men whom Melville has known and loved enfold it. It is tossed with the *Pequod* round all the seas of the ocean, yet once fairly sighted, the story of the soul's daring and of the soul's dread is never lost, but holds the reader in a grip of awful anticipation, till at the end he is left aghast at the courage of one who dares with unflinching perception follow into the heart of its uttermost ocean that quality which, in our cowardice, we call madness. [. . .]

In this story the white whale is the symbol or mask of that outer mystery, which, like a magnet, for ever attracts, and in the end overwhelms the imagination. Ahab, the monomaniac[1] captain of the *Pequod*, that godlike, godless old man, is its counterpart. He is the incarnation of the active and courageous madness that lies brooding and fierce, ever ready to spring to command, within the man of genius. He is the atheistical captain of the tormented soul. [. . .] In his heart Ahab has a glimpse of his power: "All my means are sane, my motive and object mad." To the outward world he appears to be recovered. A new leg has been made for him by the ship's carpenter of the bone of a whale's jaw. He is much changed by his suffering and mutilation, but apparently sane, though he had grown morose and fierce. On this account the owners of the *Pequod* think him the better fitted to be the captain of a Nantucket whaler. They have no suspicion of his madness, and only when the ship is far out to sea does he make his appearance. He then calls all hands upon the quarter-deck and tells them that they are upon no ordinary cruise, but that his chief purpose is to hunt and kill Moby Dick, that "great gliding demon of the seats of life." By his magnetic enthusiasm he carries with him all but Starbuck, the chief mate. Starbuck, the brave, the chivalrous, the humane honest man, the symbol of unaided virtue and right-mindedness, tragically destined to be overborne by madness, he alone protests. He calls it blasphemy to pursue a dumb brute with such vindictive rage. Ahab takes him aside, concentrating all his imaginative *puissance*[2] against Starbuck's outraged amazement. [. . .]

In this scene and throughout the story, Ahab and Starbuck present the chief elements of the drama; but there are others symbolised no less completely. There is Stubb, the second mate, whose philosophy is founded on a broad basis of good-humoured carelessness, who laughs at the most terrible auguries,[3] and

---

1    Someone with a pathological obsession (see also p. 158).
2    Power or might.
3    Signs or omens.

is undaunted not only by all the terrors of the sea, but by the subtler fears of introspection. There is Flask, the third mate, the cockney mediocrity, with "courage as fierce as fire and as mechanical," who will stoop to wanton cruelty, and will joke at the piteous terror and dumb agony of the dying whale. Yet these, and all the crew, like Starbuck, though in personality less separate and conscious than he, are drawn on by Ahab to their inevitable doom. Pip, the ship's boy, the little curly-headed negro, who went to sea by mistake, and who, terrified by the strange fierceness of life, became more and more of a coward, until frightened beyond all endurance, he lost his wits; he also is bound to furious Ahab by invisible ties of affinity. His gentle idiocy is the counterpart of the old man's fierceness, and Ahab, as his madness waxes, reads in Pip's strangely illuminated utterances oracular sayings. He takes the boy to live with him in his cabin. The two antithetical poles of human perception, the one intensified by fear, the other by courage: the one gentle and wayward, the other fierce and concentrated, live side by side, while a strange love enfolds them. On deck Fedallah watches like the hungry embodiment of a madman's purpose. For the most part he is silent, but when he speaks it is only to whisper intimations and prophecies of the end. He is feared and hated by the crew, who, in so far as they are separate from Ahab, remain sane, and whose only madness is that they are bound by his iron purpose. [. . .]

From **Frank Jewett Mather, Jr., "Herman Melville,"** Review I (August 19, 1919): 276–8 and (August 16, 1919): 298–301. Reprinted in Brian Higgins and Hershel Parker, eds, Critical Essays on Herman Melville's Moby Dick (1992), New York: Macmillan, 144–9

> Mather was a noted American critic and professor of art and archeology at Princeton. He was also art critic of the New York Evening Post, among other papers. This essay appeared on the occasion of the centennial of Melville's birth in the New York Review in August 1919. The excerpt below compares Moby-Dick to Mardi, highlighting the differences between Melville's problematic early attempt at a Romance (see **pp. 11–12**) and the more mature Moby-Dick.

[. . .] In 1849, about two years before "Moby Dick," appeared that strangest of allegories, "Mardi, and a Voyage Thither." The two works are companion pieces: "Mardi" is a survey of the universe in the guise of an imaginary voyage of discovery, "Moby Dick" is a real voyage skillfully used to illustrate the cosmos; "Mardi" is a celestial adventure, "Moby Dick" an infernal. "Mardi" is highly general—the quest of a mysterious damsel, Zillah, a sort of Beatrice,[1] a type

---

1  A character in Dante's *Divine Comedy* (*c.*1314), Beatrice leads the protagonist on a tour of Heaven. By tradition (although much debated by scholars) the character is based on the real-life Beatrice Portinari (1266–90) a Florentine noble whose great beauty inspired Dante and was for him an ideal and inspiration throughout his life.

of divine wisdom; "Moby Dick" is specific, the insanely vengeful pursuit of the dreaded white whale. The people of "Mardi" are all abstractions, those of "Moby Dick" among the most vivid known to fiction. "Mardi" was far the most ambitious effort of Melville's, and it failed. Personally I like to read in it; for its idealism tinged with a sane Rabelaisianism,[2] for its wit and rare pictorial quality, for the strange songs of Yoomy, which, undetachable, are both quaintly effective in their context, and often foreshadow oddly our modern free verse. It is often plethoric[3] and overwritten, it drops out of the Polynesian form in which it is conceived, and becomes too overt preaching and satire. It justifies the Bacchic philosopher Babbalanja's[4] aphorism—"Genius is full of trash"; but it is also full of wisdom and fine thinking. It represents an intellectual effort that would supply a small library, and I suppose it is fated to remain unread. Perhaps its trouble is its inconclusiveness. [. . .]

Upon the reader's slant towards this sort of parable will very much depend his estimate of "Moby Dick." Are we dealing with trimmings or essentials?—that is the critical question.[5] Cut out the preachments, and you will have a great novel, some readers say. Yes, but not a great Melville novel. The preachments are of the essence. The effect of the book rests on the blend of fact, fancy, and profound reflection, upon a brilliant intermingling of sheer artistry and moralizing at large. It is Kipling[6] before the letter crossed with Sir Thomas Browne,[7] it comprises all the powers and tastes of Herman Melville, is his greatest and most necessary work. So while no one is obliged to like "Moby Dick"—there are those who would hold against Dante his moralizing and against Rabelais his broad humor– let such as do love this rich and towering fabrique adore it whole-heartedly— from stem to stern, athwart ships and from maintruck to keelson.

## From **Raymond M. Weaver, "The Centennial of Herman Melville,"** Nation 109 (August 2, 1919): 146. Reprinted in Brian Higgins and Hershel Parker, eds, Critical Essays on Herman Melville's Moby Dick (1992), New York: Macmillan, 143

Weaver wrote the first biography of Melville, Herman Melville, Mariner and Mystic (1921). The review from which the excerpt below is taken was written for the New York Nation in 1919 and announces the Melville Revival to its American audience. The review both proclaims the greatness of Moby-Dick and is perhaps one of the first efforts by critics to treat the novel's structural incongruities as evidence of its organic, sui generis structure (see **p. 92**).

---

2   François Rabelais (1483–1553), French comic satirist.
3   Excessive.
4   A character in Mardi.
5   See extracts from Ward (**pp. 92–4**) and from Greenberg (**pp. 95–6**).
6   Rudyard Kipling (1865–1936). English poet, novelist and short-story writer known especially for his works set in colonial India, including The Jungle Book and Kim.
7   See n. 5, **p. 48**.

[. . .] Born in hell-fire, and baptized in an unspeakable name, "Moby-Dick, or the Whale" (1851), reads like a great opium dream. The organizing theme of the book is the hunting of Moby-Dick, the abhorred white whale, by the mono-maniac Captain Ahab. To Ahab, this ancient and vindictive monster is the incarnation of all the vast moral evil of the world; he piles on the whale's white hump the sum of all the rage and hate of mankind from the days of Eden down. There are in "Moby-Dick" long digressions, natural, historical, and philosophical on the person, habits, manners, and ideas of whales; there are long dialogues and soliloquies, such as were never spoken by mortal man in his waking senses, conversations that for sweetness, strength, and courage remind one of passages from Dekker, Webster, Massinger, Fletcher, and the other old dramatists loved by Charles Lamb;[1] perhaps a fifth of the book is made up of Melville's independent moralizings, half essay, half rhapsody; withal, the book contains some of the most finished comedy in the language. If one logically analyzes "Moby-Dick," he will be disgusted, just as Dr. Johnson, who had no analysis but the logical, was disgusted with "Lycidas."[2] And so with Melville's novel. If one will forget logic and common sense, and "abandon himself"—as Dr. Johnson would con-temptuously have said—to this work of Melville's, he will acknowledge the presence of an amazing masterpiece. But neither "Lycidas" nor "Moby-Dick" should be read by philistines or pragmatists.[3] [. . .]

From **Carl Van Doren, "Mr. Melville's Moby-Dick,"** Bookman 59 (April 1924): 154–7. Reprinted in Kevin J. Hayes, ed., The Critical Response to Herman Melville's Moby-Dick (1994), Westport, Conn.: Greenwood Press, 56–60

Van Doren published a four-page essay for the Cambridge History of American Literature in 1917 that virtually single-handedly launched the Melville Revival in the US. His essay "Mr. Melville's Moby-Dick" appeared in the New York Bookman in 1924 and usefully locates Moby-Dick at its proper point in the development of Melville as an artist.

This astounding romance is neither so sane as "Typee" and "Omoo" nor so mad as "Mardi," but occupies a fruitful ground between those two extremes of

---

1  Charles Lamb (1775–1834), poet and essayist, friend of Coleridge and Southey. The reference here is meant to align Moby-Dick with the speeches normally heard in Jacobean tragedy. Lamb was the editor of an anthology of Elizabethan and Jacobean dramatists, Specimens of English Dramatic Poets (1808).
2  A pastoral elegy by John Milton (1608–74) mourning the death of Milton's contemporary Edward King. Samuel Johnson (1709–1804), critic, scholar and poet, argued that contrary to the established purpose of the elegy, Milton's poem "will excite no sympathy" and "confer no honor" upon its subject. Weaver's point is that Johnson made the mistake of holding Milton to too rigid a generic standard. The reader of Moby-Dick who does likewise, expecting to find a realistic novel, is thus equally at fault – in effect, a philistine or someone vulgar and uncouth with no artistic taste.
3  Philistine: barbarian; pragmatist: one who is practical – here, someone who is practical to a fault, preferring only literary works which adhere closely to accepted conventions.

Herman Melville's art. It bears, indeed, the marks of a hand which moves as if it had learned its tricks during the early nineteenth century. Echoes of Carlyle[1] roar through its rhythms; the wings of transcendentalism[2] wheel over it, shutting out at times the secular sun. The narrative marches under a load of erudition, concerning whales and whalers, which recalls those simpler days when fiction and history had not agreed upon the division of labor with which each is now satisfied. Mr. Melville obviously lacks the realist's conviction that the bare facts of human life are in themselves eloquent, and so permits himself to lean a great deal upon certain misty symbols to give his meaning its rich colors and ominous shadows. For any but those among its readers who have an expert's interest in the technique of whale hunting or who take a connoisseur's delight in the manipulation of witty and poetical prose, the book is sure to seem too long, perhaps by a third. There must be plain men who would find the voyage of the story shorter than the volume. And yet, touched by certain conventions of its generation as it is, "Moby Dick" presents a face which is almost as timeless as an ocean or a heath. If there is a greater sea tale in modern literature, that tale has not yet been published.

From **H. M. Tomlinson, "A Clue to Moby-Dick,"** *Literary Review* 2 (November 5, 1921): 141–2. Reprinted in Brian Higgins and Hershel Parker, eds, *Critical Essays on Herman Melville's* Moby Dick (1992), New York: Macmillan, 172–7

Tomlinson was a leading figure of the Melville Revival in England. "A Clue to Moby-Dick" was originally published in the London *Nation and Athenæum* in 1918 and then reprinted elsewhere, including the US where it was read widely. Tomlinson was instrumental in getting other critics and authors to revisit *Moby-Dick*, and the excerpt below captures both the enthusiasm and the rigorous insight of the leading figures of the revival. The first critics were no mere amateurs and their admiration for *Moby-Dick* was due to far more than a dilettantish predilection for a strangely unique literary work.

Many years ago I was discussing the literature of the sea with a Fleet Street[1] colleague, a clever and well-read man against whose volatile enthusiasms experience had taught me to guard myself well. He began to talk of "Moby Dick." Talk! He soon became incoherent. He swept aside all other books of the

1  See also **pp. 88–90**.
2  See Transcendentalism, **pp. 41–4**.

1  Historically, the area of London where many of the leading (and not so leading) publishing houses were located. Fleet Street was also associated with low-brow, popular writing, and the reference here is perhaps tongue-in-cheek.

sea with a free, contemptuous gesture. There was only one book of the sea, and there never would be another worth mentioning. I fear that a native caution has shut me from many good things in life, so I smiled at my friend; yet, in the way of a cautious man, I smiled at him with sound reason. I had not read the White Whale; I had only heard rumors of it. But I knew "Typee" and "Omoo," and I knew my colleague even better. I may point out that a brief experience on the Somme battlefield[2] unbalanced his mind, and he died insane. Now "Typee" and its mate are brisk and attractive narratives of travel and adventure, exuberantly descriptive, lively with their honey-colored girls and palm groves, jolly with the talk of seamen in fo'castles of ships sailing waters few of us know, though we all wish we did, and full of the observation of an original mind in a tropic world that is no more. But they are not great literature. I knew perfectly well that the author of "Typee" was not the man to rise to that stellar altitude which moved my colleague to rapture and wonder. That was not Melville's plane, and having read the American writer's first two books, I thought a busy man, amid a wilderness of unread works, need not bother himself about this White Whale, for hardly a doubt it was just a whale.

I was wrong. My friend who was unbalanced by the war was right. I do not know whether Americans are aware of the position of their Melville as a writer, but I find it difficult to write of his great book within measure, for I have no doubt "Moby Dick" goes into that small company of big, extravagant, generative books which have made other writers fertile in all ages—I mean the books we cannot classify, but which must be read by every man who writes—"Gargantua and Pantagruel," "Don Quixote," "Gulliver's Travels," "Tristram Shandy," and the "Pickwick Papers."[3] That is where "Moby Dick" is, and it is therefore as important a creative effort as America has made in her history. I will sing "The Star-Spangled Banner,"[4] if that is the right hymn, with fervor and the deepest sense of debt and gratitude, at any patriotic thanksgiving service for "Moby Dick." I would assist any future body of Pilgrim Fathers to any place on earth if on their venture depended the vitality of the seed of such a book as that. The inchoate jungle of human society flowers, and in a sense is justified, in its great books, carrying in them in microcosm its fortunate future, or, if there is no future for it in the future, then its sad but heroic story.

Melville's extraordinary yarn about the White Whale came my way only recently. I had always recognized that it was a book I ought to look at, and when by chance a new edition coincided with some leisure I began to experiment upon it. I must confess that my mind to-day is not what it was in 1914. It is, as a polite alienist might say, possessed. I think all day of but one thing, and at night I dream about it. The Somme did not make me insane like my colleague, but I am not in the least surprised by his fate. I set out, with small hope, with Ahab after Moby Dick. I was at once caught in an awful adventure in which men, ships, seas,

2  Battle of the Somme (July 1, 1916–November 1916), a horrific four-month engagement along the Somme river on the western front in the First World War. The British army lost over 55,000 men on the first day alone.
3  See n. 2, p. 59.
4  See n. 3, p. 60.

harpoons, and Leviathan are but dread symbols, and in a sense I have never returned from that trip. I became missing as soon as the Pequod was out of sight of Nantucket. While the book was unfinished there was no home, there were no duties, and time and space were figments. It was an immense experience [. . .]

# *Moby-Dick* Rising: Melville Criticism 1919–70

From **William Charvat, "Melville and the Common Reader,"** *Studies in Bibliography*, XII (1958): 41–57. Reprinted in Matthew J. Bruccoli, ed., *The Profession of Authorship in America 1800–1870* (1992), Columbus, Ohio: Ohio State University Press, 262–82

> At a time when the overwhelming majority of scholars in the US were formal-ists Charvat was dutifully working to uncover the material conditions of authorship in the US and to locate major American writers more properly within the print culture of their times. The recent resurgence in interest in print culture and the so-called "history of the book," at least in the US, has recast Charvat as an important critic in his own right and a forerunner of several current critical methodologies. The excerpt below provides a concrete sense of Melville's relation to his audience and to antebellum print culture generally (see **pp. 21–7**).

Melville's career in fiction reflects almost all those tensions between the artist and society which sometimes make literature and sometimes mar it. He was, first of all, out of harmony with a predominantly female fiction-reading public. It is a crude but not misleading index to taste in his time that *Moby-Dick*, a thoroughly masculine book which few women have liked, sold only 2,500 copies in its first five years and less than 3,000 in its first twenty, whereas *The Scarlet Letter*, in identical periods, sold 10,800 and 25,200.

Second, Melville's effective career came to an end at an unfortunate moment. Though the fiction-reading audience on the Atlantic coast had begun to stratify in the 1840's, it was a decade before reader levels in the national market were clearly defined. Melville's proper level was the upper middle class, where, in the 1850's, literary taste was beginning to be interpreted and guided by the editors of national monthly magazines like *Harper's* and the *Atlantic*. Central to Melville's problem was the fact that he entered this magazine world only in 1853, when his reputation was already ruined. All his earlier work was published in book form, and was offered to an undifferentiated audience of men, women, and children among whom there was, of course, a fantastic range of sophistication and seriousness. Thus it was possible for a leading critic to label *Typee* and *Omoo* as "vendible," "venomous," and "venereous," and for a Cleveland[1] bookseller to advertise the same titles as "Books for Little Folks."

---

1   Cleveland, Ohio. A major city in the Midwestern US.

I shall be using the term "common reader" glibly, realizing that it refers to mentalities as different as "the superficial skimmer of pages" (Melville's phrase) and what Albert Guérard[2] calls "the alert non-professional reader." In Melville criticism one locates the common reader by ear, as it were. His professional readers are more easily identified. They were not university men for whom, as in our time, literature exists in its own right, but reviewers for newspapers and magazines whose first allegiance was not to art but to the immediate interest of society [. . .]

[. . .] The difference between his common readers and his critics emerges clearly in their responses to his public personality. From first to last, Melville was known by friend and foe alike as a vibrant, fascinating stylist whose moods, ranging from the gay, fanciful, playful, funny, and impudent, to the somber and meditative, were those of a living, colorful person. Because it was an intimate style, the common readers took it to be an expression of all that Melville was, and typed him as a free-wheeling bachelor-sailor with a gift for narrative. It was inevitable that they should have tried to exploit his personality ("Typee Melville" and "Mr. Omoo" were common nicknames, to his shame and annoyance), just as Wolfe and Hemingway and Dylan Thomas[3] have been exploited in our own time. The critics, on the other hand, were worried precisely because this intimate style was so palatable to readers who could be corrupted by the subversive thinking which was masked by that style. They need not have worried. All the evidence indicates that common readers skipped or ignored his persistent criticism of institutions, and did not buy those books in which thinking crowded the narrative [. . .]

From **Walter E. Bezanson, "Moby-Dick: Work of Art,"** in Tyrus Hillway and Luther S. Mansfield, eds, *Moby-Dick Centennial Essays* (1953), Dallas: Southern Methodist University Press, 30–58. Reprinted in Brian Higgins and Hershel Parker, eds, *Critical Essays on Herman Melville's Moby Dick* (1992), New York: Macmillan, 421–39

Bezanson is a seminal Melville scholar and the excerpt below represents one of the many such efforts to establish *Moby-Dick*'s merits as a work of literary art first and foremost, and only secondly as an important moment in literary history or US culture. Students should notice especially Bezanson's attempt to explain away the novel's formal and rhetorical incongruities by referring to its inherently organic structure, something recent critics ignore or have attempted to refute.

---

2   Albert Guérard (1914–2000), noted American scholar and critic. Professor at Harvard and Stanford, his students have included several major contemporary American writers, John Updike (1932–) among them.
3   Thomas Wolfe (1900–38), American novelist and author of *Look Homeward Angel* (1929); Ernest Hemingway (1898–1961), American writer and author of *Farewell to Arms* (1929); Dylan Thomas (1914–53), Welsh poet of "Do Not Go Gentle Into That Good Night" and *Under Milk Wood*.

[. . .] Some readers, looking beyond the simpler narrative, take *Moby-Dick* as *vade mecum*,[1] in our peculiarly bedeviled times searching out what its ethical imperatives may be. Still other readers help to multiply its influence through scholarship and art; for in addition to shaking down a white snowstorm of books, essays, and commentaries, *Moby-Dick* has inspired fine poems by Hart Crane and W. H. Auden, illustrations by Rockwell Kent and Boardman Robinson, paintings by Gil Wilson, a concerto by Ghedini,[2] several radio dramas, two old-time films of flickering merit (who could forget the anguished, silent groaning of John Barrymore?);[3] and from time to time good artists and directors are tempted to produce a *Moby-Dick* opera, a *Moby-Dick* ballet, and a good (if the temptations could be resisted) *Moby-Dick* movie. Then, too, readers of *Moby-Dick* are almost inevitably drawn to reading something about Melville himself: his memorable Pacific adventures, his immersion in the rich world of books and ideas, his complex spiritual and psychological history, and the nearly unique decline and recovery of his subsequent reputation.

All these matters have their attractions, and will continue to have them. Yet underlying them all is at once a simpler and a more complex attraction – the fact that the book is a work of art, and that it is a work of art of a most unusual sort. Curiously enough, it is precisely here that our reading and scholarship have been least adequate. Interest in *Moby-Dick* as direct narrative, as moral analogue, as modern source, and as spiritual autobiography has far outrun commentary on it as a work of art. A proper criticism of so complex a book will be a long time in the making and will need immense attention from many kinds of critics. In the meantime I am struck by the need just now for contributions toward a relatively impersonal criticism directed at the book itself. The surrounding areas – such as *Moby-Dick* and Melville, *Moby-Dick* and the times in which it was made – are significant just because the book is a work of art. To ask what the book means is to ask what it is about, and to ask what it is about is in turn to ask how art works in the case at hand. [. . .]

To go from *The Scarlet Letter* to *Moby-Dick* is to move from the Newtonian world-as-machine to the Darwinian world-as-organism.[4] In the older cosmology the key concepts had been law, balance, harmony, reason; in the newer, they became origin, process, development, growth. Concurrently biological images arose to take the place of the older mechanical analogies: growing plants and life forms now symbolized cosmic ultimates better than a watch or the slow-turning

---

1  A useful guidebook or reference work.
2  Hart Crane (1899–1932), American poet; W. H. Auden (1907–73), English poet; Rockwell Kent (1882–1971), noted US painter and illustrator who illustrated a now famous edition of *Moby-Dick* (1930) for Lakeside Press; Boardman Robinson (1876–1952), political cartoonist for the *New York Times* and *New York Tribune*; Gilbert Wilson (1907–91), noted American muralist who painted several paintings on various subjects taken from *Moby-Dick*; Giorgio Federico Ghedini (1892–1965), minor Italian composer who wrote a cantata (short, unacted opera) on themes from *Moby-Dick* as well as an opera based on *Billy Budd*.
3  There have been three major motion picture productions of *Moby-Dick*: *Sea Beast* (1925-silent) starring John Barrymore as Ahab; *Moby Dick* (1956) directed by John Huston and starring Gregory Peck; and a recent TV movie (1998) starring Patrick Stewart.
4  From an orderly, teleological world to one whose order is emergent and organic.

rods and gears of an eighteenth-century orrery.[5] It is enough for our purposes to note that the man who gave scientific validity to the organic world view concluded the key chapter of his great book, *The Origin of Species*,[6] with an extended image of "the great Tree of Life . . . with its ever branching and beautiful ramifications." It was a crucial simile that exploited not the tree but the tree's growth. [. . .]

Organic form is not a particular form but a structural principle. In *Moby-Dick* this principle would seem to be a peculiar quality of making and unmaking itself as it goes. The method of the book is unceasingly genetic, conveying the effect of a restless series of morphic–amorphic movements. Ishmael's narrative is always in process and in all but the most literal sense remains unfinished. For the good reader the experience of *Moby-Dick* is a participation in the act of creation. Find a key word or metaphor, start to pick it as you would a wild flower, and you will find yourself ripping up the whole forest floor. Rhetoric grows into symbolism and symbolism into structure; then all falls away and begins over again. [. . .]

The great thing about fiction, which is simply the telling of a story in written words, is that it is fiction. That it is "made up" is not its weakness but, as with all art, its greatest strength. In the successful work of fiction certain kinds of possibilities, attitudes, people, acts, situations, necessities, for the first and last time exist. They exist only through form. So it is with *Moby-Dick* – Ishmael's vast symbolic prose-poem in a free organic form. From *olim erat* to *finis*[7] is all the space and time there is.

## From **Merton M. Sealts, Jr., "Melville and Emerson's Rainbow,"** in *Pursuing Melville, 1940–1980: Chapters and Essays* (1982), Madison, Wisc. and London: University of Wisconsin Press, 267–70. Reprinted in Brian Higgins and Hershel Parker, eds, *Critical Essays on Herman Melville's Moby Dick* (1992), New York: Macmillan, 349–54

Sealts, like Bezanson, was a seminal Melvillean and the essay excerpted below remains an important starting point for understanding Melville's intellectual affinity (or difference, depending on one's reading of *Moby-Dick*) to Emerson specifically and to American Transcendentalism generally (see **pp. 41–4**).

When Melville began *Moby-Dick* early in 1850, he not only knew something of Emerson but was familiar as well with major European authors from Plato to Goethe whose works significantly influenced American Transcendentalism. Emerson once remarked of the Transcendentalists that perhaps they agreed only "in having fallen upon Coleridge and Wordsworth and Goethe, then on Carlyle, with pleasure and sympathy." By this token Melville too could be charged

---

5   A mechanical model of the solar system.
6   Charles Darwin's *The Origin of Species* appeared in 1859.
7   *Olim erat*: at one time, long ago; *finis*: the end.

with Transcendentalist leanings in 1850 and 1851, though in fact he read all of these authors as he read Emerson: with fundamental reservations.[1]

Of the four writers Emerson names, Melville had "fallen upon" Coleridge early in 1848, when he bought a two-volume edition of the *Biographia Literaria*,[2] and he also owned a heavily marked 1839 edition of Wordsworth's poetry. A direct reflection of his recent reading in 1848 and 1849 is his caricature of the "transcendental divine" in *White-Jacket*, a book written at top speed along with the earlier *Redburn* in the summer of 1849 to repair losses in standing and income attending the unpopular *Mardi*.[3] The chaplain's sermons were as "ill calculated to benefit the crew" of his vessel as *Mardi* to please the average reader. Like the author of *Mardi*, the chaplain had tasted of "the mystic fountain of Plato; his head had been turned by the Germans; and . . . White-Jacket himself saw him with Coleridge's Biographia Literaria in his hand." Both the chaplain and Melville must also have been reading Andrews Norton,[4] that distinctly *anti*transcendental divine who in 1839 had attacked Emerson's Divinity School Address[5] as "the latest form of infidelity"; the chaplain's allusion to an obscure tract by Tertullian and Ishmael's later references in *Moby-Dick* to Gnostic thought apparently come from Melville's own knowledge of Norton's *magnum opus*, *The Evidences of the Genuineness of the Gospels* (1844), as Professor Thomas Vargish[6] has demonstrated. Perhaps Melville had been reading Norton as well as Emerson while visiting the Shaws[7] during the previous winter.

In the fall of 1849, when Melville was on his way to Europe, he could hold his own in talking "German metaphysics" with a shipboard companion, George Adler,[8] whose philosophy he immediately identified as "Coleridgean." By this time he was interested enough in German writers to buy Goethe's *Auto-Biography* in London and to borrow his *Wilhelm Meister* from Duyckinck after his return to New York; during the summer of 1850, when he was already at work on *Moby-Dick*, he also borrowed three of Carlyle's writings. However much or little of Emerson Melville had read by 1850 and 1851, he obviously knew other Transcendental scripture, and it seems safe to say that his reading of one book in particular—Carlyle's *Sartor Resartus*, with its central idea of "all visible things" as "emblems" of the invisible, and of Nature itself as "*the living visible Garment of God*"—had at least as much to do with the symbolism of *Moby-Dick* as anything in the "Language" chapter of Emerson's *Nature*.

---

1   See letter to Duyckinck on **pp. 48–9**.
2   Coleridge's *Biographia Literaria* appeared in 1817 and was a philosophical and autobiographical work exploring the author's "literary life and opinions."
3   See **pp. 12–13**.
4   Noted Unitarian minister whose *Statement of Reasons for Not Believing the Doctrine of Trinitarians* (1819) was a central text of the Unitarian Church. He was a vocal critic of Emerson and Transcendentalism (see **pp. 41–4**).
5   Emerson's 1838 speech to the graduating class of the Harvard Divinity School called into question many of the school's fundamental doctrines and outraged attacks in newspapers and pamphlets ensued.
6   Thomas Vargish, "Gnostic Mythos in *Moby-Dick*," *PMLA* 81 (June 1966), 272–7.
7   Melville's in-laws.
8   George Adler (1821–68), friend of Duyckinck and a scholar of German philosophy and literature. Adler shared passage with Melville on his 1849 trip to London to negotiate the publication of *White-Jacket*.

There was a basic reservation in Melville's mind that kept him from giving more than passing allegiance to any form of philosophical idealism, whether he found it in Plato or Proclus or in their modern successors—Carlyle, Goethe, and Emerson. In *Mardi* his Babbalanja had spoken of external nature as something neutral toward mankind rather than benevolent, and in *Moby-Dick* Ishmael makes the dismaying comment that though "in many of its aspects this visible world *seems* formed in love, the invisible spheres *were* formed in fright" (emphasis added). Both Ishmael and Ahab, like idealists generally, are of course incurable analogists—so, for that matter, were Hawthorne and the supposedly anti-Transcendental Poe. But Ahab, as Leon Howard has said, is "an imperfect Transcendentalist"; "All visible objects," he agrees, "are but as pasteboard masks"—yet "sometimes" he thinks "there's naught beyond." Between such opposite negations, as walls, Melville's own being was also swung.

As Melville worked on *Moby-Dick* at Pittsfield during the fall of 1850 and most of the following year, the Hawthornes were in residence at Lenox, some seven miles away. He had a number of opportunities to discuss Emerson and Transcendentalism with both Hawthorne and his wife; Mrs. Hawthorne had known Emerson before her marriage in 1842 and the Hawthornes' occupancy of the Old Manse in Concord. On at least one occasion Melville and Hawthorne talked of Thoreau, whom Melville was reading late in 1850, and Emerson may have figured as well when they tackled what Melville called "the Problem of the Universe," discussing "metaphysics" and indulging in "ontological heroics."[9] Melville's visits to the Hawthornes' cottage sometimes lasted overnight. "He was very careful not to interrupt Mr Hawthorne's mornings," Sophia Hawthorne reported; morning was the time when her husband did his writing. Melville "generally walked off somewhere," she explained, "—& one morning he shut himself into the boudoir & read Mr Emerson's Essays in presence of our beautiful picture."

The ideas of their sometime neighbor in Concord possibly meant more to Sophia Hawthorne than to her husband, who after their marriage, as he wrote in "The Old Manse," came to admire Emerson "as a poet of deep beauty and austere tenderness, but sought nothing from him as a philosopher." Melville valued her judgment and once told her, in response to her praise of *Moby-Dick*, that with her "spiritualizing nature" she saw "more things than other people." She did not specify which of "Mr Emerson's Essays" occupied Melville during that particular morning at the cottage, which can probably be dated early in September of 1850. Although she could have meant *Essays* or *Essays: Second Series*, she could just as well have been thinking of Emerson's writings in general. By this time the Hawthornes owned presentation copies[10] of every book Emerson had then published, from the first edition of *Nature*, given her when she was Sophia Peabody, to the most recent. While telling Melville of her friendship with the Emersons, she may have shown him any or all of these books. What he read that morning, given his probable familiarity by this time with the Essays of

9 Presumably, speculative, alcohol-fueled philosophical discussion.
10 Copies given as gifts by the author.

1841 and 1844, was more likely something later—either *Nature, Addresses, and Lectures*, which had appeared in September of 1849 while he was preparing to sail for Europe, or *Representative Men*, published early in 1850 while he was still abroad. [. . .]

From **Leon Howard, "The Influence of Carlyle,"** in James Barbour and Thomas Quirk, eds, *The Unfolding of MOBY-DICK* (1987), Glassboro, N.J.: The Melville Society, 39–43. Reprinted in Brian Higgins and Hershel Parker, eds, *Critical Essays on Herman Melville's* Moby-Dick (1992), New York: Macmillan, 377–80.

> Like Sealts, Howard's piece is a vital starting point for understanding Melville's deep intellectual and stylistic indebtedness to one of *Moby-Dick*'s major influences – in this case Carlyle. Note especially Howard's discussion of Ahab and of the philosophy that emerges in the novel in several key chapters, some of which are included in Section 3.

During the latter part of 1850 Melville was also reading Carlyle. He borrowed *Sartor Resartus* and *Heroes and Hero-Worship* from Duyckinck's library shortly before he went on his vacation and Carlyle's translation of German Romances shortly before he moved to Pittsfield. He may have been interested in the last two because their titles suggested a possible usefulness in developing the Romantic elements in his book, but, though they may have had some effect upon his style, it was *Sartor Resartus* which was to have an important influence upon the evolution of *Moby-Dick*.

Like James Russell Lowell and other contemporaries, Melville appears to have been attracted by the rhetoric of Carlyle's sardonic[1] humor before becoming interested in the substance of his book. He had been attracted by Sir Thomas Browne and Robert Burton and by Duchat's translation of Rabelais while writing *Mardi* and was reading Richter[2] in translations by both Noel and Carlyle. But, though he respected Emerson as a "thought-diver," he was suspicious of Transcendental philosophy; and he had no conception of the *Bildungsroman* which Carlyle, in his own peculiar way, was introducing into English literature. Yet his own tendency toward sardonic humor and rhetorical extravagance enabled him to appreciate an author who could identify his own thoughts and emotions with a hero named Teufelsdröckh, express them in language of Shakespearean extravagance, and become the wandering outcast of his own dark mind with a sense of heroic self-confidence rather than Byronic guilt.[3] [. . .]

---

1   Cynically scornful or mocking.
2   Jean Paul Richter (1763–1825). German Romantic admired by Carlyle among others; his works incorporated dream-like elements and mysticism.
3   Lord George Byron (1788–1824). British Romantic poet whose works often depicted the hero as tortured and driven by secret guilt.

Ahab's emblematic universe was certainly more directly out of *Sartor Resartus* than out of the lecture on Mahomet. His best expression of it is in his words to Starbuck in "The Quarter-Deck":[4] "All visible objects, man, are but as pasteboard masks. But in each event—in the living act, the undoubted deed—there, some unknown but still reasoning thing puts forth the mouldings of his features from behind the unreasoning mask." This is very close to Teufelsdröckh's conviction that "all visible things are emblems; what thou seest is not there on its own account; strictly taken, it is not there at all: Matter exists only spiritually, and to represent some Idea, and *body* it forth." Furthermore, Ahab's attitude toward it came directly from *Sartor*. He did not see the material universe as God's shadow, as Mahomet did, or as the manifestation of some more abstract divine Spirit as Teufelsdröckh came to see it. He saw it through the eyes of Carlyle's hero in the first stage of an experience equivalent to a Christian "conversion"—when he became aware of evil and felt that it was the strongest force in the universe, yet was determined to resist and overcome it. Carlyle's hero followed the conventional Christian's progress through the slough of despond to the Beulah land[5] of the "Everlasting Yea." Ahab died a heroic death at the height of his defiance.

Carlyle also influenced Melville's more recognizably personal meditations on philosophical matters. If he took Carlyle's advice to close his Byron and open his Goethe, the Goethe who most affected his novel came directly from *Sartor Resartus* in the form of the Earth-spirit in *Faust* as it had appeared in Carlyle's chapter on "The World Out of Clothes." This was the image of the Creator, weaving "on the roaring Loom of Time" the visible universe as the living garment of God. Melville adopted it almost literally for his "weaver-god" in "A Bower in the Arsacides." But Melville also used it in two other chapters in an imaginative way which surely came after the literal fancy. In "The Castaway" it became the more abstract and greater god, indifferent to weal or woe, who was above and behind the demiurge[6] of *Faust* (of chap. 102); and when Pip saw "God's foot on the treadle of the loom, and spoke it," "his shipmates called him mad." In "The Mat-Maker" the god disappeared altogether, leaving "the Loom of Time" as a frame for fate, free-will, and chance as the individual used his shuttle to weave the woof of free-will into the warp of necessity while the indifferent batten tightened the weave, more or less, with its random blows. It is this sort of speculation about the three-fold possibility of causation which provides the philosophical background for Ahab's final outburst of determination, just before the chase begins: "Is Ahab, Ahab? Is it I, God, or who that lifts this arm?"[7]

[. . .] The climax of Carlyle's suggestive influence upon Melville's imagination occurred in chapter 119, "The Candles,"[8] in which his own recent personal experience, his feeling for Shakespearean drama, the literal implications of a metaphor from *Sartor*, and a Carlylean hero genuinely akin to Ahab all combined to enable him to heighten his drama and weave into it not only his romantic hero

---

4  See Chapter 36, "The Quarter-Deck" on **pp. 151–2**.
5  Promised land.
6  A powerful primary cause or source of creation.
7  See Chapter 132, "The Symphony," on **pp. 171–2**.
8  See Chapter 119 "The Candles" on **pp. 170–1**.

but also the Byronic orientalism[9] he had found difficult to manage in his earlier narrative. The chapter deals with the typhoon at the height of its awesome fury, the appearance of the corpusants or St. Elmo's fire[10] which Melville had seen for the first time on his voyage home from England, and the reappearance of the Parsee who had slipped out of the book with the beginning of the Beale section. The metaphor is contained in Carlyle's reference to Teufelsdröckh's "Spiritual New-birth" as his "Baphometic Fire-baptism" and said that "the fire-baptised soul, long so scathed and thunder-driven ... finds its own Freedom" in that feeling which was "its Baphometic Baptism." The adjective (derived from a medieval corruption of "Mahomet") was a peculiar one, but Melville would have found its metaphorical implications fully revealed in another book he had borrowed from Duyckinck at the time he borrowed *Sartor Resartus*—Carlyle's *On Heroes and Hero-Worship*. There Carlyle represented Mahomet, "The Hero as Prophet," as a "fiery mass of Life," a "strong wild man," with "a strong untutored intellect" who scorned "formulas and hearsays" and "was alone with his own soule and the reality of things." He could see the Truth behind material appearances, and his wild followers "must have seen what kind of man he *was*, let him be *called* what you like." [. . .]

From **Henry A. Murray, "In Nomine Diaboli,"** *New England Quarterly* 24 (December 1951), 435–52. Reprinted in Brian Higgins and Hershel Parker, eds, *Critical Essays on Herman Melville's* Moby Dick (1992), New York: Macmillan, 408–20.

Murray here represents attempts by critics to establish not simply how *Moby-Dick* generated its meanings but what the novel did in fact *mean* concerning philosophy, religion, politics and its various other topics (there seems no end to the list of subjects critics have identified the work as investigating). Also, perhaps more than any other essay on *Moby-Dick* up to the time of its publication, Murray's piece established an image of Melville as dark, brooding, and blasphemous – the very sort of figure in "Hawthorne and his Mosses" (**pp. 38–40**) and in his letters to Hawthorne (**pp. 49–53**) that Melville envisioned as the consummate literary artist. Compare Murray's "Melville" to that of more recent critics in *Moby-Dick* at the Millennium (**pp. 98–125**).

9 According to Edward Said's *Orientalism* (1979), orientalism is the study of the Orient as well as a style of thought based upon a distinction between "the Orient" and the "Occident." The term is often used to refer to the tendency in the West to both idealize and distort the East in its representations of it. "Byronic orientalism" refers to the ways in which Melville tried to emulate stylistically Byron's poetry dealing with eastern themes and subject matter.

10 St Elmo's Fire is the luminous discharge of electricity from some object into the atmosphere. The phenomenon occurs when the atmosphere becomes charged with enough electricity to cause a discharge between the object and the air around it. It usually appears as fiery jets extending from the tips of a ship's mast or spar, or a wing, propeller, or other part of an aircraft, or a steeple. Also known as "corposant," the appearance of St Elmo's Fire was long regarded as a bad omen.

[. . .] To me, *Moby-Dick* was Beethoven's *Eroica*[1] in words: first of all, a masterly orchestration of harmonic and melodic language, of resonating images and thoughts in varied metres. Equally compelling were the spacious sea-setting of the story, the cast of characters and their prodigious common target, the sorrow, the fury, and the terror, together with all those frequent touches, those subtle interminglings of unexampled humor, quizzical and, in the American way, extravagant, and finally the fated closure, the crown and tragic consummation of the immense yet firmly-welded whole. But still more extraordinary and portentous were the penetration and scope, the sheer audacity of the author's imagination. Here was a man who did not fly away with his surprising fantasies to some unbelievable dreamland, pale or florid, shunning the stubborn objects and gritty facts, the prosaic routines and practicalities of everyday existence. Here was a man who, on the contrary, chose these very things as vessels for his procreative powers—the whale as a naturalist, a Hunter or a Cuvier,[2] would perceive him, the business of killing whales, the whale-ship running as an oil factory, stowing-down, in fact, every mechanism and technique, each tool and gadget, that was integral to the money-minded industry of whaling. Here was a man who could describe the appearance, the concrete matter-of-factness, and the utility of each one of these natural objects, implements, and tools with the fidelity of a scientist, and, while doing this, explore it as a conceivable repository of some aspect of the human drama; then, by an imaginative tour de force, deliver a vital essence, some humorous or profound idea, coalescing with its embodiment. But still more. Differing from the symbolists[3] of our time, here was a man who offered us essences and meanings which did not level or depreciate the objects of his contemplation. On the contrary, this loving man exalted all creatures—the mariners, renegades, and castaways on board the *Pequod*—by ascribing to them "high qualities, though dark" and weaving round them "tragic graces." Here, in short, was a man with the myth-making powers of a Blake,[4] a hive of significant associations, who was capable of reuniting what science had put asunder—pure perception and relevant emotion—and doing it in an exultant way that was acceptable to skepticism. [. . .]

[. . .] Melville's clear intention was to bring not rest, but *unrest* to intrepid minds. All gentle people were warned away from his book "on risk of a lumbago or sciatica." "A polar wind blows through it," he announced.[5] He had not written to soothe, but to kindle, to make men leap from their seats, as Whitman would say, and fight for their lives. Was it the poet's function to buttress the battlements

---

1  A symphony by Beethoven written in honor of Napoleon Bonaparte (although Beethoven later retracted the dedication), significant for its great length (it was the longest symphony ever written at the time) and its formal innovation.
2  Noted nineteenth-century biologists.
3  Poets who see the immediate, unique and personal emotional response as the proper subject of art. As a result "the poet is reduced to the use of a complex and highly private kind of symbolization in an effort to give expression to an evanescent and ineffable feeling." Its practitioners include Baudelaire, Mallarmé, Yeats, and T. S. Eliot.
4  William Blake (1757–1827). English poet and painter and a primary influence on the Romantics.
5  See letter, Melville to Sarah Huyler Morewood, September 1851, pp. 53–4.

of complacency, to give comfort to the enemy? There is little doubt about the nature of the enemy in Melville's day. It was the dominant ideology, that peculiar compound of puritanism and materialism, of rationalism and commercialism, of shallow, blatant optimism and technology, which proved so crushing to creative evolutions in religion, art, and life. In such circumstances every "true poet," as Blake said, "is of the Devil's party,"[6] whether he knows it or not. Surveying the last hundred and fifty years, how many exceptions to this statement can we find? Melville, anyhow, knew that *he* belonged to the party, and while writing *Moby-Dick* so gloried in his membership that he baptized his work *In Nomine Diaboli*. It was precisely under these auspices that he created his solitary masterpiece, a construction of the same high order as the Constitution of the United States and the scientific treatises of Willard Gibbs,[7] though huge and wild and unruly as the Grand Canyon. And it is for this marvel chiefly that he resides in our hearts now among the greatest in "that small but high-hushed world" of bestowing geniuses [. . .]

## From J. A. Ward, "The Function of the Cetological Chapters in *Moby-Dick*," *American Literature* 28 (1956): 164–83

Ward's essay makes a plausible case for the function of the cetology in the novel as a whole and as one reader's account of the cumulative effect of Melville's use of fact is certainly compelling. Equally compelling, but very different in important ways, is Greenberg's account, which argues that rather than coming together in a seamless whole the cumulative effect of the cetology is to leave the reader with a sense of "epistemological fragmentation."

One of the major factors in retarding the reputation of Mr. Melville's *Moby-Dick* was the unpopularity of the chapters that methodically describe the appearance and activity of the whale and the various processes involved in whaling. Both the reading public and the literary critics found it difficult to accept what appeared to them an incongruous blend of formal exposition and traditional narration, a partial novel that could also serve as a handbook treatise on whaling, a chaotic melange of adventure, metaphysics and amateur scientific investigation. Today, however, with the increasing tendency to examine Melville's fiction as *sui generis*[1] and rather outside the main stream of the English, or, for that matter, the American novel, it is no longer orthodox even to consider Melville as an artless

---

6    From Blake's *The Marriage of Heaven and Hell* (1790): "But in Milton; the Father is Destiny, the Son, a Ratio of the five senses,/& the Holy-ghost, Vacuum!/ Note. The reason Milton wrote in fetters when he wrote of Angels/& God, and at liberty when of Devils & Hell, is because he was a true/Poet, and of the Devils party without knowing it."
7    Josiah Willard Gibbs (1839–1903), noted American mathematical physicist.

---

1    A genre unto itself.

genius ... Since recent criticism consistently defends Melville's inclusion of the unorthodox cetological chapters in *Moby-Dick*, my approach in discussing the function, techniques, and effects of the whaling passages will be analytical rather than apologetic.

In all of the novels before *Moby-Dick*, Melville reveals his interest in detailed description of things, of places, and of processes. Undoubtedly a good deal of the early expository writing stemmed from Melville's intention of satisfying a reading public with an interest in travel literature. The heavily detailed descriptions of the processes of tappa-weaving and breadfruit preparation in *Typee*, like the nearly documentary report of life on a man-of-war in *White-Jacket*, proved interesting as ends in themselves to a mid-nineteenth century reading public with a stronger relish for the remote and the exotic than for technical excellence in fiction. But to accept the taste of Melville's audience as the only explanation for the non-narrative digressions is obviously to underestimate the early fiction. For there is at least a partial thematic significance in all of the digressive passages. In *Typee* Tommo's effort to understand his environment and the nature of his captivity provides not only the suspense of the novel but also its underlying thematic movement. [. . .]

By the time he had written *White-Jacket*, Melville found the fundamental method that he was to use with most success in *Moby-Dick*. In all of the early novels there is an attempt to include everything and a developing awareness that such completeness can best be achieved by using the ship as a microcosm of the universe and by enlarging the meaning of concrete fact by metaphor and by literary, historical, and mythological allusion. Melville constantly attempted to arrive at an understanding of spiritual reality through an understanding of physical reality. It was possible for him—though he had not yet fully utilized his capabilities—to link all reality with one reality, to manufacture a network of relationships which would enable him to know everything by knowing one thing fully. He found that the material he had selected to treat in *Moby-Dick* would be ideal for metaphorical treatment, especially since the quest motif would be dominant and the object of the quest, the white whale, would serve as the object of both physical and metaphysical capture. Never before in Melville's fiction had there been such a complete union between physical object and spiritual truth; with the whale as object, as the central force and symbol in the universe from the point of view of both Ahab and Ishmael, it was possible for Melville to explore the physical dimensions and spiritual implications of the whale without hindering the movement or digressing from the theme of the book.

*Moby-Dick* is a book much more suitable for digressions than any of the earlier novels. Clearly Melville had to find some artistically satisfactory method to inject variety in his story. He had to give the effect of a long voyage, but he had to face the obvious fact that on a long whaling voyage very little happens. To concentrate entirely on action would be to multiply the Ahab scenes and thereby to create an unendurable intensity; to concentrate on the trivia, on the day-to-day activity of the seamen or on the capture of every whale would be both repetitious and monotonous. Melville chose to solve this artistic problem by punctuating the

Ahab scenes and the whaling incidents with a series of expository chapters on whales and whaling. The whale is the common denominator, both object of exposition and object of quest.

[. . .] Clearly the narrative sections of the novel would be nearly incomprehensible without the extensive descriptions of the whale and whaling processes. The whaling manual serves to make the culminating engagement with *Moby-Dick* thoroughly clear; also, of course, it functions as a means of stimulating the reader's interest in the eventual engagement, for both Ahab and Moby Dick are alternately developed as antagonists of heroic proportions. By the time the *Pequod* meets Moby Dick Melville can describe the extended action without relaxing the narrative pace, for he can take for granted that the reader has an understanding of terminology and methods, as well as a basis for accepting what otherwise would be the incredible strength and maliciousness of the white whale. [. . .]

[. . .] For, if *Moby-Dick* is on the surface a quest for the white whale, it is symbolically and essentially a quest for a knowledge of the secrets of the universe. Ahab is unsuccessful in his effort to kill the whale and Melville is unsuccessful in grasping the deep truths he seeks for. The quest itself is all-important, and through it Melville reveals his own deep interest in solving the eternal problems. In *Moby-Dick* we find a variety of attitudes toward the relationship of God and man, extending from those of Father Mapple to those of the lunatic on the *Jereboam*; we find a variety of attempts toward attaining the deepest knowledge, most noticeably the efforts of Ahab, Ishmael, and Bulkington; we also find a variety of more subtle commentaries on the value of different ways of understanding. Moby Dick himself is symbolically and actually the prime figure in the cosmos; the whale, with its great size and power, its ambiguity that can be interpreted as malice or indifference, its malignity and beneficence, is the central force in the world and symbol of all the power of nonhuman nature. William Ellery Sedgwick[2] writes that "Ahab's great heart is stretched to bursting under the ceaseless effort of his mind to lay hold of [the truth]," and that "Ahab pursues the truth as the champion of man, leaving behind him all traditional conclusions, all common assumptions, all codes and creeds and articles of faith." In terms of the novel, to "strike through the mask"[3] is to lift the veil of ambiguity that disguises the purpose, meaning, and value of life itself. Ishmael, less defiant but more contemplative than Ahab seeks also to find in the sea and more directly in the white whale the ultimate meaning of things. His various meditations in such chapters as "The Mat-Maker," "The Monkey-Rope," and "The Try-Works"[4] are milestones in his quest for understanding [. . .]

---

2   William Ellery Sedgwick (1872–1960), American editor of the *Atlantic Monthly*.
3   See Chapter 36, "The Quarter-Deck," pp. 151–2.
4   See Chapter 96, "The Try-Works," pp. 162–4.

From **Robert M. Greenberg, "Cetology: Center of Multiplicity and Discord in *Moby-Dick*,"** *ESQ: A Journal of the American Renaissance* 27.1.102 (1981): 1–13

[. . .] With respect to the cetological material, which is the concern of this essay, J. A. Ward asserts that the whale remains the unifying link with the narrative portion, that it is "the common denominator, both object of exposition and object of quest." Melville moves from story to encyclopedic exposition "without hindering the movement or digressing from the theme of the book." While Ward's is a good article, rich in insight, it too exemplifies the tendency to make certain unifying claims that ignore the texture of the material both in terms of its aesthetic effect and its philosophic import. [. . .]

In this essay, I argue that the aesthetic and philosophic goal of the cetological material is to convey a sense of epistemological fragmentation and disarray. I also stress the manner in which Melville "dramatizes" a suprahuman perspective about the manifold interactions of mind and matter. He wants to present a clashing and boundless ocean of material forms and conscious meanings at the center of life. D. H. Lawrence has Melville's penchant for abstract and paradigmatic thinking in mind when he comments that Melville "is more spell-bound by the strange slidings and collidings of Matter than by the things men do."

Melville accomplishes his goal of talking about mind and matter by introducing into his treatise on the whale an unwieldy and heterogeneous mass of subject matter and by organizing and studying this subject matter in terms of multiple theories of knowledge and types of erudition. Some of these approaches to knowledge, such as the empirical and the symbolic approach, are reconcilable: the symbolist needs a foundation in factual reality. But most other approaches are mutually exclusive. In any case, all are in turn unsatisfying and incomplete; and they are intended to speak of an epistemological disarray in the face of complex and discordant planes of experience. "I wonder, Flask, whether the world is anchored anywhere; if she is, she swings with an uncommon long cable," says Stubb to his mate as they tie down the anchor. And it is precisely the artistic equivalent, in terms of form and content, of this kinaesthetic sensation of a "world of mind" swinging from a long cable, without any points of reference or unified theory of knowledge, that Melville is seeking to communicate. [. . .]

On the whole, these chapters create a sense neither of uniformity of material nor of thematic coherence. Within the circumscribing universe of a whaling voyage, there could not be more diversity of subject matter, more microcosmic attention to factual detail, more variety of expositional situation and literary mode, more novelty of macrocosmic reference. Also, at one with this diversity is the impression of the untiring conscientiousness, the comic busyness, of the narrator trying to do justice to his superabundant, hydra-headed vision of life. Ishmael alludes to these arduous demands as he explains an aspect of the cutting-in which he overlooked at the proper time:

> In the tumultuous business of cutting-in and attending to a whale, there is much running backwards and forwards among the crew. Now hands are wanted here, and then again hands are wanted there. There is

no staying in any one place; for at one and the same time everything
has to be done everywhere. *It is much the same with him who endeavors
the description of the scene.* [emphasis Greenberg's]

The impression this unit of chapters makes, then, with its abbreviated sequences,
its abrupt shifts in venue, proximity, and mode of presentation, with its sense of
multitudinous variety and relative absence of concerted narrative action, is of a
plenum[1] of life and of an equally animated and inexhaustible versatility of mind.
If there is unity, it is unity of only the highest, most general sort. The theme of the
dangerousness of life is a unifying element; so is the mutual abundance of mind
and world, yoked together even when antagonistic, by an immanent energy, an
interrelated and multifaceted vitality, that animates everything and that the whale
both symbolizes and embodies. [. . .]

## From **Thomas Werge, "*Moby-Dick* and the Calvinist Tradition,"** *Studies in the Novel* 1.4 (1969): 484–506

Raised in the Dutch Calvinism of his mother's family Melville was well-versed in
one of the major Protestant denominations of the period, especially throughout
New York State. *Moby-Dick* itself explores the limits of such fundamental Calvinist doctrines as the innate depravity of man, free will, determinism, and the limits
of knowledge and self-knowledge especially. Werge's piece provides a useful
starting point for exploring this fundamental aspect of both *Moby-Dick* and its
author. (See also the discussion of Calvinism in Transcendentalism, **pp. 41–2**.)

[. . .] "True and substantial wisdom," begins the *Institutes*, "principally consists
of two parts, the knowledge of God, and the knowledge of ourselves." Calvin
consciously echoes Augustine here; and Edwards, at the beginning of *Freedom of
the Will*, states the same central truth: "Of all kinds of knowledge that we can
ever obtain, the knowledge of God, and the knowledge of ourselves, are the most
important."[1] Yet for Calvin as for Edwards, self-knowledge and knowledge of
God are not distinct forms of knowing, since neither can come about without the
other. Man cannot know himself until he is able to see himself in relation to God,
nor is he able to "know" God until he becomes aware of his own self as created,
fallen and dependent. This dialectic is fundamental to the Calvinist tradition and
is the starting point for and a recurring theme in the *Institutes*; while in
*Moby-Dick*, the metaphor and movement of the journey, the concrete yet
symbolic Moby-Dick and the gradual awareness of Ishmael as the journey ends

---

1    Full and diverse collection.

---

1    Calvin, *Dedication of the Institutes of the Christian Religion* (1536); St Augustine (354–430) in
     his *Confessions* (*c*. 400); Jonathan Edwards (1703–58), American Puritan minister and religious
     philosopher – his best-known work is the sermon "Sinners in the Hands of an Angry God" (1741).

are bound up with the meaning of the sea, of leviathan and of Ishmael himself. That these elements are inseparable is made clear at two related points at the outset of the narrative.

When Ishmael, fascinated by the immensity of the sea, reflects on the "mystical vibration" the seagoer experiences when no longer in sight of land, he alludes to Narcissus,[2] "who because he could not grasp the tormenting, mild image he saw in the fountain, plunged into it and was drowned. But that same image, we ourselves see in all rivers and oceans. It is the image of the ungraspable phantom of life; and this is the key to it all."[3] And before the obscure painting at the Spouter-Inn begins to assume some clarity and meaning for Ishmael, he experiences a series of "bright, but, alas, deceptive ideas[s]" of its significance: "But at last all these fancies yielded to that one portentous something in the picture's midst. *That* once found out, and all the rest were plain. But stop; does it not bear a faint resemblance to a gigantic fish? even the great leviathan himself?"[4] In each instance, this elusive and "portentous something" cannot be "known" apart from the whole impression; for, once discovered, that knowledge will inform and illuminate the meaning of all understanding.

Though Calvin in part agrees with the classical and Aristotelian dictum that all men "by nature" desire to know truth and self, he is always aware of man's inability to achieve such knowledge: "For the dulness of the human mind renders it incapable of pursuing the right way of investigating the truth; it wanders through a variety of errors, and groping, as it were, in the shades of darkness, often stumbles, till at length it is lost in its wanderings: thus in its search after truth, it betrays its incapacity to seek and find it." To this emphasis, or Calvin's "stress on the point that man's sin has impaired not only his will but his intellect," many of the clashes between Calvinist and Unitarian,[5] and, later, transcendental thought may be traced – the nature of man, the doctrine of God and the efficacy of reason and a rational knowledge of God. For Calvin, the cause of man's failure to know the true and to will the good is the Fall. Had Adam retained his innocence, man's understanding and will would have remained in harmony with God. But in the Fall, "soundness of mind and rectitude of heart were also destroyed; and this is the corruption of the natural talents." [. . .]

Calvin's doctrine of "total depravity," then, is an insistence not only on the corruption of the will but on man's utter inability to reach God and His judgments through any mode of earthly knowledge. On this issue the Enlightenment contention that the *imago Dei*[6] in man is an uncorrupted reflection of a God whose nature is "kindred" to man's – and the Unitarian conviction that God may be defined as an infinite elevation of human reason – stand in stark opposition to Calvin's epistemology. For man, according to Calvin, cannot discover certainty

---

2   In Greek mythology, a beautiful youth who refused all offers of love who, as punishment for his indifference, is made to fall in love with his own image in a mountain pool.
3   See Chapter 1, "Loomings," **pp. 131–4.**
4   See Chapter 3 "The Spouter-Inn," **pp. 134–6.**
5   Protestant denomination in US and England that denied the doctrine of the Trinity and held that reason and conscience were the only guides to religious truth.
6   Image of God.

or absolute truth. When Paul states that we know in part and "see through a glass darkly,"[7] says Calvin, he indicates "how very slender a portion of that wisdom which is truly Divine" is given to us in this life: "although these words imply, not only that faith remains imperfect as long as we groan under the burden of the flesh, but that our imperfection renders it necessary for us to be unremittingly employed in acquiring farther [*sic*] knowledge; yet he suggests, that it is impossible for our narrow capacity to comprehend that which is infinite." For "how can the infinite essence of God," asks Calvin, "be defined by the narrow capacity of the human mind, which could never yet certainly determine the nature of the . . . sun, though the object of our daily contemplation?" Calvin uses the image of the sun not to compare its illuminating rays to man's participation in the Divine Reason, as do the Neoplatonists and transcendentalists, but to emphasize man's inability to comprehend the absolute. [. . .]

Yet it is in the cetological chapters that this tendency is most clearly exemplified. For throughout these chapters, whose relevance to the coherence of *Moby-Dick* and to Melville's concern with the problem of knowledge is clear, Ishmael emphasizes the "utter confusion" that characterizes man's attempts to understand the whale. Not even the most basic step of scientific method, the classifying of an organism, is possible when leviathan is the object of study: "In some quarters," he says, "it still remains a moot point whether a whale be a fish," and though the process of classification is elaborate, it ends by "signifying nothing" (ch. 32). In attempting to categorize the whale, states Ishmael, "I promise nothing complete," for "any human thing supposed to be complete, must for that very reason infallibly be faulty" (ch. 32). Every supposedly scientific analysis of the whale serves only to reinforce its incompleteness and uncertainty.

## *Moby-Dick* at the Millennium

From **Frank Shuffelton, "Going Through the Long Vaticans: Melville's 'Extracts' in *Moby-Dick*,"** *Texas Studies in Language and Literature* 25.4 (1983): 528–40

As Shuffelton points out, *Moby-Dick* does not actually begin with its famous opening line but with the extracts that precede it by several pages. The experience of reading *Moby-Dick* thus begins before Ahab, the white whale, or even Ishmael appear in the narrative. Shuffelton's piece is thus a useful starting point for understanding and responding to Melville's use of a common nineteenth-century literary device, the epigraph. This was a motto or quotation, often from a poem, set at the beginning of a literary composition or chapter encapsulating a forthcoming theme.

---

7    1 Corinthians 13:12: "For now we see through a glass, darkly; but then face to face: now I know in part; but then shall I know even as also I am known."

We are often reminded and catch ourselves reminding others that "Call me Ishmael" is one of the greatest opening lines in the history of the novel, but we thus forget that the first sentence of *Moby-Dick* is more properly "The pale Usher—threadbare in coat, heart, body, and brain; I see him now." The first fictional characters introduced to us are, after all, the pale Usher and the Sub-Sub-Librarian, the contributors to those opening pages many readers tend to skim over in their headlong rush for the whale. More important, both of these characters are subsumed into the vision and language of that tricky narrator who, when he does come to introduce himself, adopts a confidently self-revelatory tone while simultaneously offering a masquerading name. They are here because the narrator sees them and is commentator for them, but they are in turn buried in the narrator's experience, previous versions of his presumptive self. The "late consumptive Usher" is literally buried, and the Sub-Sub is a "burrower and a grubworm." Yet the facts they supply are valuable because they point the reader to the underlying conditions of the narrative, those categories of human response and categories of the world that permit a specific human experience of the world to have imagined meaning, and their gestures are paradoxically more effective in that their offerings seems oddly irrelevant to the narrative. "Etymology" and "Extracts," on the one hand, point to the historical and imaginative background of Ishmael's developing consciousness, foreshadowing his growth from the bored, dreadridden, but naive adventurer of the first chapters into the compassionate, polysemous[1] narrator who survives to tell us not merely his experiences but the nature of ours as well. On the other hand, these two sections tease us into thought, provoking us into an attentive, reactive, and questioning reading of Ishmael's narrative.

The multifarious possibilities of "Etymology" direct the reader to the issue of language and the difficult problem noted in the quotation from Hakluyt[2] of "the signification of the word" without which "you deliver that which is not true." The "Extracts," the more extensive and important contributions I shall focus on here, prepare the reader for the central problem of *Moby-Dick*, the problem of evolving consciousness in a nonhuman world. They foreshadow the themes which illustrate that problem, and their artful ordering initiates the reader into the process which becomes the narrative order of the book. *Moby-Dick* is an account of individual men, particularly Ahab and Ishmael, in spiritual crisis, and their struggles with world and the self must be comprehended in terms of humanity's fall into alienation and self-consciousness. The "Extracts" provide a model of this fall, a historical and evolutionary frame for *Moby-Dick*'s narrative vision of death and rebirth. They are, above all, "germinous seeds" which Melville has planted in his book for eventual discovery by eagle-eyed, contemplative readers in order that they too might recreate their imaginations as they create meaning. They

---

1  Polysemous: having two or more different meanings.
2  Richard Hakluyt (1552–1616), English geographer. The quote in "Etymology" is as follows: "While you take in hand to school others, and to teach them by what name a whale-fish is to be called in our tongue, leaving out, through ignorance, the letter H, which almost alone maketh up the signification of the word, you deliver that which is not true."

are most "germinous" in being least explained, in demanding that the reader at the very outset of the novel speculate upon the meaning and purpose of what he reads, indeed question its very status as truth. [. . .]

From **Mark Niemeyer, "*Moby-Dick* and the Spirit of Revolution,"** in Kevin J. Hayes, ed., *The Critical Response to Herman Melville's* Moby-Dick (1994), Westport, Conn.: Greenwood Press, 221–35

The year 1848 was a tumultuous one in European history, and artists, politicians and intellectuals committed to democracy were enthralled and horrified by the revolutionary fervor in Europe. Niemeyer's work provides valuable insight into the revolutions that swept the Continent in the years immediately preceding Melville's work on *Moby-Dick*, and the effect such political upheavals may have had on Melville's mighty book.

In the years immediately preceding the composition of Herman Melville's *Moby-Dick*, Europe was afire with a revolutionary spirit which sparked outbreaks of varying intensities throughout the continent and in Great Britain. Inspired by hopes of grand democratic reforms, in 1848, revolutionaries in France, Germany, Italy, Hungary, and Poland organized armed insurrections designed to overthrow monarchical rule. Unfortunately for the radicals, however, their attempts to create new societies based on greater social and economic justice failed. In France, for example, the abdication of King Louis-Philippe and subsequent proclamation of the Second Republic on 25 February 1848 was followed by continued frustration on the part of many poor workers. In June, after conservatives forced the dissolution of the *Ateliers nationaux* (communal workshops organized in the first weeks of the radical takeover to reduce unemployment and eliminate hunger), socialist-inspired insurgents, many holding defensive positions behind hastily constructed barricades in Paris, were brutally attacked and suppressed by the forces of the new democratic government. In December, Louis Napoléon Bonaparte was elected President of the Republic with a large majority, primarily due to the support of conservatives. The hopes of the radicals for genuine political and social reform had been dashed; Louis Napoléon's coup d'état in 1851 and subsequent elevation to Emperor only confirmed the defeat the revolutionaries had already experienced.

What I wish to show here, is that the theme of revolution, partially inspired by the contemporary (and earlier) events in France, is pervasive throughout *Moby-Dick* and that Melville's attitude towards the spirit of revolution, while multifaceted and often ambiguous, is essentially sympathetic, the author refusing to deny the attractiveness of the notion of idealistically-inspired rebellion, of the concept of iconoclastic[1] action, of the dream of a better world. On the one hand,

---

1    An iconoclast is one who criticizes or seeks to overthrow traditional or conventional ideas or institutions.

it must be admitted that Melville's view of political revolution is tempered with a distrust in the feasibility of idealistic reform and a certain admiration for royalty. On the other hand, it seems to me, that, throughout his sixth novel, Melville never relinquishes a profound reverence for the enticing possibilities of radical change, even if some of the scenes and images in the book suggest a frustration with the intrinsically idealistic nature of the sort of hopes uprisings inspire. In *Moby-Dick*, Melville reaffirms the strength of man's desire for liberation from what he perceives as the constraints of his social condition despite the author's recognition that, as in the example of the revolutions of 1848, such a desire has a necessarily delusory aspect to its nature.

To begin with, I would like to suggest that though much of Melville's writings before the publication of *Moby-Dick* can, indeed, be interpreted as politically conservative, even in these instances he is rarely expressing opinions which could be seen as revealing hostility to a revolutionary spirit. In an 1846 letter to his brother Gansevoort, for example, Melville's reference to the Mexican War[2] seems to show a haughty disdain for the common people whom, by definition, revolutions (and other occasions of recourse to arms worthy of democratic ideals), are supposed to defend and support: "People here are all in a state of delirium about the Mexican War. A military arder pervades all ranks – Militia Colonels wax red in their coat facings – and 'prentice boys are running off to the wars by the scores. – Nothing is talked of but the 'Halls of the Montezumas' And to hear folks prate about those purely figurative apartments one would suppose that they were another Versailles[3] where our democratic rabble meant to 'make a night of it' ere long." Melville's reference to the "democratic rabble" sounds, of course, rather undemocratic. But it would be wrong, I think, to interpret this characterization as fundamentally conservative or anti-revolutionary. The Mexican War, as many Americans prefer to forget, was not conceived to free the inhabitants of the northern regions of Mexico from autocratic oppression, but to expand the American territory and, as such, remains perhaps the greatest act of imperialism ever carried out by the United States government. Thus, that Melville should criticize this action (as Theodore Parker and Henry David Thoreau, for example, also did) is neither surprising nor inconsistent with an essentially democratic view. Melville's use of the image of Versailles (referring back to the French Revolution of 1789) does suggest a certain admiration for the grandeur of the French monarchy and thus a corresponding lack of respect for the masses. But again, the tone must be carefully considered. While Melville may be betraying a genuine weakness for the splendor of the court of Louis XVI, he can also be seen to be balking at the inappropriateness and presumptuousness of a comparison between America's imperialistic actions in Mexico and the French people's more virtuous aspirations during at least the early days of the Revolution. [. . .]

---

2   Mexican–American War 1846–8 (see **p. 30** in Chronology).
3   Royal palace of the French monarchy. As Niemeyer explains shortly, this is a reference to the French Revolution of 1789.

Both the democratic and the revolutionary ideals which filled Melville at the time of the composition of *Moby-Dick* can be seen represented throughout the novel which Milton R. Stern[4] characterizes as "an act of art against totalitarianism." Among the novel's characters, it is Ishmael and Ahab who most consistently embody and support these concepts. Ishmael offers an optimistic vision of the democratic ideal; Ahab embodies the extreme form of revolutionary zeal. In the very first chapter of the book, in fact, the reader learns that though he is not a novice sailor, Ishmael has no desire to have any position of power on the ships whose crews he joins. His philosophizing on the subject suggests a profoundly democratic view of the situation of man in the world: "What of it, if some old hunks of a sea-captain orders me to get a broom and sweep down the decks? . . . Who aint a slave? Tell me that." First of all, Ishmael has no desire for power over others, and second, he does not believe that those in positions of power are in genuinely superior stations. He even fancies, using his gamesome logic, that on board a ship the common sailors (spending most of their time before the mast) have a better situation than that of the officers: "for the most part the Commodore on the quarter-deck gets his atmosphere at second hand from the sailors on the forecastle. He thinks he breathes it first; but not so." The thought leads to more general interpretations, this time with political undertones: "In much the same way do the commonalty lead their leaders in many other things, at the same time that the leaders little suspect it." Ishmael believes that it is the masses who often do, in fact, direct the affairs of society. [. . .]

To return to the conclusion of the book and the red flag which is the last visible sign of the *Pequod* before it sinks to the bottom of the sea, it seems to me, then, that this image does not represent Melville expressing "his distrust of the 'people' and his revulsion at their capacity for self-destructive violence." Viewing the work from a political point of view, the ending can, I believe, be more coherently interpreted in another way. First, Melville can be seen as simply mirroring the tragic end of the French revolutions (both of 1789 and 1848), as well as of the other revolutions of 1848, in their deadly toll and in their complete failure to achieve their more idealistic goals. Second, if he is criticizing these revolutionary activities, it is more with regret that their ideals never were fully realizable in this world and could, unfortunately, become distorted or perverted by their leaders. It is in this spirit of embracing the revolutionary challenge to accepted systems that Melville praised Hawthorne for saying "NO! in thunder"[5] and it is in this identity with the radical mind that Melville wrote to Hawthorne (in the June 1851 letter quoted above) of the probability of his developing the reputation for supporting "ruthless democracy." Finally, how else can one interpret Melville's later confession to his fellow writer, just three days after the American publication of *Moby-Dick*, "I have written a wicked book, and feel spotless as the lamb,"[6] than as an affirmation of Ahab's mad pursuit of a radical goal which middle-class

---

4    American professor and author of *The Fine Hammered Steel of Moby-Dick* (Urbana, Ill.: University of Illinois Press, 1968).
5    See p. 50.
6    See Letter, Melville to Hawthorne, November 1851, pp. 52–3.

readers would be sure to reject? Despite my own argument, I do not see *Moby-Dick* as a conscious evocation of (or support of) Marxist (or even necessarily political) revolutionary ideals. I do, however, see it as an expression (highlighted, in fact, by a certain number of consciously radical allusions) of that tension between desire and necessity (and thus, at least partly, of an embedded Marxist archetype) which resulted in the presentation of what for Melville must have been the irresistibly seductive spirit of revolution.

From **John Alvis, "*Moby-Dick* and Melville's Quarrel with America,"** *Interpretation: A Journal of Political Philosophy* 23.2 (1993): 223–47

Like Niemeyer's, Alvis's piece attempts to explore Melville's relation to the politics of his times, this time focusing on the domestic scene. American democracy was still very much a work in progress in 1850 and within a decade would be threatened with dissolution by the onset of the Civil War (see **p. 20**). Alvis sees Melville as democratic but not populist; in short, rather skeptical about the merits of a political system where one person's demagogue, we might say Ahab, is another's hero. Highly skeptical of conventional religion if not an outright atheist, Melville casts about in *Moby-Dick* for some sort of belief system upon which a truly stable democracy might ground itself.

Melville works out his thoughts on America's political character in his fifth novel, *White-Jacket* and in his sixth, *Moby-Dick*. The latter meditation is related to the former as antithesis to thesis; a hopeful confidence in his country's national purpose gives way to skeptical reflections on a dilemma inseparable from those founding principles that for Melville had once promised an enlightened and morally improved public life. In *Moby-Dick* Melville confronts a tension between the substantive and formal principles of the American regime, between a conception of the maintenance of human rights founded in nature, the nation's final cause, and the formal requirement of sovereignty, the democratic imperative of popular consent. The problem I suppose Melville to have puzzled over in the course of producing his nearest approach to a masterwork is this: How other than by appeal to Christian tradition does modern democracy produce needful restraints upon democratic will?

[. . .] The military despotism Melville anatomizes in *White-Jacket* is circumscribed and remediable by act of Congress, possibly even by executive directives. Troubles on the *Neversink* amount to an excrescence[1] upon an American body politic which, as such bodies go, Melville seems to consider essentially healthy. The earlier novel exposes bad military usages evidently on the assumption that an informed citizenry will not give their consent to unnecessarily harsh navy discipline once they know of these abuses. With *Moby-Dick*, however, we are presented

---

1  Abnormal outgrowth.

with a despotism over the spirit that relies on the consent of the very men whose lives, liberty, and pursuit of happiness will be sacrificed to the will of their leader. By thus raising the stakes the later novel calls attention to a conflict of principle latent within that Lockian-Jeffersonian political creed[2] to which the youthful narrator of *White-Jacket* had attached his hope of world redemption. [. . .]

By depicting Ahab's successful subjugation of a crew among whom we find representatives of the nation's religious heritage as well as an Ishmael widely read in the philosophic tradition, Melville dramatizes a problem implicit in that founding creed which rests upon Jefferson's espousal of Locke's doctrine of consent. Whereas for the Melville of *White-Jacket* Lockian reasoning mediated through the Declaration of Independence provides adequate political guidance, the Melville of *Moby-Dick* discerns in Jefferson's two arch-principles of inalienable rights and consent an unresolved tension: legitimate government rests upon the consent of the governed, its formal principle, and secures rights, its substantive principle. Yet what if the formal and substantive principles should prove to be at odds? Cannot the majority consent to laws that infringe rights of the minority or of individuals? Jefferson certainly thought so in his first inaugural address when he warned that Americans should "bear in mind this sacred principle, that though the will of the majority is in all cases to prevail, that will to be rightful must be reasonable." The same difficulty beset Locke, who had grounded his doctrine of the contractual origin of civil society upon the necessity of protecting rights, but had subsequently stipulated sovereignty for the majority without indicating how democratic majorities could be relied upon to respect the rights of man. Melville perceived lying at the heart of American democracy this dilemma of reconciling evidently necessary democratic means to more evidently obligatory moral ends. Moreover, *Moby-Dick* throws another shadow over the sunny political messianism voiced in *White-Jacket*. By the time he completed his greater work Melville seems to have become aware of the despotic potential implicit in the Lockian concept of society as an engine for overcoming nature's scarcity and violence. [. . .]

*Moby-Dick* leaves Melville with the problem of imagining a hero suitable to realize America's mission as "bearer of the ark of the liberties of the world" against a despotism grounded in the American doctrine of popular consent. The alliance Ishmael and Starbuck fail to arrange suggests the shape Melville judges heroic action might take in a more politically effective Christian endowed with learning or, alternatively, in a more spirited intellectual capable of appealing to Christians. Statesmanship founded in a political religion transforming passive piety into active devotion to the rights of man could suffice to meet Ahab's zeal with an equal but opposite republican temper. An appreciation of the timeliness of such a statesmanship so founded seems to have set the plan Lincoln adhered to throughout a career in which he tried to win assent to the proposition that the principle of natural rights has priority in the national purpose over the principle of consent [. . .]

---

2   Classical liberalism, or the rights of the individual as opposed to the divine right of kings.

From **David S. Reynolds, "'Its wood could only be American!':**
*Moby-Dick* **and Antebellum Popular Culture,"** in Brian Higgins
and Hershel Parker, eds, *Critical Essays on Herman Melville's* Moby Dick
(1992), New York: Macmillan, 523–44

Reynolds's essay and especially his book *Beneath the American Renaissance*
were instrumental in problematizing the image of Melville as sharply alienated
from his culture (the Isolato of the revival and of Murray's "In Nomine Diaboli,"
see **pp. 90–2**), recasting him as a writer deeply immersed in the issues and life
of his times. In the excerpt below Reynolds argues that although certainly
unconventional and critical of conventional thought, Melville was hardly a
hermit-like, tortured intellectual and artist, and that he drew heavily on popular
literary forms in even his most ambitious works.

Despite growing interest in the historical dimensions of *Moby-Dick*, it has been
difficult for scholars to dispel the longstanding myth that Melville was alienated
from his contemporary popular culture. Ever since Raymond Weaver portrayed
him as the isolated, rebellious "Devil's Advocate"[1] Melville has been generally
viewed as an uncharacteristic nay-sayer in an age of progressivist optimism, a
mythic stylist exiled from a Philistine[2] culture of utilitarianism and literal-
mindedness.

This notion of Melville's distance from his literary and social culture contra-
venes his own convictions about the symbiotic relationship between art and
society. "[G]reat geniuses are parts of the times," he proclaimed in his essay
on Hawthorne; "they themselves are the times, and possess a correspondent
coloring." He appears to have been particularly responsive to the ephemeral
literature of his time and culture. [. . .]

In fact, it was precisely Melville's *openness* to images from various contemporary cultural arenas—not, as is commonly thought, his *alienation* from
his culture—that accounts for the special complexity of *Moby-Dick*. Melville's
narrative art was one of wide-ranging assimilation and literary transformation.
It reflected his statement in "Hawthorne and His Mosses" that the American
writer was "bound to carry republican progressiveness into Literature, as well as
into Life." A principal misconception about *Moby-Dick* is that its ambiguities
stood in opposition to a popular culture that was uniformly tame and moralistic.
Actually, antebellum popular culture was full of contradictions and paradoxes
that became textually inscribed in Melville's most capacious novel.

The main types of popular writing Melville drew from in *Moby-Dick* were
Romantic Adventure fiction, dark reform literature, radical-democrat fiction,
and subversive humor. Melville had learned key images and stereotypes from
each of these modes by immersing himself in American popular culture as a writer

1   See extract from Weaver, pp. 78–9.
2   Unsophisticated, vulgar, low-brow.

for the mass market earlier in his career. Melville knew that his first two novels were, as he wrote his publisher about *Omoo*, "calculated for popular reading." After soaring to allegorical and philosophical heights in *Mardi*, he again wrote unabashedly for the popular audience in *Redburn* and *White-Jacket*, which he called "two *jobs*, which I have done for money." As dismissive as Melville was about some of this early fiction, he learned much from his forays into popular culture. Taken together, Melville's early works show him to have been a daring experimenter with popular images. The breadth of his experimentation placed him in an ideal position to produce a novel of full cultural representativeness. When Melville is studied in terms of his popular cultural backgrounds, we see the validity of a contemporary reviewer's remark that in *Moby-Dick* he seemed "resolved to combine all his popular characteristics." [. . .]

[. . .] A good amount of fiction about destructive whales or other monstrous creatures had appeared during the 1830s and 1840s. J. N. Reynolds's "Mocha Dick: or The White Whale of the Pacific," a story in the May 1839 issue of the New York *Knickerbocker*, is full of analogies to *Moby-Dick*: both works center on a dramatic chase for a white sperm whale legendary for its indestructibility; both reproduce the salty dialect of whalemen engaged in dangerous pursuit of the white whale; and both utilize this fearless pursuit as a means of illustrating the inherent democratic dignity of the unfavored trade of whaling. Another work that strikingly prefigures *Moby-Dick* is "Whaling in the Pacific. Encounter with a White Whale," a tale published 8 October 1842 in the popular Boston weekly *Uncle Sam*. This story features a dauntless Captain Coffin and his mates (one of them named Starbuck) who one day lower for a white whale that is harpooned but then crushes two whale boats with his jaws and kills several seamen in bloody revenge. [. . .]

Melville's emphasis upon the unparalleled immensity and destructiveness of his white whale can be viewed as part of a growing fascination with monsters of all varieties. There had arisen a wild one-upmanship among popular adventure writers competing against each other to see who could produce the most savage, freakish beast . . . For example, strange encounters between humans and sea monsters were standard fare in grotesque humor periodicals such as the Crockett almanacs. The 1838 Crockett almanac included a sketch, "Colonel Crockett and the Sea Sarpint," in which Davy Crockett battles a kraken said to be long enough to twist the hair of an angel who straddles the land and the sea. The 1849 Crockett almanac contained a story, "Crockett and the Great Prairie Serpent," about a huge snake, said to be larger than any kraken, whom Crockett wrestles and lashes to death. In the Crockett almanac for 1850, Crockett's nautical friend Ben Harding tells a violent story about a time he and a sailor friend harpooned a whale, climbed aboard a whale's back, and went for a dizzying ride until at last the whale vindictively rammed against their ship, which was saved only when the whale was killed by a lance. The largest monster in antebellum literature was the kraken depicted in Eugene Batchelder's *Romance of the Sea-Serpent, or The Ichthyosaurus* (1849), a bizarre narrative poem about a sea serpent that terrorizes the coast of Massachusetts, destroys a huge ship in mid-ocean, repasts on human remains gruesomely with sharks and whales, attends a Harvard commencement (where he has been asked to speak), shocks partygoers by appearing at a Newport ball, and at last is hunted and killed by a fleet of Newport sailors. [. . .]

The capacity for a richly imagistic work such as *Moby-Dick* had been inherent in American popular culture since the early 1830s, when vehement reformers began coining larger-than-life, mythic metaphors for the social vices they fiercely denounced. Virtually every reform movement of the day—temperance, anti-slavery, antiprostitution, naval reform, utopian socialism—became notably sensationalized in the hands of popular reformers competing for the attention of an American public increasingly taken with Dark Adventure novels and crime-filled penny newspapers. [. . .]

But in all these cases, precise meaning matters less than the dazzling ability of Melville's characters and symbols to radiate meanings. Melville's comprehensive pillaging of classic religious and literary sources reveals his overarching interest in adding resonance and suggestiveness to popular cultural chronotopes that were formless, neutral, or contradictory in their native state. The *Pequod*'s quest for the whale is ultimately self-destructive and the book's truth remains tantalizingly elusive; but this does not place *Moby-Dick* at odds with American culture, as is commonly believed. What distinguishes this novel from its many popular proto-types is that it absorbs numerous American images and treats them not frivolously or haphazardly, as did the popular texts, but instead takes them seriously, salvages them from the anarchically directionless and gives them new intensity and mythic reference. Melville's quest is dangerous, but it is also exhilarating and finally joyful. Upon completing the novel Melville could express his paradoxical feeling of danger and peace by writing to Hawthorne: "I have written a wicked book, and feel spotless as the lamb. Ineffable socialities are in me."[3] Having written a novel that fully absorbed the subversive forces of his culture, Melville could nonetheless feel warmly calm because he had produced a lasting testament to the creative spirit.

From **Sheila Post-Lauria, "Originality: The Case of *Moby-Dick*,"** in *Correspondent Colorings: Melville in the Marketplace* (1996), Amherst, Mass.: University of Massachusetts Press, 101–22

Like Reynolds, Post-Lauria is interested in the popular literary forms Melville drew on as he composed *Moby-Dick*. Compare her account of the work as a "mixed form" novel to the other accounts of the book's complex structure, especially early critics such as Bezanson (see **pp. 83–5**). Taken together Reynolds's and Post-Lauria's work represents a sort of historicized formalist approach to working through the problems presented by the novel's bewildering use of a variety of discourses.

---

3  Letter, Melville to Hawthorne, November 1851, pp. 52–3.

While most textual critics assert that Melville planned his "market" novels, *Redburn* and *White-Jacket*, by deliberately employing popular forms of the day, they locate Melville's "creativity" and "originality" instead in his "unplanned" works. In these critics' view, creativity and originality bear little relation to compositional planning and indeed seem antithetical to it. For these reasons, genetic theorists have continued to endorse the idea that Melville did not plan what is considered his most original and creative work, *Moby-Dick*. [. . .]

The heterogeneity of *Moby-Dick*—often attributed to the author's "soared ambition," "fluid consciousness," "shifting . . . conceptions," and even "lessons of craft from Shakespeare"—actually reflects a narrative license of the times. The metaphysical discussions, genre shifts, use of Shakespearean conventions, and the mixture of facts and romance, typically considered Melville's improvisations, also appear in "mixed form" narratives, a genre (in)famous at midcentury but now largely overlooked. Through this heterogeneous form, Melville links his work to a popular yet subversive trend in both English and American antebellum literary cultures. Indeed, Melville's debt to "mixed form"—which Eigner calls a subgenre of the romance—is central to understanding the narrative form and Melville's intentions and method in *Moby-Dick*. Recovering this complex narrative form represents the first necessary step to reconsidering Melville's actual creativity, as well as resolving the disparate readings by contextualist and genetic scholars of *Moby-Dick*.

The genre of the mixed form novel emerged in transatlantic literary circles as a response to early nineteenth-century critical strictures on literary realism. Praise for a literary work by reviewers supportive of realistic fiction almost always included the positive comparison of the author's representational approach with seventeenth-century Dutch realist painting. With this genre as the model of portraiture in mid-nineteenth-century culture, realist writers depicted their fictional worlds with the minute detail of a Rembrandt, Vermeer, or Steen.[1] They observed a strict fidelity with almost daguerreotype[2] accuracy. [. . .]

Recognizing the forms of the conventional metaphysical narrative of *Moby-Dick*, we may now "consider this matter" of narrative form in a larger perspective. Melville's demonstration of the multiplicity of literature encourages a reconsideration of existing genetic theories of his work. The "two" and "three *Moby-Dicks*" theories should be revised to include an understanding of Melville's commitment to the metaphysical narrative. The hypothesis, posited by the editors of the Northwestern Newberry edition,[3] that "it seems most likely that Melville started to write *Moby-Dick* on the pattern of his five earlier books, as a sailor voyager's firsthand account of his experience and observations" seems unlikely, given the foregoing insights into Melville's growing allegiance to the metaphysical narrative. Mixed form assumes as a basic premise that the "unnecessary dupli-

---

1   Dutch genre painters (see **n. 2, p. 68**).
2   An early photographic technology.
3   The accepted, standardized edition of *Moby-Dick* (see **p. 181** in Further Reading).

cates" Hayford[4] has conjectured regarding Melville's compositional method are actually necessary. They stress the varying perspectives that are essential to reading and comprehending the narrative form of *Moby-Dick*. Rather than "unintentional," "flawed," or "blurred," Melville's concept of narrative form in *Moby-Dick*, based on mixed form, helps us understand its intentionality and distinction in depicting the disparate segments of experience—or as Ishmael proclaims in *Moby-Dick*, the "separate citation of items" (203). The suggestion by the Northwestern-Newberry editors that Melville built "better than he knew" (to borrow Emerson's phrase) should be reformulated to suggest that Melville built better than *we* knew. [. . .]

This emphasis on perception induces modern readers to reconsider their own perception of *Moby-Dick*. Melville's orchestration of many forms liberates the novel from restrictive categories. Mixed form is an aesthetic foundation that stimulated the remarkable artistic creativity portrayed in *Moby-Dick*. The author's masterpiece simply reflects, and yet transcends, genre. In the hands of the author, the mixed form of *Moby-Dick* is a catalyst to this timely—and timeless—mixture.

## From **Elizabeth Schultz, "The Sentimental Subtext of *Moby-Dick*: Melville's Response to the 'World of Woe,'"** ESQ: A Journal of the American Renaissance 42.1 (1996): 29–49

Sentimental fiction was hugely popular in Melville's day and represented his biggest competition in the marketplace. The so-called "cult of sentimentality" emerged at the end of the eighteenth century in a response to the emphasis on reason and rationality during the Enlightenment. Women writers especially touted a return to the knowledge – especially moral knowledge – to be deduced from one's emotional barometer. Although among serious writers and critics the term "sentimental" was pejorative as early as 1800, there was a huge demand for literary works that evoked strong emotional responses to their – more often than not – conventional and melodramatic plots and themes. Yet as Schultz argues it would be wrong to think of *Moby-Dick* with its all-male cast as representing, in her words, "a stand against sentimentality." Like the essays by Reynolds and Post-Lauria, Schultz's piece provides an important discussion of one of the main literary contexts for key scenes in *Moby-Dick*.

As early as 1929, Lewis Mumford[1] identified *Moby-Dick* as a master narrative, intent upon valorizing a masculine culture: "All Melville's books about the sea have the one anomaly and defect of the sea from the central, human point of

---

4    One of the editors of the Northwestern–Newberry edition.

---

1    One of the revivalists; "The Significance of Herman Melville," *The New Republic* 56 (October 10, 1928), 212–14.

view: one-half of the race, woman, is left out of it. Melville's world, all too literally, is a man-of-war's world … One looks for some understanding of woman's lot and woman's life in Moby-Dick; and one looks in vain." If one looks at the "little lower layer" of sentimentality in Moby-Dick, however, one discovers a subtext clearly reflecting "some understanding of woman's lot and woman's life." This subtext, drawing on and at times subverting the rhetoric of nineteenth-century sentimental literature, shows Melville in Moby-Dick as sensitive not only to the "watery world of woe," which, according to Father Mapple, "bowled over" Jonah[2] and which ultimately bowls over the entire crew of the Pequod. It also shows him as sensitive to the woe of women and children at home and to the necessity of responding with sympathy and care. Moby-Dick's sentimental subtext works to reinforce and expand its nineteenth-century reader's awareness of the gender-structured domestic sphere as the locus simultaneously of anguish and of the tenderness that anguish calls up.

Some critics have declared that Melville, in his attention to defining and redefining masculinity in Moby-Dick, takes a stance against the sentimentality of the mid-nineteenth century. But sentimentality, when broadly defined as "an orientation toward feeling" that manifests "an irresistible impulse toward human connection," can be seen to comprise a significant dimension of Moby-Dick. Noting that "[t]o voice feeling, for Ishmael and Ahab, is to experience pain," David Leverenz contends that their masculine response to pain is anger, hatred, hysteria, violence, and self-loathing. I will argue that the sentimental layer of Moby-Dick, which illuminates the vulnerable position of women and children in nineteenth-century American society, proposes alternative feelings: sympathy and care. While in the process of composing the novel, Melville announced his allegiance to this sentimental tradition by stating emphatically to Hawthorne, "I stand for the heart." [ … ]

Following his daytime labors upstairs, as Merton M. Sealts Jr.[3] speculates, Melville probably would have rejoined the female-dominated family circle around the fireplace downstairs and, given his tired eyes, listened gratefully "to whatever work was being read aloud, in accordance with long-standing custom." Thus in addition to his own heterogeneous and unorthodox reading, he would have become familiar with what the women in his family were reading. Included in this reading might have been works by Dickens, in which Melville took particular pleasure. Not only did Melville read Pickwick Papers en route to England in 1849, but in mid-January 1851, at the very time the "whale" was "in his flurry," the Melville family commenced a reading of the two-volume edition of David Copperfield, just published by the New York house of Putnam in 1850

---

2   The book of Jonah (Old Testament) describes how the prophet Jonah defies God's command to go to Nineveh, the capital of Assyria, to preach repentance. He attempts to flee by booking passage on a ship to Tarshish, only to have his escape attempt thwarted by a divinely ordained storm. Thrown overboard and swallowed by a great fish, Jonah is vomited up on shore after three days and nights. He then obeys God's command and preaches in Nineveh, where the population promptly repents. God thus changes his plan to destroy the city, demonstrating that divine mercy is available to all – Jew and Gentile alike. Allusions to the story occur in the New Testament, where it serves to prefigure the resurrection of Jesus.
3   American critic and seminal Melvillean (see pp. 85–8).

and brought home by Melville's wife, Elizabeth, following a stay in Boston. Of all the sentimental fiction Melville would have known, *David Copperfield* most significantly resonates in *Moby-Dick*.

So long as Ishmael, Melville's narrator, remains on land (in the novel's first twenty-two chapters) and among women, he objectifies them. Queequeg, after all, takes a woman's place in his life on land. It is as though Ishmael, like Melville during his work among them, cannot hear women in these early chapters and consequently represents them in stereotypical and misogynistic terms: as cruel stepmother, as potentially castrating hotel owner, as threatening interloper in the bachelors' paradise of the whaleship. When Ishmael leaves for the sea, however, he shifts his perspective to include women as subjects and to perceive their share in the world's woe. As the *Pequod*'s crew members set sail from Nantucket, Peleg emphasizes their masculinity and, in effect, denies their connection to women by commending them as "sons of bachelors" (103). But at sea, this connection becomes stronger for Ishmael. By sending his narrator away from the land—away from home, family, women—Melville gives him, and his readers, the opportunity to look more closely at those whom he left behind. Rather than forgetting the domestic scene, Ishmael thinks of it frequently. In "The Lee Shore" (chap. 23),[4] he presents his well-known catalog of the benefits and pleasures to be found at home, on land: "[I]n the port is safety, comfort, hearth-stone, supper, warm blankets, friends, all that's kind to our mortalities" (106). In "A Squeeze of the Hand" (chap. 94), he extends this early list to include "the wife, the heart, the bed, the table, the saddle, the fire-side, the country" (416). As the dramatic intensity of Ishmael's relationship with Queequeg subsides and the narrative of Ahab's quest quickens after chapter 22, the subtext projecting the sentimental values implicit in these catalogs begins to manifest itself in the novel's expository chapters—in counterpoint to the dominant quest narrative.

Extracted from their contexts, Ishmael's catalogs suggest the vision of domestic bliss conventionally attributed to mid-nineteenth-century American writers and readers. However, as recent critics emphasize, home life at Arrowhead was not blissful,and as Nina Baym[5] observes, home life in the sentimental novels the Melville family would have been reading aloud is in fact "presented, over-whelmingly, as unhappy. There are very few intact families in this literature," Baym asserts, "and those that are intact are unstable or locked into routines of misery.... Domestic setting and description ... do not by any means imply domestic idyll." Melville's sentimental subtext in *Moby-Dick* points to the suffering of the women and children confined to this depressing domestic sphere and assigns responsibility for their unhappiness to gender differentiation in the nineteenth-century home. In his comparison of Michelangelo's representation of God with representations of Christ by unidentified Italian painters, he clearly spells out this difference: whereas God embodies masculine power, Christ reveals

---

4   See excerpt from Chapter 23, "The Lee Shore" **pp. 144–5.**
5   Well-known scholar of American literature. Her "Melville's Quarrel with Fiction," *Publications of the Modern Language Association* 94 (1979), 909–21, is an important discussion of Melville's theory of language.

"divine love" and the negative of power, the "feminine" traits of "submission and endurance" (376). Far from responding with hostility or dread, indifference or scorn to women (interpretations of Melville's attitude that have dominated recent critical discourse), he represents their lives on "the slavish shore" (107) as steeped in suffering. Portrayed as victimized by their sexual and legal status, women, submitting and enduring, are nonetheless associated in *Moby-Dick* with caring relationships. [. . .]

The abandonment of women and children in *Moby-Dick* reveals Melville's decided strategy of drawing on familiar images and themes from popular fiction in the interest of expanding his readers' range of sympathies. The condition of the orphan, unlike that of the "isolato," is not chosen but imposed, usually upon the young, innocent, and vulnerable child. It also comes to be the defining circumstance for many nineteenth-century bildungsromans, including *David Copperfield* as well as Susan Warner's best-selling *Wide, Wide World*, published a year before *Moby-Dick* in 1850. That Melville was aware of his culture's commodification of both widows and orphans is suggested by Bildad's cynical justification, early in the novel, of the low wages assigned to Ishmael and other crew members of the *Pequod*: "[T]hou must consider . . . the other owners of this ship—widows and orphans, many of them—and that if we too abundantly reward the labors of this young man, we may be taking the bread from those widows and those orphans" (77). [. . .]

"*It was the devious-cruising Rachel,*[6] *that in her retracing search after her missing children, only found another orphan*" (573). In the striking last phrase of his epilogue, Ishmael echoes an identical phrase in *David Copperfield*. Recently orphaned himself, David is introduced to Em'ly and Ham, also parentless, as yet "another orphan" (141). The only survivor of the *Pequod*, Ishmael, orphaned from the beginning of the novel, is orphaned again with the loss of his entire community at the end. By identifying Ishmael in his final words as "*another orphan*," Melville associates him with other literary orphans, including those in *David Copperfield*, and accordingly assigns him the sympathy culturally guaranteed the child bereft of parents. From the beginning of the novel Ishmael himself has expressed a consciousness of the cruel "step-mother world," and his devastating experiences of loss at the conclusion would appear to magnify his woes. Yet the homeless, orphaned youth is saved by his friend's coffin, embraced by the grieving and maternal *Rachel*, and thus reunited with his fellows. His rescue is the basis for his capacity to feel that "while ponderous planets of unwaning woe revolve round [him], deep down and deep inland there [he] still bathe[s] . . . in eternal mildness of joy" (389). It might also be argued that this rescue, which connects him to the sympathetic and caring human family, is the basis for his capacity to empathize with the world's woe.

---

6  Rachel is the wife of Jacob (see Genesis 29:6) and is traditionally considered the spiritual mother of Israel.

From **Leland S. Person Jr., "Melville's Cassock: Putting on Masculinity in *Moby-Dick*,"** *ESQ: A Journal of the American Renaissance* 40.1 (1994): 1–26

Surprisingly, there has been relatively little work done on *Moby-Dick* and gender, and Person's piece is one of the few attempts to deal with the topic in light of the book's immediate social and historical contexts. And as Person argues, it is clear that far from simply accepting and reinforcing conventional gender roles and constructs, Melville puts them to the same rigorous examination he does every other subject in his book. In this instance, like many others in the work, the effect is more comic than it is serious.

Writing to Sarah Morewood about the forthcoming *Moby-Dick*, Herman Melville warned: "Dont you buy it—dont you read it, when it does come out, because it is by no means the sort of book for you. It is not a peice of fine feminine Spitalfields silk—but is of the horrible texture of a fabric that should be woven of ships' cables & hausers."[1] In a later letter to Sophia Hawthorne, who had read *Moby-Dick* and written him a "highly flattering" letter, Melville claimed to be "really amazed" that she had found "any satisfaction" in the book. "It is true that some *men* have said they were pleased with it," he said, "but you are the only *woman*—for as a general thing, women have small taste for the sea." Critics have generally agreed that *Moby-Dick* is a man's book and that Melville's representation of seafaring manhood inscribes a patriarchal, anti-female ideology that reinforces nineteenth-century gender separatism—a manhood based on differentiation from women. Ann Douglas has argued that the "book was written for men, or at least from a self-consciously masculine viewpoint," that Melville portrays women and "domestic virtues" as "what is forgotten, over-ridden, whether for good or bad." Richard H. Brodhead calls *Moby-Dick* "so outrageously masculine that we scarcely allow ourselves to do justice to the full scope of its masculinism." And Nancy Fredricks asserts that the novel "represents a bastion of masculinist aesthetics" and exemplifies the "segregation of the sexes in nineteenth-century America."[2]

Instead of seeing the male exclusivity of *Moby-Dick* as a limitation, I want to do justice to the full scope of Melville's "masculinism." Where Douglas argues that "Melville wishes to explore rather than challenge the meaning of masculine authority," I think Melville both explores and challenges a traditional, essentially phallocentric masculinity (individualistic, instrumental, projective, competitive). To a degree, he tries to "unman Man." "[S]mall erections may be finished by their first architects," Ishmael observes about the Cathedral of Cologne, but "grand ones, true ones, ever leave the copestone to posterity. God keep me from ever completing anything."[3] Even constructions based on phallic metaphors, he

---

1   Letter, Melville to Sarah Huyler Morewood, September 1851, pp. 53–4.
2   Douglas, Brodhead and Fredricks are US scholars of American literature.
3   Melville saw the cathedral in 1849 on his brief tour of Europe.

implies, must be incomplete—potentially multiple rather than one—in order to be grand and true. Consistently destabilizing any single construct of male identity, Melville conducts a discursive experiment on manhood. He does for sailors what Whitman tries to do for other working men: to cross and confuse the gender lines that bracket acceptable male behavior and to expand the range and reach of manhood. Much as the mincer turns the foreskin of the whale's severed penis inside out in order to put it on and inhabit it, Melville tries on or "tries out" various masculinities that men—even sea-men—can "put on."

[. . .] Although Melville does not represent female desires in *Moby-Dick*, this absence does not automatically lead to the reinscription of "the" phallus as the "central signifier of erotic relations." Indeed, eliding female desires from the novel, as many feminist utopian writers exclude male desires, enables masculinity to be disassociated from its "difference" and interrogated—and the phallus to be decentered, rather than reinscribed, as the primary signifier of male experience. Instead of reinforcing the gender separatism of his culture, Melville creates a male utopia in *Moby-Dick* in order to liberate masculinity from its position in a binary opposition (as "not-woman"). Paradoxically, by separating his sailors from women, by putting them literally and figuratively at sea, he can more readily destabilize a manhood predicated on difference. In my view, Melville not only deconstructs conventional masculinity by demonstrating the dangers of phallocentric manhood but also explores alternative constructions of maleness. Gender and sexuality, as psychological or cultural constructs, are essentially unstable and fluid like the sea. Ishmael says that the desire of "every robust healthy boy" to go to sea is a prerequisite of manhood (5), but the sea represents not so much an exclusively male sphere that reinforces patriarchal authority as a fluid realm in which all constructs dissolve.

In "The Cassock" (chap. 95),[4] Melville suggests, by the mincer's severing of the phallus from the whale's body in order to put it on, that any masculine construct represents a castration, a reduction of male identity to a particular physical embodiment. To wear the skin of the whale's penis is to take the place of the penis, but this act of surrogation requires killing the whale, disembodying the phallus, and, as Martin points out, inhabiting an "empty phallus." The act of investing the male self in the phallus, in other words, means killing male potentiality, robbing it of its vitality and making it coterminous[5] with its sign. From this point of view, *Moby-Dick* turns on the paradox of chasing an ever-elusive, ideal manhood and trying to become a man. As Melville puts it in "Knights and Squires" (chap. 26), there is a difference between "man, in the ideal," and "men," who "may seem [as] detestable as joint stock companies and nations" (117). In positing the existence of an "immaculate manliness . . . within ourselves, so far within us, that it remains intact though all the outer character seem gone," Melville distinguishes between the idea of manliness and any single masculine role or "investiture" that men can "put on." This is not to say, however, that Melville is reductively essentialistic or that he offers a program for achieving such

---

4   See Chapter 95, "The Cassock," **pp. 161–2.**
5   Contained within the same boundaries; coextensive.

"immaculate manliness." Rather, by disassociating "immaculate manliness" from any single investiture, Melville destabilizes masculinity in order to open the possibility of multiple male identities and roles.

The tendency to view *Moby-Dick* through limited gender categories seems strange in view of the way that Melville himself confuses gender identities in the novel and repeatedly blurs the boundaries that mark gender differences. In the bawdy section of "The Tail" (chap. 86), for example, Melville comically deconstructs, as well as celebrates, this obviously phallic symbol and goes out of his way to emphasize its feminine, as well as masculine, qualities. In the tail the "confluent measureless force of the whole whale seems concentrated to a point" (376), Melville notes, apparently echoing the phallocentrism and privileged unicity that many feminist scholars have identified with manhood—what Jane Gallop calls the patriarchal "economy of the One." But Melville does not allow the "tail" to rest securely in its muscular oneness. The tail's "amazing strength" does not "cripple the graceful flexion of its motions," he notes, for the member becomes a site "where infantileness of ease undulates through a Titanism of power" (376), a locus of "daintiness," "delicacy," "tenderness," and even "maidenly gentleness" (377). While he feminizes the whale's tail, Melville masculinizes Christ, who has been excessively feminized in the "soft, curled, hermaphroditical Italian pictures." Such pictures, Melville argues, "so destitute as they are of all brawniness, hint nothing of any power, but the mere negative, feminine one of submission and endurance" (376). Although Melville does seem to be working with conventional gender characteristics in this chapter, the effect of his descriptions is to destabilize their applicability to either sex. He seems to agree with Margaret Fuller's assertion in *Woman in the Nineteenth Century* (1845)[6] that "[t]here is no wholly masculine man, no purely feminine woman," because "male" and "female" are "perpetually passing into one another." [. . .]

From **Sterling Stuckey, "The Tambourine in Glory: African Culture and Melville's Art,"** in Robert S. Levine, ed., *The Cambridge Companion to Herman Melville* (1998), Cambridge: Cambridge University Press, 37–64

Conventional wisdom on Melville's handling of race in *Moby-Dick* is that the book is far from racist, and is by even twenty-first century standards a provocative exploration of race and racial ideology. Yet any discussion of the thematic aspects of Melville's handling of race and of his depiction of his characters of color should be preceded by an understanding of the racial milieu in which Melville lived and worked. Stuckey's piece does just this, providing a concrete sense of the lived realities of African-Americans to which Melville would have been exposed in New York City and growing up in Albany.

---

6   Noted American Transcendentalist and editor of *The Dial*; friend of Hawthorne.

In his first eleven years, Herman Melville lived in an environment in which slavery was being gradually legislated out of existence, its shadow receding across New York State. Despite the movement to abolish slavery, however, denials of freedom less severe but no less real were much in evidence. There was, for that matter, little indication that racial equality was being considered by northern whites, most of whom did not oppose southern slavery.

Melville was born in August 1819, a time when slave music and dance enjoyed brilliantly ironic expression in public and private, North as well as South. In New York City and across the state, slaves were observed dancing and making music on street corners and in marketplaces, as if preparing for the Pinkster Festival[1] that, once a year in May for several days and at times in multiple locations, engaged the attention of white spectators. As in expressions of black culture in America generally, participants in festivals revealed but a portion of their art because it was dangerous to communicate clear signs of African spirituality.

The appreciation of irony allowed slaves to conceal, beneath a protective covering of improvisation, that which was unpalatable to whites, thereby preserving what was proper to them by almost endlessly changing its face. In other words, harsh reality encouraged experimentation to alter cherished values in order to protect them at their core. Slaves, then, mainly perceived reality as flux artistically, and therefore in a religious sense as well, for the distinction between the sacred and the secular was not often drawn by them and has long been the least understood quality of their culture.

Melville's family was wonderfully placed, residentially, to be exposed to black celebrations in nineteenth-century New York City. The address at which he was born, No. 6 Pearl Street, faced the "tip of Manhattan Island, on one side, and on the other the wharves and shipping offices of the South Street waterfront." Though slaves were known to entertain whites along the wharves of New York and to reach such destinations in skiffs, only in time did such settings, with respect to African culture, become important to Melville. However, celebrations of blacks along Broadway were, from an early age, impossible for him to ignore, the music alone commanding attention, as did the rhythmic march/dance of those in processions.

Until he was ten, Melville's addresses were located in sections of the city either near or on Broadway, with one at 55 Cortlandt that was ideal for hearing or attending Broadway celebrations. From that address a procession celebrating the coming abolition of slavery in New York almost certainly was heard, for its path brought it within hearing distance of the southern Broadway area in which the celebrants made music that to the young might seem as natural as the sound

---

1   A holiday celebrated by African-American and Dutch New Yorkers of the Hudson valley, starting in the early 1700s and extending well into the nineteenth century. "Pinkster" is the Dutch name for Pentecost, a Christian holiday observed seven weeks after Easter. Because of its timing Pinkster was also closely associated with Spring and renewal. Slave owners would give African-Americans time off and many would use Pinkster as an opportunity to reunite with loved ones and family members, often journeying from rural areas to New York City. By the mid-1700s, markets in New York and Brooklyn attracted large gatherings at Pinkster time.

of rain or the play of sunlight. Melville's exposure to black music was especially full in his youth: he was but six in 1825 when the "great procession of negroes, some of them well-dressed" paraded, "two by two, preceded by music and a flag . . . down Broadway." The parade held the attention of onlookers:

> An African club, called the Wilberforce Society, thus celebrated the . . . abolition of slavery in New York, and concluded the day by a dinner and ball. The colored people of New York, belonging to this society, have a fund, contained of their own, raised by weekly subscription, which is employed in assisting sick and unfortunate blacks. This fund, contained in a sky-blue box, was carried in the procession; the treasurer holding in his hand a large gilt key; the rest of the officers wore ribands [sic] of several colors, and badges like the officers of free masons; marshals with long staves walked outside the procession. During a quarter of an hour, scarcely any but black faces were to be seen in Broadway.

This was part of the cultural world of New Yorkers, who had little inclination to deny that the music of blacks was substantially different from that of white Americans. The Wilberforce Society was known to march with its own band, and its style of marching in 1825 did not substantially differ from what it was before or following the celebration of that year. In this regard, it is more than coincidence that many of its members, whether born in Africa or in America, referred to themselves as "Africans."

The 55 Cortlandt address was but a ten-minute walk from City Hall and the Commons, the latter a staging area for parades and for celebrations like Pinkster. Moreover, the Negros Burial Ground, in which 20,000 African women, men, and children were buried, was part of the Commons, a sacred place revered by people of African descent that attracted African dancers and musicians and storytellers throughout the year. It is doubtful that Melville, when no more than six or seven, would have been unaware of Pinkster activity at the Commons, or at its burial ground, since both were in his own neighborhood.

Reports of firearms and displays of firecrackers announced 4th of July celebrations for whites in New York City, signaling for blacks their own day of celebration or regret to follow, except that in 1827 their celebration was special. On that July 5, the New York Emancipation Day parade, beginning at City Hall near 55 Cortlandt and continuing down Broadway to the Battery, won the attention of most who glanced in its direction: The Grand Marshal for the day was Samuel Hardenburgh, "a splendid looking man, in cocked hat and drawn sword, mounted on a milk-white steed . . . his aids on horseback dashing up and down the line. . . ." A sacred occurrence and a time of jubilee, the participants assembled just a block from the Negros Burial Ground, around which hundreds of Africans gathered while waiting for thousands more before following the line of march toward the southern terminus of Broadway.

It does not greatly matter whether Melville observed this particular celebration of the abolition of slavery, for many white children in attendance were his cohorts, and just as black youth remembered the event long after it occurred, it also remained a part of the consciousness of young whites who saw and heard the jubilant marchers. Yet Melville might have been standing, chaperoned, among them on the Broadway sidewalk, hearing and observing resplendently dressed – "in scarfs of silk with gold-edgings" – members of black mutual aid societies "with colored bands of music and their banners appropriately lettered and painted: 'The New York African Society for Mutual Relief,' 'The Wilberforce Benevolent Society,' and 'The Clarkson Benevolent Society.' " Then followed "the people five or six abreast, from grown men to small boys." Also marching were members of the various African marine societies, who when not at home were at sea on ships out of New York port. [. . .]

One of the great festivals of New York, Pinkster was thought to be more robust in Melville's mother's hometown, Albany, than anywhere else in New York State. His mother's family knew the festival from the time Africans began dominating its cultural forms in the late colonial period. More especially, Maria Gansevoort's patrician family was connected to Pinkster as few others were. Though one cannot speak of the connection with great certitude, the most noted Pinkster drummer, Jackie Quackenboss, may well have been owned by the Quackenboss family that married into the Gansevoort family in the late eighteenth century, when "every family of wealth and distinction owned one or more slaves." Jackie was such a dramatic figure in Albany's cultural history that family lore concerning him would have been relished by one of Melville's imagination, and there is no reason to suppose it would have been withheld. In allowing Jackie to drum at Pinkster, the Quackenboss family provided crucial support to the festival and must have been proud that he bore their name. [. . .]

Pinkster's special relationship to his family on his mother's side in Albany, together with his family's location in New York near Pinkster Commons and its burial ground, meant that it was virtually impossible for Melville to avoid, over nearly twenty years, contact with African culture – and issues – before first voyaging from the United States. Moreover, he enriched his knowledge of black culture by reading travelers' accounts of African culture, which gave him special insight into how blacks were affected by life in America and how their values affected others. His interest in foreign places, through travel no less than through reading, is convincing evidence that Melville was more prone than most Americans to immerse himself in different values: Newton Arvin writes that names of travelers such as Captain Cook, Krusenstern, Ledyard, Vancouver, and Mungo Park[2] "scintillated before him like constellations

---

2    Captain James Cook (1728–79), noted English navigator and explorer whose journals were published in several volumes; Adam Johann von Krusenstern (1770–1846), Russian navigator who surveyed the North Pacific Coast of America and published an account of his travels in 3 vols (1809–13); John Ledyard (1750–89), navigator and explorer who witnessed the death of Captain Cook and authored *Narrative of the Third and Last Expedition of Capt. James Cook* (1798); George Vancouver (1758–98), explorer on his own as well as a companion of Cook, his *A Voyage of Discovery to the North Pacific* (1798) was published after his death; Mungo Park (1771–1806), trained Scottish botanist and explorer noted for his exploration of the Niger river in Africa which he chronicled in his *Travels in the Interior Districts of Africa* (1799).

during his whole boyhood, as the names of great soldiers do before other boys. . . ." [. . .]

His presence on the *Acushnet* during a later voyage afforded him an opportunity to explore cultural interaction between black and white sailors. The *Acushnet* had "the usual mixture of free Negroes, Portuguese, and strays from the north of Europe" together with a majority "with good New England names," which made for a cultural laboratory in which Melville might thrive as a student of that difference he increasingly came to value. Being at sea tested, in a highly focused manner, his cultural as well as other perceptions. In this regard, one must not underestimate the degree to which African influences in music and dance remained with free Negroes, resulting in artistic and spiritual qualities that, in some instances, clearly distinguished them from other sailors. [. . .]

And so in "Midnight Forecastle" Melville translates his knowledge of black dance and music into literary art. Moreover, when reading *Moby-Dick*, we revisit with him scenes of his youth in Albany and in New York City and rediscover what scholars have largely failed even to reflect on – the presence of black culture in the North and the African aesthetic that informs it. While we encounter whites who are fascinated by the culture of people said to be their inferiors, it is now clear that Melville's depiction of African music and dance is a convincing representation – and here is the great irony – of American art in *Moby-Dick*.

From **Joseph Andriano, "Brother to Dragons: Race and Evolution in *Moby-Dick*,"** *American Transcendental Quarterly* 10.2 (1996): 141–53

Andriano's piece complements nicely the work of Stuckey by providing both an overview of the critical history of discussions of *Moby-Dick* and race and a discussion of the dominant ideologies of race in the US at mid-century. Andriano makes a compelling case for *Moby-Dick* as a thinly veiled but powerful critique of the major "theories" of race in the period.

The question of race in *Moby-Dick* has been a vexed one since the early 1960s, when Charles Foster first "reinterpreted" the text as an indictment of the Fugitive Slave Law and the Compromise of 1850.[1] Since Carolyn Karcher's *Shadow over the Promised Land* (1980), the consensus has been that Melville, though occasionally succumbing to culturally ingrained racist stereotyping, created in *Moby-Dick* a radically anti-racist text. Ishmael's discourse is often calculated to undercut the myth of white supremacy, asserting that society's survival may ultimately depend on the acceptance of Ishmael's democratic vision (seeing equality in diversity) and a rejection of Ahab's tyrannical one (seeing only white). [. . .]

---

1   See **p. 31** in Chronology and **p. 27** in Melville and Antebellum America.

In 1850, while Melville was writing *Moby-Dick* and pondering Hawthorne's "blackness ten times black," he may have read Louis Agassiz's[2] article in *The Christian Examiner*, "The Diversity of Origin of the Human Races," which purports to demonstrate with empirical evidence and inductive logic that black and other "colored" people are not Sons and Daughters of Adam and Eve—that, indeed, they *may* even be a different species from whites. Although he leaves it up to the reader to decide whether his findings have any connection with "the political condition of the negroes," Agassiz in his disclaimer obviously implies that his "science" may be used to justify slavery.

Melville undermined such scientific rationalizations when he created the "colored" characters of *Moby-Dick*—especially Queequeg and Daggoo. Even if he did not read the article, he was certainly familiar with the school of thought Agassiz represented, which started from the assumption that "the white race" was superior to all others. Queequeg and Daggoo—even Pip and Fleece—all give eloquent testimony to refute Louis Agassiz and the whole school of scientific racism. In denying a hierarchic structure of races, Melville ironically comes closer to the world view of modern natural history, which has supplanted the Scale of Nature, or Ladder of Perfection, with the Tree of Life.

Agassiz claimed not to deny the essential "unity of mankind"; he believed that it was possible for humanity to be "unified" even if the races had separate origins. His idea of unity is actually the Ladder of Perfection, with whites at the top rung of the human segment, just below the angels. He takes comfort in the observation that "men of the same nation" bond together in a recognition of "that higher relation arising from the intellectual constitution of man." That he means to exclude blacks from this vision of brotherhood becomes obvious later when he puts them at the bottom of the ladder: "Are not these facts [that blacks are "submissive, obsequious," and "inferior," suffering from a "peculiar apathy, a peculiar indifference to the advantages afforded by civilized society"] indications that the different races do not rank upon one level in nature . . . ?"

Queequeg represents all colored races—he is presumably Polynesian; he has yellow tattoos; and he worships a black "Congo idol." [. . .] So Melville has Ishmael bond most thoroughly with Queequeg, refuting Agassiz in one way—by eliminating "rank"—and ironically demonstrating that his comments about white brotherhood perfectly describe Ishmael's relationship with dark Queequeg: "[W]ho would consider the difference in their physical features as an objection to their being more intimately connected than other men who in features resemble them more . . . ?" Those who consider all other races inferior to whites "marvelled that two fellow-beings [Queequeg and Ishmael] could be so companionable; as though a white man were anything more dignified than a whitewashed negro."

Melville is not content to assert the equal humanity of the "colored" races; he often inverts the Scale of Nature, savaging the white man (e.g. Stubb) and

---

2    Jean Louis Rodolphe Agassiz (1807–73), Swiss-American zoologist and botanist who, once he emigrated to the US, was a popular teacher and lecturer, as well as a professor at Harvard. He had many fields of interest and became involved in the discourse on race in the US by advocating a "scientific" justification for slavery and the inherent inferiority of Africans.

elevating the "savage." One way he does this is by satirizing characters who treat "sons of darkness" like animals (to Captain Peleg, for example, Queequeg is no better than a quohog, or clam; another is to turn the tables by having the white man be the lower animal: Ishmael even imagines himself as a barnacle cleaving to the "noble savage."

It could of course be argued that Melville's participation in the "noble savage" myth[3] is just as racist, say, as his occasional indulgence in "romantic racialism." He seems compelled to undercut the myth, however, by creating the character of Fedallah, an ignoble pagan. Moreover, by the end of the book, Melville has revealed the essential savagery of the entire human race, regardless of color. While it may be true, he implies, that for every noble savage there is an ignoble one, it is also true that for every great white man (Ahab), there is a mediocre one (Flask). And for every civilized white man (Starbuck), there is a savage one (Stubb). Ishmael is a pagan Christian who constantly destroys dichotomies between white and black, Christian and cannibal, human and animal. [. . .]

The "savages" in *Moby-Dick*, including that white savage Ishmael, provide a link between human and animal. But they do so in a way that implicitly denies the notion of rank. Agassiz had clearly placed American Indians higher up the ladder of races than blacks; Melville, in vivid contrast, equalizes the colors by creating a trinity of Queequeg, Tashtego, and Daggoo. Our last view of them is on the three mastheads of the sinking Pequod (—with Tashtego at the mainmast not because he is superior to the others but because he represents the Vanishing American, as the name of the Pequod itself does). Earlier, when Tashtego falls into the "cistern" (the decapitated head of a slain sperm whale), Daggoo attempts to save him, but fails. Why couldn't Melville allow the "imperial negro" to save the Indian? Although it would have provided a perfect rebuttal to Agassiz, the symbolism would perhaps have been too race-specific. So Queequeg, epitome of all non-white races, comes to the rescue instead. In any event, all three colored harpooneers are associated here with the inside of the whale's head. They provide a link between human and whale.

But Melville relentlessly reminds white readers that they too are animals, sometimes no less bestial than sharks. Indeed, to hunt the whale, as Captain Peleg reminds Ishmael, one must at least be able to "talk shark" if not to *be* one, like Stubb, who is more of a shark than "Massa Shark himself." The black cook Fleece is our authority here. He is perhaps the most controversial figure in the book: to many readers, he has too much of the blackface minstrel stereotype about him to be taken seriously as an anti-racist symbol. But his sermon, despite Melville's lamentable attempt at Black English Vernacular, is indeed the black response to white Father Mapple's sermon. Fleece presents a naturalist's vision to cross the theological one. [. . .]

3   For further discussion of the Noble Savage, see p. 140.

From **Paul Giles, "'Bewildering Intertanglement': Melville's Engagement with British Culture,"** in Robert S. Levine and Andrew Delbanco, eds, *The Cambridge Companion to Herman Melville* (1998), Cambridge: Cambridge University Press, 224–49

Giles's piece is an excellent overview of the influence of English culture and literature on Melville, of the role of British critics in the Melville Revival, and of the place of Melville and of *Moby-Dick* in the British sensibility generally.

[. . .] Melville's relative invisibility within the field of later-twentieth-century British culture is all the more telling given his cult status among various maverick thinkers in Britain around the end of the Victorian era. Hershel Parker,[1] in fact, has suggested that the initial "revival of Melville's reputation was almost exclusively a British phenomenon," arising out of a general interest in the American author among various groups of artistic and political rebels, notably the Pre-Raphaelites and, later, the Fabian Socialists.[2] In the 1860s and 1870s, poets like Dante Gabriel Rossetti and James Thomson were attracted to Melville because of the way his broad cultural iconoclasm seemed to be linked, at some vital level, with an ambience of sexual freedom, an issue that greatly concerned British radicals of this era. A few years later, Thomson's influence helped indirectly to generate an admiring circle of Melville acolytes[3] in the provincial town of Leicester, guided by James Billson, a political and religious iconoclast who worked in the legal profession. In 1884, Billson wrote to the American author of how "here in Leicester your books are in great request . . . as soon as one is discovered (for that is what it really is with us) it is eagerly read and passed round a rapidly increasing knot of 'Melville readers.'" Another of this Leicester set, J. W. Barrs, was friendly with Henry S. Salt, who has been described by Parker as the first "Melville scholar" since he published two diligently researched essays on the American writer in the *Scottish Art Review* of November 1889 and the *Gentleman's Magazine* in 1892.

In cultural terms, Salt might be seen in many ways as the typical British champion of Melville's writing around the turn of the twentieth century. After a traditional upbringing, he returned to spend nine years as a master at his old school, Eton, before creating such a stir by his interest in rebellious figures like Shelley, Swinburne, and Thoreau[4] that he was obliged to leave this bastion of

1  One of Melville's most recent biographers and editor of several volumes on Melville and on *Moby-Dick*.
2  Pre-Raphaelites, a movement in painting that arose in reaction to and defiance of established ideas about art in the mid-nineteenth century; Fabian Socialists, British socialist organization founded in 1883.
3  Disciples.
4  Percy Bysshe Shelley (1792–1822), British Romantic poet; Algernon Charles Swinburne (1837–1909), poet, playwright, novelist and critic whose works frequently challenged Victorian mores; Henry David Thoreau (1817–62), American man of letters and Transcendentalist (see pp. 41–4).

educational conservatism. He then forged links with the Fabian Society and the newly emerging Labour Party, and became a proselytizer for causes such as vegetarianism and the Humanitarian League. He continued to publish widely on British authors whom he could cast as outsiders – William Godwin, Thomas De Quincey[5] – as well as vigorously promoting American authors like Emerson, Hawthorne, Poe, and Whitman, in addition to Melville. He also developed friendships with other intellectuals who shared his recalcitrant[6] tendencies: William Morris, George Bernard Shaw, Edward Carpenter, Havelock Ellis.[7] Ellis himself corresponded briefly with Melville in 1890, when the pioneering psychologist was, as he put it, "making some investigations into the ancestry of distinguished English & American poets and imaginative writers, with reference to the question of race."

All of these bohemian characters looked to Melville as an emblem of authentic nature, as an untrammeled spirit who seemed to offer an exuberant alternative to the stuffy principles of British society. A similar pattern was repeated, on a less intellectually self-conscious level, by maritime authors like W. Clark Russell and John Masefield[8] – Masefield spoke in 1912 about Melville's "picturesqueness and directness" – as well as by fantasists like J. M. Barrie,[9] who cherished *Typee* and *Omoo* as an escape back into the adventure world of boyhood. These British enthusiasts were impressed by the way Melville's fictional heroes fail to accommodate themselves to the landlocked preoccupations of an insular society, and their nonconformist sympathies anticipate the line taken by the most famous British advocate of Melville in the early twentieth century, D. H. Lawrence. *Studies in Classic American Literature* (1923) evokes the spirit of the New World as a welcome escape from the repressive confines of British culture, specifically celebrating Melville's "slithery" and "uncanny magic" and going on to describe him as "a futurist long before futurism found paint." Lawrence's whole style of articulation involves something new, of course, but it is worth emphasizing that the provincial, antiestablishment milieu from which Lawrence himself emerged had been remarking upon the qualities of Melville for some forty years. [. . .]

---

5  William Godwin (1756–1836), English philosopher and novelist, father of Mary Shelley and husband of Mary Wollstonecraft; Thomas De Quincey (1785–1859), prose writer.
6  Stubbornly resistant to control or guidance.
7  William Morris (1834–96), English poet, artist and designer who was also a socialist activist critical of industrial society; George Bernard Shaw (1856–1950), Irish playwright who was a committed Fabian socialist and whose plays often examined political themes; Edward Carpenter (1844–1929), ordained minister, author and Fabian who wrote several works on social reform including *Towards Democracy* (1883–1902), a long unrhymed poem heavily influenced by American poet Walt Whitman; Havelock Ellis (1859–1939), English psychologist who published a controversial study of human sexuality resulting in obscenity and pornography charges against its author.
8  W. Clark Russell (1844–1911), British merchant seaman who upon retiring wrote over fifty novels, most of them fictional sea adventures; John Masefield (1878–1967), English poet, novelist, dramatist and journalist who was named Poet Laureate in 1930.
9  J. M. Barrie (1860–1937), Scottish playwright and novelist best remembered for his play *Peter Pan* (1904).

In general, though, it is noticeable how British critics in the first half of the twentieth century tended to focus upon Melville's earlier narratives – *Typee, Omoo, Redburn, Moby-Dick* – and to emphasize their romantic, atavistic[10] energies. There was relatively little conception of how Melville's fiction might be intricately interwoven with issues of hierarchical authority and control, and it could be that his texts were considered acceptable to British readers as long as they could be said simply to embody "the stark forces of nature," as E. L. Grant Watson suggests in a 1920 issue of the London *Mercury*.[11] When, however, a later generation of scholars began unpacking more assiduously the cultural implications and undercurrents of Melville's work, British readers who were quite at home with the reflective ironies and social ambiguities of James or Hawthorne found themselves less comfortable with the more profane implications of Melville's aggressive irreverence. [. . .]

[. . .] In biographical terms, the influence of English literature on the composition of *Moby-Dick* is well known. Six months after beginning to write the novel, Melville started to reconceive its shape in the light of his recent readings in Shakespeare and Thomas Carlyle. He greatly admired Shakespeare – though not, he insisted, the vacuous elitism that went along with the Bard's reputation, as indicated by "the number of the *snobs* who burn their tuns of rancid fat at his shrine." Indeed, in the essay[12] extolling the "power of blackness" in the "hither side of Hawthorne's soul," the very essay that campaigns fiercely against "literary flunkyism towards England," we find Melville seeking to reinvent Shakespeare as another exponent of "deep far-away things," with a putatively Calvinistic feeling for "dark characters" who find themselves "[t]ormented into desperation." Whatever the merits of this as a critique of the English dramatist, it is not difficult to see how *Moby-Dick* appropriates Shakespeare in an attempt self-consciously to grapple with what the author takes to be universal themes. The multilayered dramatic interludes and Shakespearean soliloquies, as well as the metaphysical speculations with which the text is larded, testify to Melville's desire to overcome a cultural "anxiety of influence" by projecting his novel beyond American provincialism into the "unshored, harborless immensities" of world literature. [. . .]

Besides censoring the section on how the ceremonial oil for royal coronations derives from the profane practices of whaling, the editor at the publishing house of Richard Bentley made a sizable number of other excisions when Melville's novel was first published in England as *The Whale* on 18 October 1851. (Melville had changed his mind about the title in September 1851, too late for Bentley, though not for Harper and Brothers in New York, which brought it out as *Moby-Dick* on 14 November.)[13] The English edition omitted most of the supposedly indecorous references to the Bible: thus, farcically enough, "that's Christianity" became "that's the right sort," while "Providence" is recast as "those three mys-

---

10  Reversion or "throwback" to an earlier stage of development.
11  See extract from Grant Watson, **pp. 75–7**.
12  See extract from "Hawthorne and His Mosses," **pp. 38–40**.
13  See Melville's Career and the Writing of Moby-Dick, **pp. 17–19**.

terious ladies." Likewise, the "crucifixion on Ahab's face" was toned down, becoming the blander "eternal anguish in his face." Other alleged obscenities were simply omitted, including references to Nature "painting like the harlot," the "back parts, or tail" of the whale, and so on.

Such editorial caution, however, failed to prevent *The Whale* from being harangued by English reviewers for its blasphemy and indecency. The anonymous contributor to *John Bull*, for instance, complained of "some heathenish, and worse than heathenish talk" in the novel, which was, he said, "calculated to give ... serious offence." This writer was appalled that Melville "should have defaced his pages by occasional twists against revealed religion which add nothing to the interest of his story, and cannot but shock readers accustomed to a reverent treatment of whatever is associated with sacred subjects." Other English reviewers equated these moral transgressions with Melville's apparently wild and lawless rhetoric, a literary style of "eccentricity" (*Britannia*), "purposeless extravagance" (*Illustrated London News*), or "rhapsody run mad" (*Spectator*). The London *Morning Chronicle* of 20 December 1851 epitomizes this early English reception of *The Whale*, with the reviewer associating the "strange contents" of Melville's epic with its willful rejection of Anglo-Saxon empiricism. The profligate author is said to display his "old extravagance, running a perfect muck throughout the three volumes, raving and rhapsodizing in chapter after chapter – unchecked, as it would appear, by the very slightest remembrance of judgment or common sense." [. . .]

# 3

# Key Passages

# Introduction

The excerpts below do not attempt to represent an abridged edition of the primary text. Rather, they have been selected because they are passages critics have returned to time and again when discussing *Moby-Dick* no matter what the topic or methodology. As well, for the first-time reader of *Moby-Dick* the excerpts and the introductions which accompany them should prove extremely helpful in moving beyond the work's plot to the more compelling issues the text raises – many of which are addressed by the critics in Section 2 in detail. Some passages were easy choices. No reader can ignore the thematic importance of Chapter 42: "The Whiteness of the Whale," or of Chapter 99: "The Doubloon" to both the plot of the *Pequod* and to the ideational significance of the hunt for the whale itself. *Moby-Dick* is about many things and, as Ishmael tells us at the end of "The Whiteness of the Whale," "of all these things the Albino whale was the symbol. Wonder ye then at the fiery hunt?" Some passages that individual readers have found particularly compelling will no doubt have been left out. But it is hoped that the issues raised in the discussions which follow will serve as useful guides for coming to grips with any such passages, and thus to *Moby-Dick* as a whole.

## Principal Biblical Allusions

Melville was steeped in the Bible and biblical allusions abound in *Moby-Dick*. The following list aims to provide a starting point, providing short explanatory notes on the major allusions only. For more on Melville's use of the Bible see **p. 183** in Further Reading.

**Ahab**  Historical King of Israel who in the Bible turns from worshiping the one true God and, influenced by his Philistine wife Jezebel, erects temples to Baal. The prophet Elijah confronts Ahab and prophesies his eventual destruction. Ahab is eventually killed in battle.

**Bildad**  In the Book of Job Bildad is one of three friends who come to Job to try and comfort him in his trial by God, reassuring Job that God does not punish the righteous and warning him not to curse God in his despair.

**Elijah**   Appears before Ahab and prophesies a three-year drought in Israel, declaring that Jehovah will seek vengeance for the apostasy[1] of the king.

**Gabriel**   One of the archangels who in Christian tradition intercedes with God to show mercy on certain of his subjects.

**Ishmael**   In the book of Genesis Abraham has a son by his wife's servant Hagar after his wife is unable to conceive. After Abraham and his wife are able to bear a child successfully, Ishmael and Hagar are turned out of Abraham's house to wander the wilderness. In Judeo-Christian tradition, Ishmael is believed to have been chosen by God to found the twelve tribes of Israel. In Islam, Ishmael is considered a prophet and Muslims recognize Arabs as Ishmael's descendants, thus distinguishing them from the Israelites who are considered descended from Abraham. The Bible, however, provides little unambiguous evidence supporting either tradition.

**Jeroboam**   The first ruler of the ten tribes of Israel who like Ahab turns from the one true God, in this case to worshiping golden calves. He is punished by God with the loss of his power and of his son.

**Job**   From the book of Job in the Old Testament, Job is a pious man tested almost beyond endurance by God and who questions his own faith, passing the test and remaining pious and observant in the end.

**Rachel**   The wife of Jacob and traditional spiritual mother of Israel.

---

1   Abandonment of one's faith.

# Key Passages

## Chapter 1: Loomings

The famous opening line "Call me Ishmael" is full of both portent and ambiguity. Its use of the second person calls attention to the utterance itself, self-consciously asking the reader to see it as significant even as it leaves it up to the reader to determine its allusive (one might say *illusive*) meaning. In the Bible Ishmael is the son of the exiled Hagar and an ostracized wanderer. In Genesis 16:12 he is described as follows: "he will be a wild man; his hand will be against every man, and every man's hand against him; and he shall dwell in the presence of all his brethren." Yet Ishmael is merely a name *Moby-Dick*'s narrator takes for himself; his real identity remains undisclosed. Melville thus immediately signals that this is no ordinary literary voice. As both first-person narrator and a character in the story he recounts (what narratologists call a homodiegetic narrator) Ishmael's voice is more fully foregrounded perhaps than any other character save Ahab and yet he is far from omniscient. An aloof, seriocomic observer of the plight of the *Pequod* and its crew, Ishmael's is a privileged viewpoint but limited at the same time. He observes firsthand the truth of the story of the *Pequod* but like all tellers of tales must use language to tell his story in retrospect. As a book that tackles (among other things) the obstacles that one faces in any effort to grasp and to communicate "the unfathomable phantom of life," language and perspective are two of *Moby-Dick*'s primary subjects. From the opening lines of the story of the *Pequod* then, the book's very frame becomes one of its many interpretive problems. Ishmael's attempt to tell the truth about the *Pequod*, its captain, and about Moby Dick are thus put to the same tests and subject to the same limits as those Ishmael raises explicitly in the narrative itself.

Equally important in the opening chapter is Ishmael's effort to equate the sea and seafaring with truth and the quest for truth respectively. This is no ordinary sea tale. Over the course of the first chapter Ishmael is used to entice the reader to read on, to conjure up interest in this wandering seafarer and his story, and

> to see that the story and the hunt for the white whale Moby Dick, are full of
> import. For as every one knows, "meditation and water are wedded for ever."

Call me Ishmael.[1] Some years ago—never mind how long precisely—having little or no money in my purse, and nothing particular to interest me on shore, I thought I would sail about a little and see the watery part of the world. It is a way I have of driving off the spleen,[2] and regulating the circulation. Whenever I find myself growing grim about the mouth; whenever it is a damp, drizzly November in my soul; whenever I find myself involuntarily pausing before coffin warehouses, and bringing up the rear of every funeral I meet; and especially whenever my hypos[3] get such an upper hand of me, that it requires a strong moral principle to prevent me from deliberately stepping into the street, and methodically knocking people's hats off—then, I account it high time to get to sea as soon as I can. This is my substitute for pistol and ball. With a philosophical flourish Cato[4] throws himself upon his sword; I quietly take to the ship: There is nothing surprising in this. If they but knew it, almost all men in their degree, some time or other, cherish very nearly the same feelings towards the ocean with me.

There now is your insular city of the Manhattoes, belted round by wharves as Indian isles by coral reefs—commerce surrounds it with her surf. Right and left, the streets take you waterward. Its extreme down-town is the Battery,[5] where that noble mole is washed by waves, and cooled by breezes, which a few hours previous were out of sight of land. Look at the crowds of water-gazers there.

Circumambulate the city of a dreamy Sabbath afternoon. Go from Corlears Hook to Coenties Slip, and from thence, by Whitehall, northward.[6] What do you see?—Posted like silent sentinels all around the town, stand thousands upon thousands of mortal men fixed in ocean reveries. Some leaning against the piles; some seated upon the pier-heads; some looking over the bulwarks of ships from China; some high aloft in the rigging, as if striving to get a still better seaward peep. But these are all landsmen; of week days pent up in lath and plaster—tied to counters, nailed to benches, clinched to desks. How then is this? Are the green fields gone? What do they here?

But look! here come more crowds, pacing straight for the water, and seemingly bound for a dive. Strange! Nothing will content them but the extremest limit of the land; loitering under the shady lee of yonder warehouses will not suffice. No. They must get just as nigh the water as they possibly can without falling in. And

---

1  See p. 130.
2  Organ of the body traditionally thought to be the home of the emotions and violent passions; here, to drive off feelings of anger and melancholy.
3  Short for hypochondrias, vague psychological afflictions or negative states of mind.
4  Cato of Utica (95–46 BC), also known as Cato the Younger, Roman statesman who opposed Julius Caesar and who committed suicide following the military defeat of one of his close allies by Caesar's forces. He was a staunch Republican who refused to compromise his principles and who is often seen as a symbol of integrity in public life. The allusion here is meant to be humorously mock-heroic.
5  Extreme southern tip of Manhattan Island, now Battery Park.
6  All were fairly well-known landmarks of nineteenth-century Manhattan, and are now in the extreme lower part of the borough.

there they stand—miles of them—leagues. Inlanders all, they come from lanes and alleys, streets and avenues—north, east, south, and west. Yet here they all unite. Tell me, does the magnetic virtue of the needles of the compasses of all those ships attract them thither?

Once more. Say, you are in the country; in some high land of lakes. Take almost any path you please, and ten to one it carries you down in a dale, and leaves you there by a pool in the stream. There is magic in it. Let the most absent-minded of men be plunged in his deepest reveries—stand that man on his legs, set his feet a-going, and he will infallibly lead you to water, if water there be in all that region. Should you ever be athirst in the great American desert,[7] try this experiment, if your caravan happen to be supplied with a metaphysical professor. Yes, as every one knows, meditation and water are wedded for ever.

But here is an artist. He desires to paint you the dreamiest, shadiest, quietest, most enchanting bit of romantic landscape in all the valley of the Saco.[8] What is the chief element he employs? There stand his trees, each with a hollow trunk, as if a hermit and a crucifix were within; and here sleeps his meadow, and there sleep his cattle; and up from yonder cottage goes a sleepy smoke. Deep into distant woodlands winds a mazy way, reaching to overlapping spurs of mountains bathed in their hill-side blue. But though the picture lies thus tranced, and though this pine-tree shakes down its sighs like leaves upon this shepherd's head, yet all were vain, unless the shepherd's eye were fixed upon the magic stream before him. Go visit the Prairies[9] in June, when for scores on scores of miles you wade knee-deep among Tiger-lilies—what is the one charm wanting?—Water—there is not a drop of water there! Were Niagara[10] but a cataract of sand, would you travel your thousand miles to see it? Why did the poor poet of Tennessee,[11] upon suddenly receiving two handfuls of silver, deliberate whether to buy him a coat, which he sadly needed, or invest his money in a pedestrian trip to Rockaway Beach?[12] Why is almost every robust healthy boy with a robust healthy soul in him, at some time or other crazy to go to sea? Why upon your first voyage as a passenger, did you yourself feel such a mystical vibration, when first told that you and your ship were now out of sight of land? Why did the old Persians hold the sea holy? Why did the Greeks give it a separate deity, and make him the own brother of Jove?[13] Surely all this is not without meaning. And still deeper the meaning of that story of Narcissus,[14]

---

7  Extremely arid region in the southwest US encompassing parts of several states.
8  The allusion here is to the Hudson River School of Thomas Cole and others, a nineteenth-century American movement in painting whose principal subjects were epic romantic landscapes of the American frontier, especially upstate New York and the Hudson River valley. The valley of the Saco, which Melville visited, is in New Hampshire.
9  An extremely large and bountiful but treeless region of the Midwestern US encompassing several entire states and large parts of several others. It is primarily agricultural with scattered industrial cities. The tone here is comic and ironic – although they lack large bodies of water the Prairies are sufficient in themselves for what they are and the comparison as a whole is thus inappropriate.
10 Niagara Falls in upstate New York near Buffalo on the Canadian–US border where Lake Erie empties into Lake Ontario.
11 Presumably a fictional poet; no direct reference has been established.
12 Resort town on the coast of Long Island, New York.
13 The allusion here is confused. Jove is the supreme father-deity of Roman religion; Poseidon is the Greek god of the sea.
14 See n. 2, p. 48.

who because he could not grasp the tormenting, mild image he saw in the fountain, plunged into it and was drowned. But that same image, we ourselves see in all rivers and oceans. It is the image of the ungraspable phantom of life; and this is the key to it all. [. . .]

Though I cannot tell why it was exactly that those stage managers, the Fates, put me down for this shabby part of a whaling voyage, when others were set down for magnificent parts in high tragedies, and short and easy parts in genteel comedies, and jolly parts in farces—though I cannot tell why this was exactly; yet, now that I recall all the circumstances, I think I can see a little into the springs and motives which being cunningly presented to me under various disguises, induced me to set about performing the part I did, besides cajoling me into the delusion that it was a choice resulting from my own unbiased freewill and discriminating judgment.

Chief among these motives was the overwhelming idea of the great whale himself.[15] Such a portentous and mysterious monster roused all my curiosity. Then the wild and distant seas where he rolled his island bulk; the undeliverable, nameless perils of the whale; these, with all the attending marvels of a thousand Patagonian[16] sights and sounds, helped to sway me to my wish. With other men, perhaps, such things would not have been inducements; but as for me, I am tormented with an everlasting itch for things remote. I love to sail forbidden seas, and land on barbarous coasts. Not ignoring what is good, I am quick to perceive a horror, and could still be social with it—would they let me—since it is but well to be on friendly terms with all the inmates of the place one lodges in.

By reason of these things, then, the whaling voyage was welcome; the great flood-gates of the wonder-world swung open, and in the wild conceits that swayed me to my purpose, two and two there floated into my inmost soul, endless processions of the whale, and, midmost of them all, one grand hooded phantom, like a snow hill in the air.

## Chapter 3: The Spouter-Inn

Chapter 3 finds Ishmael in New Bedford, Massachusetts, looking for a place to spend the night. Here he encounters Queequeg for the first time, and the chapter as a whole is one of the most comic in the book. The passages below, however, focus on two significant moments only. The picture Ishmael sees and ruminates over in "The Spouter-Inn" is a trope in miniature of one of the novel's major topics: the search for truth and the role of interpretation and of observation and perspective in that search. The "boggy, soggy, squitchy" picture figures the various attempts made throughout the book to observe, reason through, and eventually arrive at some

15  See especially extract from Chapter 42, "The Whiteness of the Whale," pp. 155–8.
16  Region of southern South America encompassing parts of Chile and Argentina; it is cold and mountainous.

Entering that gable-ended Spouter-Inn, you found yourself in a wide, low, straggling entry with old-fashioned wainscots,[1] reminding one of the bulwarks[2] of some condemned old craft. On one side hung a very large oil-painting so thoroughly besmoked, and every way defaced, that in the unequal cross-lights by which you viewed it, it was only by diligent study and a series of systematic visits to it, and careful inquiry of the neighbors, that you could any way arrive at an understanding of its purpose. Such unaccountable masses of shades and shadows, that at first you almost thought some ambitious young artist, in the time of the New England hags,[3] had endeavored to delineate chaos bewitched. But by dint of much and earnest contemplation, and oft repeated ponderings, and especially by throwing open the little window towards the back of the entry, you at last came to the conclusion that such an idea, however wild, might not be altogether unwarranted.

But what most puzzled and confounded you was a long, limber, portentous, black mass of something hovering in the centre of the picture over three blue, dim, perpendicular lines floating in a nameless yeast. A boggy, soggy, squitchy picture truly, enough to drive a nervous man distracted. Yet was there a sort of indefinite, half-attained, unimaginable sublimity about it that fairly froze you to it, till you involuntarily took an oath with yourself to find out what that marvelous painting meant. Ever and anon a bright, but, alas, deceptive idea would dart you through.—It's the Black Sea in a midnight gale.—It's the unnatural combat of the four primal elements.—It's a blasted heath.—It's a Hyperborean[4] winter scene.— It's the breaking-up of the ice-bound stream of Time. But at last all these fancies yielded to that one portentous something in the picture's midst. *That* once found out, and all the rest were plain. But stop; does it not bear a faint resemblance to a gigantic fish? even the great leviathan himself?

In fact, the artist's design seemed this: a final theory of my own, partly based upon the aggregated opinions of many aged persons with whom I conversed upon the subject. The picture represents a Cape-Horner[5] in a great hurricane; the half-foundered ship weltering there with its three dismantled masts alone visible;

---

1    Paneling applied to the walls of a room for decorative purposes.
2    Part of the ship's side above the deck forming the wall of the ship's deck area.
3    The reference is to the witch trials of seventeenth-century New England, especially Salem, Massachusetts.
4    Pertaining to the far north.
5    A ship rounding Cape Horn.

and an exasperated whale, purposing to spring clean over the craft, is in the enormous act of impaling himself upon the three mast-heads. [. . .]

A tramping of sea boots was heard in the entry; the door was flung open, and in rolled a wild set of mariners enough. Enveloped in their shaggy watch coats,[6] and with their heads muffled in woollen comforters, all bedarned and ragged, and their beards stiff with icicles, they seemed an eruption of bears from Labrador.[7] They had just landed from their boat, and this was the first house they entered. No wonder, then, that they made a straight wake for the whale's mouth—the bar—when the wrinkled little old Jonah,[8] there officiating, soon poured them out brimmers all round. One complained of a bad cold in his head, upon which Jonah mixed him a pitch-like potion of gin and molasses, which he swore was a sovereign cure for all colds and catarrhs[9] whatsoever, never mind of how long standing, or whether caught off the coast of Labrador, or on the weather side of an ice-island.

The liquor soon mounted into their heads, as it generally does even with the arrantest topers[10] newly landed from sea, and they began capering about most obstreperously.[11]

I observed, however, that one of them held somewhat aloof, and though he seemed desirous not to spoil the hilarity of his shipmates by his own sober face, yet upon the whole he refrained from making as much noise as the rest. This man interested me at once; and since the sea-gods had ordained that he should soon become my shipmate (though but a sleeping-partner one, so far as this narrative is concerned), I will here venture upon a little description of him. He stood full six feet in height, with noble shoulders, and a chest like a coffer-dam.[12] I have seldom seen such brawn in a man. His face was deeply brown and burnt, making his white teeth dazzling by the contrast; while in the deep shadows of his eyes floated some reminiscences[13] that did not seem to give him much joy. His voice at once announced that he was a Southerner, and from his fine stature, I thought he must be one of those tall mountaineers from the Alleganian Ridge[14] in Virginia. When the revelry of his companions had mounted to its height, this man slipped away unobserved, and I saw no more of him till he became my comrade on the sea. In a few minutes, however, he was missed by his shipmates, and being, it seems, for some reason a huge favorite with them, they raised a cry of "Bulkington! Bulkington! where's Bulkington?" and darted out of the house in pursuit of him. [. . .]

---

6  Long, usually woolen coats worn in adverse weather while on duty ("watch").
7  A peninsular region of eastern Canada composed of portions of Quebec and Newfoundland provinces, it is a high, arid and generally frigid plateau.
8  See n. 2, p. 111.
9  Inflammation of the mucous membranes of the nose and throat.
10  Chronic excessive drinkers.
11  In an excessively boisterous manner.
12  Large, water-tight enclosure attached to the side of a ship to facilitate repairs below the water line.
13  Memories.
14  Mountainous region encompassing parts of both West Virginia and Virginia, part of the Alleghany plateau.

# Chapter 9: The Sermon

Father Mapple is believed to be based on the real-life Father Edward Taylor, a prominent Boston minister and/or Reverend Enoch Mudge, pastor of the New Bedford Seaman's Bethel (chapel), which Melville visited before sailing on the *Acushnet* in 1841. Whatever the case, Melville's fictional Father Mapple plays a short but important role. The books of Jonah and Job are the two most prominent biblical sources for *Moby-Dick*. Steeped in the Bible, especially the characters and stories of the Old Testament, and raised in the Dutch Calvinism he eventually rejected, Melville in *Moby-Dick* draws on both biblical narratives in a variety of ways, secularizing them but at the same relying on them to give his own story a sense of history. Melville wants the reader to imagine that Ishmael's story and Ahab's struggle with the whale have been going on for ages. God's adjuration to Jonah to preach truth in the face of falsehood becomes for the religious skeptic Melville simply an a priori desire to get at the truth, to, in Ahab's words, "strike through the mask" of mere appearances (see **p. 152**). And much like Jonah Ishmael is a sort of prophet, isolated and outcast because he defies convention to get at the very "axis of reality." In "The Sermon" Melville is thus able to frame Ishmael's struggle to tell the tale of the *Pequod* within the larger context of man's ongoing struggle to understand his place in the cosmos. Melville's use and transformation of his biblical sources are in this chapter paradigmatic of his use of biblical sources throughout *Moby-Dick*.

Father Mapple rose, and in a mild voice of unassuming authority ordered the scattered people to condense. "Starboard gangway, there! Side away to larboard—larboard gangway to starboard! Midships! midships!"

There was a low rumbling of heavy sea-boots among the benches, and a still slighter shuffling of women's shoes, and all was quiet again, and every eye on the preacher. [. . .]

[. . .] A brief pause ensued; the preacher slowly turned over the leaves of the Bible, and at last, folding his hand down upon the proper page, said: "Beloved shipmates, clinch the last verse of the first chapter of Jonah—'And God had prepared a great fish to swallow up Jonah.'[1]

"Shipmates, this book, containing only four chapters—four yarns—is one of the smallest strands in the mighty cable[2] of the Scriptures. Yet what depths of the soul does Jonah's deep sea-line sound! what a pregnant lesson to us is this prophet! What a noble thing is that canticle[3] in the fish's belly! How billow-like and boisterously grand! We feel the floods surging over us; we sound with him to the kelpy bottom of the waters; sea-weed and all the slime of the sea is

---

1   See **n. 2, p. 110**.
2   Large rope woven of many strands.
3   Chant or song.

about us! But *what* is this lesson that the book of Jonah teaches? Shipmates, it is a two-stranded lesson; a lesson to us all as sinful men, and a lesson to me as a pilot of the living God. As sinful men, it is a lesson to us all, because it is a story of the sin, hard-heartedness, suddenly awakened fears, the swift punishment, repentance, prayers, and finally the deliverance and joy of Jonah. As with all sinners among men, the sin of this son of Amittai[4] was in his wilful disobedience of the command of God—never mind now what that command was, or how conveyed—which he found a hard command. But all the things that God would have us do are hard for us to do—remember that—and hence, he oftener commands us than endeavors to persuade. And if we obey God, we must disobey ourselves; and it is in this disobeying ourselves, wherein the hardness of obeying God consists.

"With this sin of disobedience in him, Jonah still further flouts at God, by seeking to flee from Him. He thinks that a ship made by men, will carry him into countries where God does not reign, but only the Captains of this earth. He skulks about the wharves of Joppa,[5] and seeks a ship that's bound for Tarshish. There lurks, perhaps, a hitherto unheeded meaning here. By all accounts Tarshish could have been no other city than the modern Cadiz.[6] That's the opinion of learned men. And where is Cadiz, shipmates? Cadiz is in Spain; as far by water, from Joppa, as Jonah could possibly have sailed in those ancient days, when the Atlantic was an almost unknown sea. Because Joppa, the modern Jaffa, shipmates, is on the most easterly coast of the Mediterranean, the Syrian; and Tarshish or Cadiz more than two thousand miles to the westward from that, just outside the Straits of Gibraltar.[7] See ye not then, shipmates, that Jonah sought to flee world-wide from God? Miserable man! Oh! most contemptible and worthy of all scorn; with slouched hat and guilty eye, skulking from his God; prowling among the shipping like a vile burglar hastening to cross the seas. So disordered, self-condemning is his look, that had there been policemen in those days, Jonah, on the mere suspicion of something wrong, had been arrested ere he touched a deck. How plainly he's a fugitive! no baggage, not a hat-box, valise, or carpet-bag,—no friends accompany him to the wharf with their adieux.[8] At last, after much dodging search, he finds the Tarshish ship receiving the last items of her cargo; and as he steps on board to see its Captain in the cabin, all the sailors for the moment desist from hoisting in the goods, to mark the stranger's evil eye. Jonah sees this; but in vain he tries to look all ease and confidence; in vain essays his wretched smile. Strong intuitions of the man assure the mariners he can be no innocent. In their gamesome but still serious way, one whispers to the other— 'Jack, he's robbed a widow;' or, 'Joe, do you mark him; he's a bigamist;'[9] or,

---

4    Father of Jonah.
5    Now Jaffa, a port that is part of Tel Aviv, Israel.
6    City in Spain on the bay of Cadiz.
7    Narrow body of water in extreme southwest Spain that separates the European continent from North Africa.
8    Adieux: French for "farewells" or "goodbyes."
9    Bigamy: having more than one wife.

'Harry lad, I guess he's the adulterer that broke jail in old Gomorrah, or belike, one of the missing murderers from Sodom.'[10] Another runs to read the bill that's stuck against the spile upon the wharf to which the ship is moored, offering five hundred gold coins for the apprehension of a parricide,[11] and containing a description of his person. He reads, and looks from Jonah to the bill; while all his sympathetic shipmates now crowd round Jonah, prepared to lay their hands upon him. Frighted Jonah trembles, and summoning all his boldness to his face, only looks so much the more a coward. He will not confess himself suspected; but that itself is strong suspicion. So he makes the best of it; and when the sailors find him not to be the man that is advertised, they let him pass, and he descends into the cabin. [. . .]

"Shipmates, God has laid but one hand upon you; both his hands press upon me. I have read ye by what murky light may be mine the lesson that Jonah teaches to all sinners; and therefore to ye, and still more to me, for I am a greater sinner than ye. And now how gladly would I come down from this mast-head and sit on the hatches there where you sit, and listen as you listen, while some one of you reads *me* that other and more awful lesson which Jonah teaches to *me*, as a pilot of the living God. How being an anointed pilot-prophet, or speaker of true things, and bidden by the Lord to sound those unwelcome truths in the ears of a wicked Nineveh,[12] Jonah, appalled at the hostility he should raise, fled from his mission, and sought to escape his duty and his God by taking ship at Joppa. But God is everywhere; Tarshish he never reached. As we have seen, God came upon him in the whale, and swallowed him down to living gulfs of doom, and with swift slantings tore him along 'into the midst of the seas,' where the eddying depths sucked him ten thousand fathoms down, and 'the weeds were wrapped about his head,' and all the watery world of woe bowled over him. Yet even then beyond the reach of any plummet—'out of the belly of hell'—when the whale grounded upon the ocean's utmost bones, even then, God heard the engulfed, repenting prophet when he cried. Then God spake unto the fish; and from the shuddering cold and blackness of the sea, the whale came breeching up towards the warm and pleasant sun, and all the delights of air and earth; and 'vomited out Jonah upon the dry land;' when the word of the Lord came a second time; and Jonah, bruised and beaten—his ears, like two sea-shells, still multitudinously murmuring of the ocean—Jonah did the Almighty's bidding. And what was that, shipmates? To preach the Truth to the face of Falsehood! That was it!"[13] [. . .]

---

10 Murder was just one of the many sins for which the city of Sodom was destroyed by God, according to the Old Testament. The point here is that Jonah is seen by the crew as a sinner who may possibly have escaped Sodom and they are thus justified in throwing him overboard.
11 Murderer of one's father, mother, or other near relative.
12 Ancient capital city of the Assyrian Empire mentioned frequently in the Bible (Assyria was known to the Jews as the "Land of Nimrod"). Although not as infamous as Sodom or Gomorrah, Nineveh is usually associated with Babylon and the Jewish exile and captivity; in short, a place whose people did not worship the one true God.
13 Compare this chapter to Melville's discussion of the "Great Art of Telling the Truth" in the extract from "Hawthorne and His Mosses" (1850), p. 39.

# Chapter 10: A Bosom Friend

"George Washington cannibalistically developed," thus Ishmael describes Queequeg in Chapter 10. Conventional critical wisdom has thus maintained that Queequeg is a perfect example of the "Noble Savage"—an eighteenth-century term used to describe "primitive" non-European people of color, and the theoretical basis for representations of Indians, Africans, African-Americans, and indigenous peoples generally by European and American writers in the nineteenth century. Based on the natural law of the Enlightenment and on the writings of eighteenth-century French philosopher Jean-Jacques Rousseau, the Noble Savage myth held that man in a state of nature was uncorrupted by civilization and thus more innately "good" than civilized man. American writers in the nineteenth century were also heavily influenced by the Stadialist Model of historical progress. This theory of historical causality, a product of eighteenth-century Scottish common philosophy and historiography, held that all civilizations evolved through four stages of development: (1) a "savage" stage based on hunting and fishing; (2) a "barbarian" stage based on herding; (3) a stage considered "civilized" and based mainly on agriculture; (4) a stage based on commerce and manufacturing and which was typically considered "over-civilized" and thus characteristic of a society in decline. Although mildly pejorative, "savage" is thus closer to "primitive" than "barbaric" in meaning.

For many contemporary critics, the Noble Savage is often seen as a con-descending if not racist stereotype. Yet as the essay by Andriano in Section 2 suggests (pp. 119–21), Melville's handling of race, and especially his delineation of his non-Euro-American characters, is rarely conventional. And as the passage below illustrates, although Queequeg is certainly "primitive," Ishmael's comic description of the blossoming of his friendship with him plays havoc with nineteenth-century assumptions about race, religion, and the characteristic distinctions between civilized and noncivilized societies and persons.

Equally important are Melville's use of sentiment, which forms the basis for Ishmael's egalitarian relationship with Queequeg, and the thinly veiled homoeroticism of the chapter's final image: "in our hearts' honeymoon lay I and Queequeg—a cosy, loving pair."

[. . .] With much interest I sat watching him. Savage though he was, and hideously marred about the face—at least to my taste—his countenance[1] yet had a something in it which was by no means disagreeable. You cannot hide the soul. Through all his unearthly tattooings, I thought I saw the traces of simple honest heart; and in his large, deep eyes, fiery black and bold, there seemed tokens of a spirit that would dare a thousand devils. And besides all this, there was a certain lofty bearing[2] about the Pagan, which even his uncouthness could not altogether

1  Facial appearance.
2  Noble or lofty bearing or demeanor.

maim. He looked like a man who had never cringed and never had had a creditor. Whether it was, too, that his head being shaved, his forehead was drawn out in freer and brighter relief, and looked more expansive than it otherwise would, this I will not venture to decide; but certain it was his head was phrenologically[3] an excellent one. It may seem ridiculous, but it reminded me of General Washington's head, as seen in the popular busts of him. It had the same long regularly graded retreating slope from above the brows, which were likewise very projecting, like two long promontories thickly wooded on top. Queequeg was George Washington cannibalistically developed. [. . .]

After supper, and another social chat and smoke, we went to our room together. He made me a present of his embalmed head; took out his enormous tobacco wallet, and groping under the tobacco, drew out some thirty dollars in silver;[4] then spreading them on the table, and mechanically dividing them into two equal portions, pushed one of them towards me, and said it was mine. I was going to remonstrate; but he silenced me by pouring them into my trowsers'[5] pockets. I let them stay. He then went about his evening prayers, took out his idol, and removed the paper fireboard. By certain signs and symptoms, I thought he seemed anxious for me to join him; but well knowing what was to follow I deliberated a moment whether, in case he invited me, I would comply or otherwise.

I was a good Christian; born and bred in the bosom of the infallible Presbyterian Church. How then could I unite with this wild idolator in worshipping his piece of wood? But what is worship? thought I. Do you suppose now, Ishmael, that the magnanimous God of Heaven and earth—pagans and all included—can possibly be jealous of an insignificant bit of black wood? Impossible! But what is worship?—to do the will of God—*that* is worship. And what is the will of God?—to do to my fellow man what I would have my fellow man to do to me—*that* is the will of God. Now, Queequeg is my fellow man. And what do I wish that this Queequeg would do to me? Why, unite with me in my particular Presbyterian form of worship. Consequently, I must then unite with him in his; ergo, I must turn idolator.[6] So I kindled the shavings; helped prop up the innocent little idol; offered him burnt biscuit with Queequeg; salamed[7] before him twice or thrice; kissed his nose; and that done, we undressed and went to bed, at peace with our own consciences and all the world. But we did not go to sleep without some lively chat.

How it is I know not; but there is no place like a bed for confidential disclosures between friends. Man and wife, they say, there open the very bottom of their

---

3  Phrenology was a popular but absurd nineteenth-century "science" purporting to be able to determine one's character attributes and personality by studying the shape and peculiarities of one's skull.
4  An allusion to the thirty pieces of silver the high priests paid Judas to betray Christ (Matthew 26:15).
5  Trousers or pants.
6  The "logic" here is specious and highly blasphemous, and the whole scene comic and not serious. Parker argues that making Ishmael a Presbyterian was Melville's revenge for the attacks on him as a result of his scathing condemnations of Protestant missionary work in *Typee*. One of the most vicious attacks on Melville appeared in the Presbyterian New York *Evangelist* (see **p. 69**).
7  Bowed low in salutation or greeting.

souls to each other; and some old couples often lie and chat over old times till nearly morning. Thus, then, in our hearts' honeymoon, lay I and Queequeg—a cosy, loving pair.

## Chapter 16: The Ship

In Chapter 16 the reader is first introduced to both the *Pequod* and to Ahab. The ship itself is a sort of Noble Savage, named after an extinct New England Indian tribe; she is a "cannibal of a craft" and in Ishmael's long description the ship becomes a complex symbol laden with all sorts of connotations and meanings historical, political, religious and literary, most of which are annotated in the excerpt that follows.

As well, Ishmael and the reader learn about the *Pequod*'s captain for the first time. Ishmael and Peleg's exchange explicitly addresses the allusive dimensions of Ahab's name, but Peleg's insistence that unlike the biblical Ahab (a vile and wicked king) the captain of the *Pequod* "has his humanities" suggests that Ahab is both hero and anti-hero. He is a "grand, ungodly, god-like man" whose pursuit of the whale, although ultimately fatal to himself and his crew and ship, is far from easily condemned. The apparent contradiction of such a figure remains one of the deepest attractions and problems for the modern reader of *Moby-Dick*: how can a character be both so deeply heroic and tragic at the same time?

[. . .] You may have seen many a quaint craft in your day, for aught I know;— square-toed luggers; mountainous Japanese junks; butter-box galliots,[1] and what not; but take my word for it, you never saw such a rare old craft as this same rare old Pequod. She was a ship of the old school, rather small if anything; with an old fashioned claw-footed[2] look about her. Long seasoned and weather-stained in the typhoons and calms of all four oceans, her old hull's complexion was darkened like a French grenadier's, who has alike fought in Egypt and Siberia.[3] Her venerable bows looked bearded. Her masts—cut somewhere on the coast of Japan, where her original ones were lost overboard in a gale—her masts stood stiffly up like the spines of the three old kings of Cologne.[4] Her ancient decks were worn and wrinkled, like the pilgrim-worshipped flag-stone in Canterbury Cathedral where Becket bled.[5] But to all these her old antiquities, were added new

---

1  Various small, awkward looking (and awkward sailing) ships.
2  Like eighteenth-century furniture, long thin legs with slightly heavier feet, usually carved to resemble animal claws. The point is that certain parts of the *Pequod* were out of proportion to other parts.
3  French soldiers, probably alluding to two of Napoleon's major campaigns.
4  Melville visited Cologne in 1849. The Cathedral's reliquary purportedly contained the bones of the three wise kings present at the nativity.
5  Thomas à Becket (1118–70), Archbishop of Canterbury who fell into disfavor with Henry II because of his opposition to the king's policies, especially the appointment of Henry's son as Archbishop of York. He was eventually murdered by loyalists to the king in Canterbury Cathedral.

and marvelous features, pertaining to the wild business that for more than half a century she had followed. Old Captain Peleg, many years her chief-mate, before he commanded another vessel of his own, and now a retired seaman, and one of the principal owners of the Pequod,—this old Peleg, during the term of his chief-mateship, had built upon her original grotesqueness, and inlaid it, all over, with a quaintness both of material and device, unmatched by anything except it be Thorkill-Hake's carved buckler or bedstead.[6] She was appareled like any barbaric Ethiopian emperor, his neck heavy with pendants of polished ivory. She was a thing of trophies. A cannibal of a craft, tricking herself forth in the chased bones of her enemies. All round, her unpanelled, open bulwarks were garnished like one continuous jaw, with the long sharp teeth of the sperm whale, inserted there for pins, to fasten her old hempen thews[7] and tendons to. Those thews ran not through base blocks of land wood, but deftly travelled over sheaves of sea-ivory. Scorning a turnstile wheel at her reverend helm, she sported there a tiller; and that tiller was in one mass, curiously carved from the long narrow lower jaw of her hereditary foe. The helmsman who steered by that tiller in a tempest, felt like the Tartar,[8] when he holds back his fiery steed by clutching its jaw. A noble craft, but somehow a most melancholy! All noble things are touched with that. [. . .]

"And what dost thou want of Captain Ahab? It's all right enough; thou art shipped."

"Yes, but I should like to see him."

"But I don't think thou wilt be able to at present. I don't know exactly what's the matter with him; but he keeps close inside the house; a sort of sick, and yet he don't look so. In fact, he ain't sick; but no, he isn't well either. Any how, young man, he won't always see me, so I don't suppose he will thee. He's a queer man, Captain Ahab—so some think—but a good one. Oh, thou'lt like him well enough; no fear, no fear. He's a grand, ungodly, god-like man, Captain Ahab; doesn't speak much; but, when he does speak, then you may well listen. Mark ye, be forewarned; Ahab's above the common; Ahab's been in colleges, as well as 'mong the cannibals; been used to deeper wonders than the waves; fixed his fiery lance in mightier, stranger foes than whales. His lance! aye, the keenest and the surest that, out of all our isle! Oh! he ain't Captain Bildad; no, and he ain't Captain Peleg; *he's Ahab*, boy; and Ahab of old, thou knowest, was a crowned king!"

"And a very vile one. When that wicked king was slain, the dogs, did they not lick his blood?"[9]

"Come hither to me—hither, hither," said Peleg, with a significance in his eye that almost startled me. "Look ye, lad; never say that on board the Pequod. Never say it anywhere. Captain Ahab did not name himself. 'Twas a foolish, ignorant

---

6   Icelandic Viking hero whose exploits were carved on his furniture and other belongings.
7   Sinew or muscle, here made of rope.
8   Before the 1920s Russians used the term "Tartar" to designate the Azerbaijani Turks and several tribes of the Caucasus with whom they were usually at war. Here, "Tartar" connotes a fierce warrior who most often fought on horseback.
9   I Kings 16:29 to I Kings 22:53 recounts the tale of Ahab's reign over Israel and his apostasy and destruction by God. In I Kings 21:19 the prophet Elijah warns Ahab "Thus says the Lord, 'In the place where dogs licked up the blood of Naboth shall dogs lick your own blood.'"

whim of his crazy, widowed mother, who died when he was only a twelvemonth old. And yet the old squaw Tistig, at Gay-head,[10] said that the name would somehow prove prophetic. And, perhaps, other fools like her may tell thee the same. I wish to warn thee. It's a lie. I know Captain Ahab well; I've sailed with him as mate years ago; I know what he is—a good man—not a pious, good man, like Bildad, but a swearing good man—something like me—only there's a good deal more of him. Aye, aye, I know that he was never very jolly; and I know that on the passage home, he was a little out of his mind for a spell; but it was the sharp shooting pains in his bleeding stump that brought that about, as any one might see. I know, too, that ever since he lost his leg last voyage by that accursed whale, he's been a kind of moody—desperate moody, and savage sometimes; but that will all pass off. And once for all, let me tell thee and assure thee, young man, it's better to sail with a moody good captain than a laughing bad one. So good-bye to thee—and wrong not Captain Ahab, because he happens to have a wicked name. Besides, my boy, he has a wife—not three voyages wedded—a sweet, resigned girl. Think of that; by that sweet girl that old man has a child: hold ye then there can be any utter, hopeless harm in Ahab? No, no, my lad; stricken, blasted, if he be, Ahab has his humanities!" [. . .]

## Chapter 23: The Lee Shore

"The Lee Shore" marks the departure of Bulkington and the ostensive transference of his function in the narrative to Ishmael, awkward as this is. The quest for truth is given added heroic significance here, and Melville's vision of the seeker of truth as hero perhaps its most explicit articulation. "Take heart, take heart, O Bulkington! Bear thee grimly, demigod! Up from the spray of thy ocean-perishing—straight up, leaps thy apotheosis!" Here, Moby Dick becomes an exalted, glorified ideal of Ishmael's claim that "in landlessness alone resides the highest truth." The white whale's resistance to Ishmael's attempts to explain him, and to Ahab's attempts to destroy him are here made tropes of "the intrepid effort of the soul to keep the open independence of her sea; while the wildest winds of heaven and earth conspire to cast her on the treacherous, slavish shore."

Some chapters back, one Bulkington was spoken of, a tall, new-landed mariner, encountered in New Bedford at the inn.

When on that shivering winter's night, the Pequod thrust her vindictive bows into the cold malicious waves, who should I see standing at her helm but Bulkington! I looked with sympathetic awe and fearfulness upon the man, who in midwinter just landed from a four years' dangerous voyage, could so unrestingly push off again for still another tempestuous term. The land seemed scorching to

10  On Martha's Vineyard, an island off of the coast of Massachusetts.

his feet. Wonderfullest things are ever the unmentionable; deep memories yield no epitaphs; this six-inch chapter is the stoneless grave of Bulkington. Let me only say that it fared with him as with the storm-tossed ship, that miserably drives along the leeward land.[1] The port would fain give succor; the port is pitiful; in the port is safety, comfort, hearthstone, supper, warm blankets, friends, all that's kind to our mortalities.[2] But in that gale, the port, the land, is that ship's direst jeopardy; she must fly all hospitality; one touch of land, though it but graze the keel, would make her shudder through and through. With all her might she crowds all sail off shore; in so doing, fights 'gainst the very winds that fain would blow her homeward; seeks all the lashed sea's landlessness again; for refuge's sake forlornly rushing into peril; her only friend her bitterest foe!

Know ye, now, Bulkington? Glimpses do ye seem to see of that mortally intolerable truth; that all deep, earnest thinking is but the intrepid effort of the soul to keep the open independence of her sea; while the wildest winds of heaven and earth conspire to cast her on the treacherous, slavish shore?

But as in landlessness alone resides the highest truth,[3] shoreless, indefinite as God—so, better is it to perish in that howling infinite, than be ingloriously dashed upon the lee, even if that were safety! For worm-like, then, oh! who would craven crawl to land! Terrors of the terrible! is all this agony so vain? Take heart, take heart, O Bulkington! Bear thee grimly, demigod! Up from the spray of thy ocean-perishing—straight up, leaps thy apotheosis![4]

## Chapter 26: Knights and Squires

Each character in *Moby-Dick* has a different but vital importance to the unfolding of the narrative's themes. An important starting place for drawing one's own conclusions about what each character contributes is understanding that each of the main members of the crew – Ishmael, Ahab, Starbuck, Stubb, Flask, the various harpooneers – represents a different attitude toward the pursuit of the whale and toward Ahab's obsession. Ahab's revenge embodies, among other things, an angry, perhaps justifiable but ultimately destructive rage against the conditions of human existence. Chief among these of course is the inscrutability of an ambivalent and malignant universe. Starbuck's piety and Stubb's black humor contrast sharply with Ahab's rage. Collectively, the crew represent the diverse ways in which humankind deals with the trials and ambiguities of

---

1   "Leeward" designates the direction in which the wind is blowing and thus driving the ship. During a storm, a shoreline to "lee" is dangerous because the ship is threatened with being blown on to shore and thus sunk. In such a case, what is normally a place of refuge becomes precisely that which the ship and crew must flee in order to survive.
2   The things which make us mortal, i.e., our limitations, which often result in suffering or deprivation.
3   Again see extract from Melville's "Hawthorne and His Mosses" (1850), pp. 38–40, and the letters to Hawthorne on pp. 49–53.
4   The culmination or highest stage of development; a glorified ideal.

existence. If Ahab is Job tested beyond endurance in a universe where God is absent, enraged by his suffering but impotent to do much about it, Starbuck and the other characters offer alternative ways of coping with the trials we all face as we try to come to terms with our place in the world.

The chief mate of the Pequod was Starbuck, a native of Nantucket, and a Quaker by descent.[1] He was a long, earnest man, and though born on an icy coast, seemed well adapted to endure hot latitudes, his flesh being hard as twice-baked biscuit. Transported to the Indies, his live blood would not spoil like bottled ale. He must have been born in some time of general drought and famine, or upon one of those fast days for which his state is famous. Only some thirty arid summers had he seen; those summers had dried up all his physical superfluousness. But this, his thinness, so to speak, seemed no more the token of wasting anxieties and cares, than it seemed the indication of any bodily blight. It was merely the condensation of the man. He was by no means ill-looking; quite the contrary. His pure tight skin was an excellent fit; and closely wrapped up in it, and embalmed with inner health and strength, like a revivified Egyptian, this Starbuck seemed prepared to endure for long ages to come, and to endure always, as now; for be it Polar snow or torrid sun, like a patent chronometer,[2] his interior vitality was warranted to do well in all climates. Looking into his eyes, you seemed to see there the yet lingering images of those thousand-fold perils he had calmly confronted through life. A staid, steadfast man, whose life for the most part was a telling pantomime of action,[3] and not a tame chapter of words. Yet, for all his hardy sobriety and fortitude, there were certain qualities in him which at times affected, and in some cases seemed well nigh to overbalance all the rest. Uncommonly conscientious for a seaman, and endued with a deep natural reverence, the wild watery loneliness of his life did therefore strongly incline him to superstition; but to that sort of superstition, which in some organizations seems rather to spring, somehow, from intelligence than from ignorance. Outward portents and inward presentiments[4] were his. And if at times these things bent the welded iron of his soul, much more did his far-away domestic memories of his young Cape wife[5] and child, tend to bend him still more from the original ruggedness of his nature, and open him still further to those latent influences which, in some honest-hearted men, restrain the gush of dare-devil daring, so often evinced by others in the more perilous vicissitudes[6] of the fishery. "I will have no man in my boat,"

1    Denoting a devout, disciplined but peculiar disposition.
2    Timepiece.
3    Pantomime used here to refer to a type of play, hence Starbuck is depicted as a man of action and
     not words whose life has been a drama or play of many adventures.
4    Here, forebodings. That is, Starbuck interprets both external signs and inward mental and physical
     states as having supernatural significances.
5    Cape Cod, Massachusetts.
6    Dangerous random events.

said Starbuck, "who is not afraid of a whale." By this, he seemed to mean, not only that the most reliable and useful courage was that which arises from the fair estimation of the encountered peril, but that an utterly fearless man is a far more dangerous comrade than a coward. [. . .]

## Chapter 27: Knights and Squires

Stubb was the second mate. He was a native of Cape Cod; and hence, according to local usage, was called a Cape-Cod-man. A happy-go-lucky; neither craven[1] nor valiant; taking perils as they came with an indifferent air; and while engaged in the most imminent crisis of the chase, toiling away, calm and collected as a journeyman joiner[2] engaged for the year. Good-humored, easy, and careless, he presided over his whale-boat as if the most deadly encounter were but a dinner, and his crew all invited guests. He was as particular about the comfortable arrangement of his part of the boat, as an old stage-driver is about the snugness of his box. When close to the whale, in the very death-lock of the fight, he handled his unpitying lance coolly and off-handedly, as a whistling tinker[3] his hammer. He would hum over his old rigadig[4] tunes while flank and flank with the most exasperated monster. Long usage had, for this Stubb, converted the jaws of death into an easy chair. What he thought of death itself, there is no telling. Whether he ever thought of it at all, might be a question; but, if he ever did chance to cast his mind that way after a comfortable dinner, no doubt, like a good sailor, he took it to be a sort of call of the watch[5] to tumble aloft, and bestir themselves there, about something which he would find out when he obeyed the order, and not sooner. [. . .]

The third mate was Flask, a native of Tisbury, in Martha's Vineyard.[6] A short, stout, ruddy young fellow, very pugnacious[7] concerning whales, who somehow seemed to think that the great Leviathans had personally and hereditarily affronted him; and therefore it was a sort of point of honor with him, to destroy them whenever encountered. So utterly lost was he to all sense of reverence for the many marvels of their majestic bulk and mystic ways; and so dead to anything like an apprehension of any possible danger from encountering them; that in his poor opinion, the wondrous whale was but a species of magnified mouse, or at least water-rat, requiring only a little circumvention and some small application of time and trouble in order to kill and boil. This ignorant, unconscious fearlessness of his made him a little waggish in the matter of whales; he followed these fish for

1  Cowardly.
2  Joiner: carpenter.
3  A traveling mender of metal household utensils.
4  Variant of "rigadoon," or lively dance usually in double-time.
5  Crews on ships were organized into units or "watches," each watch bearing responsibility for the ship over a certain interval, usually four hours. When more hands were needed additional watches would be called up from below ships to assist with the labor of sailing and maintaining the ship.
6  Island off the southern coast of Massachusetts.
7  Combative.

the fun of it; and a three years' voyage round Cape Horn[8] was only a jolly joke that lasted that length of time. As a carpenter's nails are divided into wrought nails and cut nails; so mankind may be similarly divided. Little Flask was one of the wrought ones; made to clinch tight and last long. They called him King-Post on board of the Pequod; because, in form, he could be well likened to the short, square timber known by that name in Arctic whalers; and which by the means of many radiating side timbers inserted into it, serves to brace the ship against the icy concussions of those battering seas. [. . .]

Next was Tashtego,[9] an unmixed Indian from Gay Head, the most westerly promontory of Martha's Vineyard, where there still exists the last remnant of a village of red men, which has long supplied the neighboring island of Nantucket with many of her most daring harpooneers. In the fishery, they usually go by the generic name of Gay-Headers. Tashtego's long, lean, sable hair, his high cheek bones, and black rounding eyes—for an Indian, Oriental in their largeness, but Antarctic in their glittering expression—all this sufficiently proclaimed him an inheritor of the unvitiated blood of those proud warrior hunters, who, in quest of the great New England moose, had scoured, bow in hand, the aboriginal forests of the main. But no longer snuffing in the trail of the wild beasts of the woodland, Tashtego now hunted in the wake of the great whales of the sea; the unerring harpoon of the son fitly replacing the infallible arrow of the sires. To look at the tawny brawn of his lithe snaky limbs, you would almost have credited the superstitions of some of the earlier Puritans, and half believed this wild Indian to be a son of the Prince of the Powers of the Air.[10] Tashtego was Stubb the second mate's squire.

Third among the harpooneers was Daggoo, a gigantic, coal-black negro-savage, with a lion-like tread—an Ahasuerus[11] to behold. Suspended from his ears were two golden hoops, so large that the sailors called them ring-bolts, and would talk of securing the top-sail halyards to them. In his youth Daggoo had voluntarily shipped on board of a whaler, lying in a lonely bay on his native coast. And never having been anywhere in the world but in Africa, Nantucket, and the pagan harbors most frequented by whalemen; and having now led for many years the bold life of the fishery in the ships of owners uncommonly heedful of what manner of men they shipped; Daggoo retained all his barbaric virtues, and erect as a giraffe, moved about the decks in all the pomp of six feet five in his socks. There was a corporeal humility in looking up at him; and a white man standing before him seemed a white flag come to beg truce of a fortress. Curious to tell, this imperial negro, Ahasuerus Daggoo, was the Squire of little Flask, who

8  Extreme southern tip of South America, also known as the "cape of storms." Passage around the cape between the Atlantic Ocean and the Pacific is nearly always perilous as the weather and seas are notoriously unpredictable and often dangerous.
9  Compare all the descriptions of the harpooneers to the discussion of race and the Noble Savage in the extract from Andriano on pp. 119–21.
10  The Devil. From Ephesians 2:1–2:2, "And you he made alive, when you were dead through the trespasses and sins in which you once walked, following the course of this world, following the prince of the power of the air, the spirit that is now at work in the sons of disobedience."
11  In the Bible, Hebrew form of Xerxes, King of Persia (see Esther 1.1).

looked like a chess-man beside him. As for the residue of the Pequod's company, be it said, that at the present day not one in two of the many thousand men before the mast employed in the American whale fishery, are Americans born, though pretty nearly all the officers are. Herein it is the same with the American whale fishery as with the American army and military and merchant navies, and the engineering forces employed in the construction of the American Canals and Railroads.[12] The same, I say, because in all these cases the native American liberally provides the brains, the rest of the world as generously supplying the muscles. No small number of these whaling seamen belong to the Azores,[13] where the outward bound Nantucket whalers frequently touch to augment their crews from the hardy peasants of those rocky shores. In like manner, the Greenland whalers sailing out of Hull or London, put in at the Shetland Islands, to receive the full complement of their crew. Upon the passage homewards, they drop them there again. How it is, there is no telling, but Islanders seem to make the best whalemen. They were nearly all Islanders in the Pequod, *Isolatoes* too, I call such, not acknowledging the common continent of men, but each *Isolato* living on a separate continent of his own. Yet now, federated along one keel, what a set these Isolatoes were! An Anacharsis Clootz[14] deputation from all the isles of the sea, and all the ends of the earth, accompanying Old Ahab in the Pequod to lay the world's grievances before that bar from which not very many of them ever come back. Black Little Pip—he never did! Poor Alabama boy! On the grim Pequod's forecastle, ye shall ere long see him, beating his tambourine; preclusive of the eternal time, when sent for, to the great quarter-deck on high, he was bid strike in with angels, and beat his tambourine in glory; called a coward here, hailed a hero there!

## Chapter 28: Ahab

Ishmael's long description of his reaction to seeing Ahab for the first time functions as a powerful delineation of Ahab's character. It shapes the reader's reaction to the action that follows in important ways as Ahab appears in all his ragged glory as both heroic and menacing, a formidable presence on board ship, in Ishmael's imagination, and in the mind of the reader. The tension created as a result of Ishmael's admiration for and fear of Ahab is sustained throughout the novel – and perhaps never resolved. As first defined by Aristotle (384–322 BCE)

---

12  See Melville and Antebellum America, p. 28.
13  Group of islands in the mid-Atlantic west of Spain.
14  Of mixed races and nationalities. Anacharsis Clootz (1755–94), French revolutionary and an ardent supporter of the liberation of Europe in the name of the ideals of the Revolution. According to Parker (see **p. 182** in Further Reading) the reference is to when Clootz led a motley crew from various nations into the French National Assembly in 1790 to symbolize international support for the French Revolution. Melville had read about Clootz in Carlyle's *French Revolution* (1837). Clootz was killed during the Reign of Terror in 1794.

in his *Poetics*, a dramatic tragedy presents a causally related series of events in the life of a person of significance culminating in an unhappy catastrophe, the whole of which is treated with dignity and seriousness. The audience of a tragic drama thus experiences both fear and pity as they bear witness to the destruction of the tragic hero. It is useful to see Ahab as a tragic hero in that Ishmael's admiration and fear of Ahab are easily reconciled thereby. Yet the reader of *Moby-Dick* should remain cognizant that Melville rarely drew on established literary conventions without altering them in important and provocative ways. Glossing over the complex emotions evoked by the fate of the *Pequod*, its crew, and its captain thus risks overlooking what Melville was able to do with the central character of the book. For example, Ahab sees many things in *Moby-Dick*, the least important of which is that he was maimed by the white whale in a previous encounter. Ahab's thirst for revenge against the whale that "dismasted" him thus functions as a trope for, among other things, a type of existential and Job-like rage against an ambivalent but malignant cosmos. His wound is more psychological than physical.

[. . .] It was one of those less lowering, but still grey and gloomy enough mornings of the transition, when with a fair wind the ship was rushing through the water with a vindictive sort of leaping and melancholy rapidity, that as I mounted to the deck at the call of the forenoon watch, so soon as I levelled my glance towards the taffrail,[1] foreboding shivers ran over me. Reality outran apprehension; Captain Ahab stood upon his quarter-deck.

There seemed no sign of common bodily illness about him, nor of the recovery from any. He looked like a man cut away from the stake, when the fire has overrunningly wasted all the limbs without consuming them, or taking away one particle from their compacted aged robustness. His whole high, broad form, seemed made of solid bronze, and shaped in an unalterable mould, like Cellini's cast Perseus.[2] Threading its way out from among his grey hairs, and continuing right down one side of his tawny scorched face and neck, till it disappeared in his clothing, you saw a slender rod-like mark, lividly whitish. It resembled that perpendicular seam sometimes made in the straight, lofty trunk of a great tree, when the upper lightning tearingly darts down it, and without wrenching a single twig, peels and grooves out the bark from top to bottom, ere running off into the soil, leaving the tree still greenly alive, but branded. Whether that mark was born with him, or whether it was the scar left by some desperate wound, no one could certainly say. By some tacit consent, throughout the voyage little or no allusion was made to it, especially by the mates. But once Tashtego's senior, an old Gay-Head Indian among the crew, superstitiously asserted that not till he was full forty years old did Ahab become that way branded, and then it came

1    The rail around the stern or back end of the ship.
2    Noted bronze statue by Benvenuto Cellini (1500–71) depicting Perseus holding the head of Medusa whom he has just slain. Perseus is depicted as strikingly strong, athletic, and handsome.

upon him, not in the fury of any mortal fray, but in an elemental strife at sea. Yet, this wild hint seemed inferentially negatived, by what a grey Manxman[3] insinuated, an old sepulchral man,[4] who, having never before sailed out of Nantucket, had never ere this laid eye upon wild Ahab. Nevertheless, the old sea-traditions, the immemorial credulities,[5] popularly invested this old Manxman with preternatural powers of discernment. So that no white sailor seriously contradicted him when he said that if ever Captain Ahab should be tranquilly laid out—which might hardly come to pass, so he muttered—then, whoever should do that last office for the dead, would find a birth-mark on him from crown to sole. [. . .]

[. . .] Ahab stood erect, looking straight out beyond the ship's ever-pitching prow. There was an infinity of firmest fortitude, a determinate, unsurrenderable wilfulness, in the fixed and fearless, forward dedication of that glance. Not a word he spoke; nor did his officers say aught to him; though by all their minutest gestures and expressions, they plainly showed the uneasy, if not painful, consciousness of being under a troubled master-eye. And not only that, but moody stricken Ahab stood before them with a crucifixion[6] in his face; in all the nameless regal overbearing dignity of some mighty woe.[7] [. . .]

# Chapter 36: The Quarter-Deck

Perhaps the most famous and most important moment in the novel, in the excerpt below Ahab articulates in the lofty rhetoric of Shakespearean drama just what Moby Dick represents to him and just why he is driven beyond reason to pursue and destroy the white whale. Nowhere else in the novel is the hunt for the whale so thoroughly and metaphorically linked to the search for truth. Recall that most scholars now agree that at a certain point in its development Melville shifted the focus of his Romance of the whale fishery from a sort of "*Mardi*-an" discussion of whaling with Bulkington as its central character to a much more ambitious exploration of the "very axis of reality" (see **p. 38**). In this scene, a result of Melville's reading of Shakespeare undertaken in 1850, Ahab most fully emerges as the modern Lear, a psychically wounded hero committed to striking through the mask of appearances to discover what lies beyond it – even if there is "naught beyond."

---

3  A person from the Isle of Man, an island off the west coast of England.
4  A sepulchre is a tomb. Here, a "sepulchral man" is a gloomy man.
5  A Melvillean neologism, here meaning those things commonly held to be true.
6  This would have been considered by many nineteenth-century readers as blasphemous.
7  Possibly an allusion to Ecclesiastes 1:18: "For with much wisdom comes much sorrow; the more knowledge, the more grief." Compare also to Chapter 96: "The Try-Works," where Ishmael exclaims, "The truest of all men was the Man of Sorrows, and truest of all books is Solomon's, and Ecclesiastes is the fine hammered steel of woe." The Man of Sorrows is Christ. Solomon, King of Israel after his father David, was the builder of the Temple of Jerusalem. The books of the Bible traditionally attributed to him include Ecclesiastes, Song of Solomon and parts of Proverbs.

It is important to note too that the conflict between Ahab and Starbuck, between an ungodly but god-like tragic seeker of truth and the quiet desperate piety of the first mate, is here brought into high relief. Ahab, however, convinces the crew to join him in his quest, isolating Starbuck and allowing his quest to proceed.

[. . .] "Hark ye yet again,—the little lower layer. All visible objects, man, are but as pasteboard masks. But in each event—in the living act, the undoubted deed— there, some unknown but still reasoning thing puts forth the mouldings of its features from behind the unreasoning mask. If man will strike, strike through the mask![1] How can the prisoner reach outside except by thrusting through the wall? To me, the white whale is that wall, shoved near to me. Sometimes I think there's naught beyond. But 'tis enough. He tasks me; he heaps me; I see in him outrageous strength, with an inscrutable malice sinewing it. That inscrutable thing is chiefly what I hate; and be the white whale agent, or be the white whale principal, I will wreak that hate upon him. Talk not to me of blasphemy, man; I'd strike the sun if it insulted me. For could the sun do that, then could I do the other; since there is ever a sort of fair play herein, jealousy presiding over all creations. But not my master, man, is even that fair play. Who's over me? Truth hath no confines. Take off thine eye! more intolerable than fiends' glarings is a doltish stare! So, so; thou reddenest and palest; my heat has melted thee to anger-glow. But look ye, Starbuck, what is said in heat, that thing unsays itself. There are men from whom warm words are small indignity. I meant not to incense thee. Let it go. Look! see yonder Turkish cheeks of spotted tawn—living, breathing pictures painted by the sun. The Pagan leopards—the unrecking and unworshipping things, that live; and seek, and give no reasons for the torrid life they feel! The crew, man, the crew! Are they not one and all with Ahab, in this matter of the whale? See Stubb! he laughs! See yonder Chilian! he snorts to think of it. Stand up amid the general hurricane, thy one tost[2] sapling cannot, Starbuck! And what is it? Reckon it. 'Tis but to help strike a fin; no wondrous feat for Starbuck. What is it more? From this one poor hunt, then, the best lance out of all Nantucket, surely he will not hang back, when every foremast-hand has clutched a whetstone? Ah! constrainings seize thee; I see! the billow lifts thee! Speak, but speak!—Aye, aye! thy silence, then, *that* voices thee.[3] *(Aside)* Something shot from my dilated nostrils, he has inhaled it in his lungs. Starbuck now is mine; cannot oppose me now, without rebellion."

"God keep me!—keep us all!" murmured Starbuck, lowly. [. . .]

---

1   Again, see extract from Melville's "Hawthorne and His Mosses" (pp. 38–40) and the letters to
    Hawthorne (pp. 49–53).
2   Tossed.
3   By remaining silent Starbuck acquiesces to Ahab's quest.

# Chapter 41: Moby Dick

"A wild, mystical, sympathetical feeling was in me; Ahab's quenchless feud seemed mine" – so Ishmael describes the complex combination of admiration and fear evoked in him by Ahab and his quest. Chapter 41 establishes both the story of Ahab's "dismasting" – the encounter with Moby Dick that left him maimed – but as well and perhaps most importantly the full import of that wounding for Ahab. As Ishmael tells the reader, Ahab eventually comes to associate Moby Dick with all his "intellectual and spiritual exasperations . . ." Ahab's hatred for the whale is not simply a matter of personal revenge – it powerfully figures the problems of human existence, in Melville's words "the very axis of reality," that the author was most interested in exploring (see Melville's Career and the Writing of *Moby-Dick*, **pp. 15–16**). In his monomania Ahab heaps all that tortures and haunts the human psyche onto the whale's white hump, instilling it with meanings personal and universal. Moby Dick becomes thus a "Job's whale"[1] pursued by Ahab in a vindictive and destructive attempt to right all the wrongs suffered by man "from Adam down." Ishmael knows that to literally see in the whale all the psychological and spiritual doubts and torments Ahab suffers is insane – and yet he strongly empathizes with Ahab, willfully choosing to follow and aid him in his pursuit to the very last, declining even to pass final judgment as he floats mid-Pacific in the Epilogue.

I, Ishmael, was one of that crew; my shouts had gone up with the rest; my oath had been welded with theirs; and stronger I shouted, and more did I hammer and clinch my oath, because of the dread in my soul. A wild, mystical, sympathetical feeling was in me; Ahab's quenchless feud seemed mine. With greedy ears I learned the history of that murderous monster against whom I and all the others had taken our oaths of violence and revenge. [. . .]

His three boats stove around him, and oars and men both whirling in the eddies;[2] one captain, seizing the line-knife from his broken prow, had dashed at the whale, as an Arkansas duellist at his foe, blindly seeking with a six inch blade to reach the fathom-deep life of the whale. That captain was Ahab. And then it was, that suddenly sweeping his sickle-shaped lower jaw beneath him, Moby Dick had reaped away Ahab's leg, as a mower a blade of grass in the field. No turbaned Turk, no hired Venetian[3] or Malay, could have smote him with more

---

1  In the Old Testament Job is a pious man tested beyond endurance by God. Tormented in ways he can't understand, he eventually questions his own faith but falls short of outright blasphemy, remaining pious and observant in spite of his unjust suffering. For Melville, Job is a literary and philosophical reference point. A figure he can point to in order to illustrate the profundity of Ahab's rage in a universe where God is at best absent and possibly nonexistent.
2  Currents in water or air.
3  An allusion to *Othello* Act 5, Scene 2, 407–12, where just after killing Desdemona and just prior to killing himself Othello declares: "Set you down this / And say besides, that in Aleppo once, / Where a malignant and a turban'd Turk / Beat a Venetian and traduc'd the state, / I took by the throat the circumcised dog, / And smote him thus."

seeming malice. Small reason was there to doubt, then, that ever since that almost fatal encounter, Ahab had cherished a wild vindictiveness against the whale, all the more fell for that in his frantic morbidness he at last came to identify with him, not only all his bodily woes, but all his intellectual and spiritual exasperations. The White Whale swam before him as the monomaniac[4] incarnation of all those malicious agencies which some deep men feel eating in them, till they are left living on with half a heart and half a lung. That intangible malignity which has been from the beginning; to whose dominion even the modern Christians ascribe one-half of the worlds; which the ancient Ophites[5] of the east reverenced in their statue devil;—Ahab did not fall down and worship it like them; but deliriously transferring its idea to the abhorred white whale, he pitted himself, all mutilated, against it. All that most maddens and torments; all that stirs up the lees of things; all truth with malice in it; all that cracks the sinews and cakes the brain; all the subtle demonisms of life and thought; all evil, to crazy Ahab, were visibly per-sonified, and made practically assailable in Moby Dick. He piled upon the whale's white hump the sum of all the general rage and hate felt by his whole race from Adam down; and then, as if his chest had been a mortar,[6] he burst his hot heart's shell upon it.

It is not probable that this monomania in him took its instant rise at the precise time of his bodily dismemberment. Then, in darting at the monster, knife in hand, he had but given loose to a sudden, passionate, corporal animosity;[7] and when he received the stroke that tore him, he probably but felt the agonizing bodily laceration, but nothing more. Yet, when by this collision forced to turn towards home, and for long months of days and weeks, Ahab and anguish lay stretched together in one hammock, rounding in mid winter that dreary, howling Patagonian Cape;[8] then it was, that his torn body and gashed soul bled into one another; and so interfusing, made him mad. That it was only then, on the homeward voyage, after the encounter, that the final monomania seized him, seems all but certain from the fact that, at intervals during the passage, he was a raving lunatic;[9] and, though unlimbed of a leg, yet such vital strength yet lurked in his Egyptian chest, and was moreover intensified by his delirium, that his mates were forced to lace him fast, even there, as he sailed, raving in his hammock. In a strait-jacket, he swung to the mad rockings of the gales. And, when running

---

4   Monomania was a nineteenth-century clinical term from faculty psychology, the dominant model and science of the mind at the time Melville was writing *Moby-Dick*. It denotes a pathological obsession with one idea or object. (See also extract from Chapter 44; "The Chart" on pp. 158–9.)
5   A Gnostic sect, dualistic and philosophic movement of the late Hellenistic and early Christian periods, known for extreme cultism and inverted morality.
6   A mortar is a hard shell or receptacle used to grind substances down to a paste or very small particles. Here, Ahab's heart is "burst" or ground down in the mortar of his chest.
7   An anger emerging from his very physical being.
8   The extreme southern tip of South America is known as Cape Horn or the Cape of Storms. Prior to the construction of the Panama Canal any vessel sailing between the Atlantic and Pacific oceans had to pass around it. South of it lies Antarctica and its weather is notoriously dangerous and unpredictable, offering no safe haven for any vessel. Here Melville likens the storms typical of the Cape to the storm in Ahab's psyche.
9   See Chapter 44, "The Chart," pp. 158–9.

into more sufferable latitudes, the ship, with mild stun' sails[10] spread, floated across the tranquil tropics, and, to all appearances, the old man's delirium seemed left behind him with the Cape Horn swells, and he came forth from his dark den into the blessed light and air; even then, when he bore that firm, collected front, however pale, and issued his calm orders once again; and his mates thanked God the direful madness was now gone; even then, Ahab, in his hidden self, raved on. [. . .]

Here, then, was this grey-headed, ungodly old man, chasing with curses a Job's whale[11] round the world, at the head of a crew, too, chiefly made up of mongrel renegades, and castaways—and cannibals—morally enfeebled also, by the incompetence of mere unaided virtue or right-mindedness in Starbuck, the invulnerable jollity of indifference and recklessness in Stubb, and the pervading mediocrity in Flask. Such a crew, so officered, seemed specially picked and packed by some infernal fatality to help him to his monomaniac revenge. How it was that they so aboundingly responded to the old man's ire—by what evil magic their souls were possessed, that at times his hate seemed almost theirs; the White Whale as much their insufferable foe as his; how all this came to be—what the White Whale was to them, or how to their unconscious understandings, also, in some dim, unsuspected way, he might have seemed the gliding great demon of the seas of life,—all this to explain, would be to dive deeper than Ishmael can go. The subterranean miner that works in us all, how can one tell whither leads his shaft by the ever shifting, muffled sound of his pick? Who does not feel the irresistible arm drag? What skiff in tow of a seventy-four[12] can stand still? For one, I gave myself up to the abandonment of the time and the place; but while yet all a-rush to encounter the whale, could see naught in that brute but the deadliest ill.

## Chapter 42: The Whiteness of the Whale

If for Ahab the white whale is a "Job's whale," for Ishmael it is this and something more: it is ambiguity incarnate, a physical and symbolic embodiment of a malignant and ambivalent universe. Ahab's projection is feverish and personal, as idiosyncratic as it is maniacal. Ishmael's estimation of the portentousness of the white whale is in contrast rational, panhistorical,[1] and modern. The long catalogue of whiteness and what it has represented throughout the ages allows Ishmael to locate his own attitude toward the whale's symbolic meanings in a

---

10 Sails set in good weather in addition to the mainsails
11 A "Job's whale" because Ahab is tormented and tested by Moby Dick beyond endurance, as Job is tested by God. See also Job 41:1: "Can you draw out Leviathan with a fishhook, or press down his tongue with a cord?"
12 Nautical term for a large warship, referring to the number of cannon it carried.

---

1 Of or pertaining to all histories.

historical narrative dating back to the Ancient Greeks. He thus grounds his reading of the whale in material fact and not in some physical, existential or psychic wound – he does not take Moby Dick personally and so remains aloof and thus better able to render his experience on the *Pequod* intelligible for his audience. If more abstract than Ahab's hatred for the whale, Ishmael's fear of the nameless void embodied by Moby Dick is not any less profound or disturbing. Ahab's rage is the rage of Achilles in Homer's *Iliad* – epic, outside of history, a personal defiance of the gods.[2] Ishmael's is modern man's fear and revulsion at the ambiguity if not meaningless of life. He admires Ahab for a will he himself does not possess, an epic defiance his cosmopolitanism and erudition[3] do not allow him to adopt. Making a definitive choice and thus committing to a struggle like Ahab's is not an option for the jaded and cynical Ishmael. But he will join Ahab's quest as a bemused observer, basking in the glow of Ahab's sun, safe from actually committing himself to a fray he knows is doomed from the outset.

What the white whale was to Ahab, has been hinted; what, at times, he was to me, as yet remains unsaid.

Aside from those more obvious considerations touching Moby Dick, which could not but occasionally awaken in any man's soul some alarm, there was another thought, or rather vague, nameless horror concerning him, which at times by its intensity completely overpowered all the rest; and yet so mystical and well nigh ineffable was it, that I almost despair of putting it in a comprehensible form. It was the whiteness of the whale that above all things appalled me. But how can I hope to explain myself here; and yet, in some dim, random way, explain myself I must, else all these chapters might be naught.

Though in many natural objects, whiteness refiningly enhances beauty, as if imparting some special virtue of its own, as in marbles, japonicas,[4] and pearls; and though various nations have in some way recognized a certain royal pre-eminence in this hue; even the barbaric, grand old kings of Pegu[5] placing the title "Lord of the White Elephants" above all their other magniloquent[6] ascriptions of dominion; and the modern kings of Siam[7] unfurling the same snow-white quadruped in the royal standard; and the Hanoverian[8] flag bearing

2    Achilles is the hero of Homer's *Iliad* (*c.* 700 BCE), an epic Greek poem that recounts events set during the Trojan War (*c.* 1200 BCE). Achilles' rage at being slighted by his ally Agamemnon results in his own death and the deaths of thousands of his men.
3    Cosmopolitan: sophisticated and broad minded; erudite: deeply learned.
4    Japonica refers to the camellia plant, one species of which is known for its beautiful white flowers.
5    Pegu, now Bago, a regional capital of South Myanmar, formerly Burma, in Southeast Asia on the Bay of Bengal.
6    Lofty and extravagant in speech.
7    Siam, now Thailand.
8    Hanover, former kingdom of Lower Saxony in what is now Northern Germany.

the one figure of a snow-white charger; and the great Austrian Empire, Cæsarian heir to overlording Rome[9] having for the imperial color the same imperial hue; and though this pre-eminence in it applies to the human race itself, giving the white man ideal mastership over every dusky tribe;[10] and though, besides all this, whiteness has been even made significant of gladness, for among the Romans a white stone marked a joyful day; and though in other mortal sympathies and symbolizings, this same hue is made the emblem of many touching, noble things— the innocence of brides, the benignity of age; though among the Red Men of America the giving of the white belt of wampum was the deepest pledge of honor; though in many climes, whiteness typifies the majesty of Justice in the ermine[11] of the Judge, and contributes to the daily state of kings and queens drawn by milk-white steeds; though even in the higher mysteries of the most august religions it has been made the symbol of the divine spotlessness and power; by the Persian fire worshippers, the white forked flame being held the holiest on the altar; and in the Greek mythologies, Great Jove himself being made incarnate in a snow-white bull; and though to the noble Iroquois, the midwinter sacrifice of the sacred White Dog was by far the holiest festival of their theology, that spotless, faithful creature being held the purest envoy they could send to the Great Spirit with the annual tidings of their own fidelity; and though directly from the Latin word for white,[12] all Christian priests derive the name of one part of their sacred vesture, the alb or tunic, worn beneath the cassock; and though among the holy pomps of the Romish faith, white is specially employed in the celebration of the Passion of our Lord; though in the Vision of St. John,[13] white robes are given to the redeemed, and the four-and-twenty elders stand clothed in white before the great white throne, and the Holy One that sitteth there white like wool; yet for all these accumulated associations, with whatever is sweet, and honorable, and sublime, there yet lurks an elusive something in the innermost idea of this hue, which strikes more of panic to the soul than that redness which affrights in blood. [. . .]

Is it that by its indefiniteness it shadows forth the heartless voids and immensities of the universe, and thus stabs us from behind with the thought of annihilation, when beholding the white depths of the milky way? Or is it, that as in essence whiteness is not so much a color as the visible absence of color, and at the same time the concrete of all colors; is it for these reasons that there is such a dumb

---

9 Reference is to the Holy Roman Empire, the political entity that originated at the coronation, as emperor, of the German king Otto I (962 CE) and which existed until the renunciation of the imperial title by Francis II in 1806. It encompassed much of what is now Western Europe and speciously claimed it was rightfully descended from the Roman Empire of the Caesars. The tone here is ironic.

10 See extract from Andriano, pp. 119–21.

11 A fur-bearing animal whose expensive fur turns white in winter and which has traditionally lined the robes of royalty and later judges, symbolizing purity.

12 "Albus" is Latin for "white."

13 In Revelations 4 John is shown a vision of God's throne in heaven: "4 Surrounding the throne were twenty-four other thrones, and seated on them were twenty-four elders. They were dressed in white and had crowns of gold on their heads. 5 From the throne came flashes of lightning, rumblings and peals of thunder. Before the throne, seven lamps were blazing. These are the seven spirits of God. 6 Also before the throne there was what looked like a sea of glass, clear as crystal."

blankness, full of meaning, in a wide landscape of snows—a colorless, all-color of atheism from which we shrink? And when we consider that other theory of the natural philosophers,[14] that all other earthly hues—every stately or lovely emblazoning—the sweet tinges of sunset skies and woods; yea, and the gilded velvets of butterflies, and the butterfly cheeks of young girls; all these are but subtle deceits, not actually inherent in substances, but only laid on from without; so that all deified Nature absolutely paints like the harlot, whose allurements cover nothing but the charnel-house within; and when we proceed further, and consider that the mystical cosmetic which produces every one of her hues, the great principle of light, for ever remains white or colorless in itself, and if operating without medium upon matter, would touch all objects, even tulips and roses, with its own blank tinge—pondering all this, the palsied universe lies before us a leper; and like wilful travellers in Lapland,[15] who refuse to wear colored and coloring glasses upon their eyes, so the wretched infidel gazes himself blind at the monumental white shroud that wraps all the prospect around him. And of all these things the Albino whale was the symbol. Wonder ye then at the fiery hunt?

## Chapter 44: The Chart

Faculty psychology was the dominant model of the human mind for much of the nineteenth century. According to this model the mind was composed of three separate abilities or "faculties": the will, the emotions, and the intellect. Some theorists also included the moral faculty as one of these abilities. "Monomania" was a clinical term describing any pathological obsession with an idea or object. The relationship of the mind to the body was a relatively new field of inquiry with profound ethical, religious and philosophical implications which theologians, proto-psychologists as well as American writers like Melville, Edgar Allan Poe, and Hawthorne explored throughout the period. Faculty psychology thus forms the most immediate context for working through the complex representation of Ahab's psyche in Chapter 44, from which the excerpt below is taken.

[. . .] Often, when forced from his hammock by exhausting and intolerably vivid dreams of the night, which, resuming his own intense thoughts through the day, carried them on amid a clashing of phrensies, and whirled them round and round in his blazing brain, till the very throbbing of his life-spot became insufferable anguish; and when, as was sometimes the case, these spiritual throes in him

14 Empirical philosophers such as Hume and Locke (see p. 43 in Transcendentalism).
15 Large region of northern Europe, mostly in the Arctic Circle, encompassing parts of several European countries.

heaved his being up from its base, and a chasm seemed opening in him, from which forked flames and lightnings shot up, and accursed fiends beckoned him to leap down among them; when this hell in himself yawned beneath him, a wild cry would be heard through the ship; and with glaring eyes Ahab would burst from his state room, as though escaping from a bed that was on fire. Yet these, perhaps, instead of being the unsuppressable symptoms of some latent weakness, or fright at his own resolve, were but the plainest tokens of its intensity. For, at such times, crazy Ahab, the scheming, unappeasedly steadfast hunter of the white whale; this Ahab that had gone to his hammock, was not the agent that so caused him to burst from it in horror again. The latter was the eternal, living principle or soul in him; and in sleep, being for the time dissociated from the characterizing mind, which at other times employed it for its outer vehicle or agent, it spontaneously sought escape from the scorching contiguity of the frantic thing, of which, for the time, it was no longer an integral. But as the mind does not exist unless leagued with the soul, therefore it must have been that, in Ahab's case, yielding up all his thoughts and fancies to his one supreme purpose; that purpose, by its own sheer inveteracy of will, forced itself against gods and devils into a kind of self-assumed, independent being of its own. Nay, could grimly live and burn, while the common vitality to which it was conjoined, fled horror-stricken from the unbidden and unfathered birth. Therefore, the tormented spirit that glared out of bodily eyes, when what seemed Ahab rushed from his room, was for the time but a vacated thing, a formless somnambulistic[1] being, a ray of living light, to be sure, but without an object to color,[2] and therefore a blankness in itself. God help thee, old man, thy thoughts have created a creature in thee; and he whose intense thinking thus makes him a Prometheus;[3] a vulture feeds upon that heart for ever; that vulture the very creature he creates.

## Chapter 70: The Sphynx

Modeled on the soliloquies of Shakespearean drama, Ahab's address to the head of a recently killed sperm whale hanging on the side of the *Pequod* allows Melville to continue to explore the intricacies of whaling but at the same time integrate the book's larger concerns with the "cetological center" (see extracts from Ward and Greenberg on **pp. 92–4** and **95–6**, respectively). The smooth segue from cetological description to the high rhetoric and philosophizing

---

1 Sleepwalker-like.
2 Critics point to this passage in particular when discussing Melville and faculty psychology – is the soul coloring the mind or the mind the soul here? In short, what is the relation between the two?
3 In Greek mythology Prometheus was the son of a Titan who stole fire from the gods and gave it to mankind. His punishment was to be chained to a rock where a vulture gnawed out his liver. In one variant of the legend Prometheus is credited with manufacturing man out of water and clay. Melville seems to be combining the two ideas here, the obsession becoming a sort of golem or homunculus feeding on Ahab's heart, punishing him thereby.

of Ahab is just the thing critics point to when claiming that the work has a grand organic unity. And Ahab's final exclamation links the entire passage to Emerson and his correspondence theory of language described in *Nature* (see **pp. 46–8**).

[. . .] It was a black and hooded head; and hanging there in the midst of so intense a calm, it seemed the Sphynx's in the desert. "Speak, thou vast and venerable head," muttered Ahab, "which, though ungarnished with a beard, yet here and there lookest hoary with mosses; speak, mighty head, and tell us the secret thing that is in thee. Of all divers, thou hast dived the deepest.[1] That head upon which the upper sun now gleams, has moved amid this world's foundations. Where unrecorded names and navies rust, and untold hopes and anchors rot; where in her murderous hold this frigate earth is ballasted with bones of millions of the drowned; there, in that awful water-land, there was thy most familiar home. Thou hast been where bell[2] or diver never went; hast slept by many a sailor's side, where sleepless mothers would give their lives to lay them down. Thou saw'st the locked lovers when leaping from their flaming ship; heart to heart they sank beneath the exulting wave; true to each other, when heaven seemed false to them. Thou saw'st the murdered mate when tossed by pirates from the midnight deck; for hours he fell into the deeper midnight of the insatiate maw;[3] and his murderers still sailed on unharmed—while swift lightnings shivered the neighboring ship that would have borne a righteous husband to outstretched, longing arms. O head! thou hast seen enough to split the planets and make an infidel of Abraham,[4] and not one syllable is thine!"

"Sail ho!" cried a triumphant voice from the main-mast-head.

"Aye? Well, now, that's cheering," cried Ahab, suddenly erecting himself, while whole thunder-clouds swept aside from his brow. "That lively cry upon this deadly calm might almost convert a better man.—Where away?"

"Three points on the starboard bow, sir, and bringing down her breeze to us!"[5]

"Better and better, man. Would now St. Paul would come along that way, and to my breezelessness bring his breeze![6] O Nature, and O soul of man! how far beyond all utterance are your linked analogies! not the smallest atom stirs or lives in matter, but has its cunning duplicate in mind."[7]

1   See pp. 48–9, letter to Duyckinck describing Melville's reaction to seeing Emerson lecture.
2   A diving bell.
3   Maw, "mouth"; "insatiate maw," here, death.
4   By tradition the historical and spiritual father of the Hebrews. In short, even the most devout would lose their faith.
5   Coming towards the ship with the wind at her back, i.e., very rapidly.
6   The allusion is difficult to decipher. A useful possibility is that it is simply a broad reference to St Paul as an inspiring figure. Paul preached the gospel tirelessly to skeptics and doubters before being martyred by the Romans. The record of his life comes down to us in Acts and in his letters (the Pauline Epistles), including Corinthians, Galatians, and Romans among others. Accordingly, Ahab here expresses a longing for spiritual and epistemological guidance to inspire him and to assuage his doubt.
7   Compare this passage especially to the ideas espoused in the extract from Emerson's "*Nature*: Chapter IV. Language" on **pp. 46–8**.

# Chapter 95: The Cassock

As Person suggests in the essay excerpted in Section 2 (see **pp. 113–15**), "The Cassock" is central to any discussion of Melville and gender, and especially to a discussion of the ways in which Melville comically interrogates masculine identity. The chapter excerpted below in its entirety also exhibits all the characteristics of the Melvillean comic style in *Moby-Dick*: mock-serious tone, word play, and thinly disguised sexual double entendre.

Had you stepped on board the Pequod at a certain juncture of this post-mortemizing[1] of the whale; and had you strolled forward nigh the windlass,[2] pretty sure am I that you would have scanned with no small curiosity a very strange, enigmatical object,[3] which you would have seen there, lying along lengthwise in the lee scuppers.[4] Not the wondrous cistern[5] in the whale's huge head; not the prodigy of his unhinged lower jaw; not the miracle of his symmetrical tail; none of these would so surprise you, as half a glimpse of that unaccountable cone,—longer than a Kentuckian is tall,[6] nigh a foot in diameter at the base, and jet-black as Yojo, the ebony idol of Queequeg. And an idol, indeed, it is; or, rather, in old times, its likeness was. Such an idol as that found in the secret groves of Queen Maachah in Judea; and for worshipping which, king Asa, her son, did depose her, and destroyed the idol, and burnt it for an abomination at the brook Kedron, as darkly set forth in the 15th chapter of the first book of Kings.[7]

   Look at the sailor, called the mincer, who now comes along, and assisted by two allies, heavily backs the grandissimus,[8] as the mariners call it, and with bowed shoulders, staggers off with it as if he were a grenadier carrying a dead comrade from the field. Extending it upon the forecastle deck, he now proceeds cylindrically to remove its dark pelt, as an African hunter the pelt of a boa. This done he turns the pelt inside out, like a pantaloon leg; gives it a good stretching,

---

1    A Melvillean neologism suggesting both dissection and forensic autopsy.
2    Mechanism used to lift the anchor.
3    Like an enigma, something obscure and puzzling. Here, the whale's penis.
4    Scuppers, an opening at the rear (lee) of the ship allowing water on deck to escape.
5    Large receptacle.
6    Kentucky was part of the American frontier in the first half of the nineteenth century and "tall tales" about Kentucky woodsmen – exaggerated stories of adventurous exploits in the wilderness – abounded, some forming the bases for America's burgeoning dime novel industry by mid-century.
7    The allusion here, mock-serious in tone, is meant to impart a sense of the mock-heroic. According to I Kings 15: 9–15 "In the twentieth year of Jeroboam king of Israel, Asa became king of Judah, 10 and he reigned in Jerusalem forty-one years. His grandmother's name was Maacah daughter of Abishalom. 11 Asa did what was right in the eyes of the Lord, as his father David had done. 12 He expelled the male shrine prostitutes from the land and got rid of all the idols his fathers had made. 13 He even deposed his grandmother Maacah from her position as queen mother, because she had made a repulsive Asherah pole. Asa cut the pole down and burned it in the Kidron Valley. 14 Although he did not remove the high places, Asa's heart was fully committed to the Lord all his life."
8    The whale's penis.

so as almost to double its diameter; and at last hangs it, well spread, in the rigging, to dry. Ere long, it is taken down; when removing some three feet of it, towards the pointed extremity, and then cutting two slits for arm-holes at the other end, he lengthwise slips himself bodily into it. The mincer now stands before you invested in the full canonicals of his calling. Immemorial to all his order, this investiture alone will adequately protect him, while employed in the peculiar functions of his office.

That office consists in mincing the horse-pieces of blubber for the pots; an operation which is conducted at a curious wooden horse, planted endwise against the bulwarks,[9] and with a capacious tub beneath it, into which the minced pieces drop, fast as the sheets from a rapt orator's desk. Arrayed in decent black; occupying a conspicuous pulpit; intent on bible leaves; what a candidate for an archbishoprick, what a lad for a Pope were this mincer!*

*Bible leaves! Bible leaves! This is the invariable cry from the mates to the mincer. It enjoins him to be careful, and cut his work into as thin slices as possible, inasmuch as by so doing the business of boiling out the oil is much accelerated, and its quantity considerably increased, besides perhaps improving it in quality.

# Chapter 96: The Try-Works

Both the description of the ship as the "the material counterpart of her monomaniac commander's soul" and of Ishmael falling asleep at the tiller of the ship during the midnight watch revisit and develop aspects of the book's themes introduced in earlier chapters and discussed above in the introductions to several excerpts. In addition, nowhere perhaps is Melville's use of the conventions of Gothic literature more apparent than in the nightmarish vision of the stokers in front of the tryworks. As many critics have noted, Chapter 96 is a testament to just how powerfully Melville was able to imaginatively transform his experiences on a whaleship, turning everyday scenes into powerfully suggestive and symbolic mises-en-scène or arranged set pieces, similar to Dutch genre paintings.[1] Finally, this chapter forms the principal textual evidence for discussions of *Moby-Dick*, Plato and philosophical idealism generally, alluding as it does so explicitly to the cave allegory from the

9  Walls of the ship which encircle the deck.

1  French, literally "placed on stage," i.e., arranged. Genre painting is the depiction of subjects and scenes from everyday life, ordinary folk and common activities. It achieved its greatest popularity in the seventeenth century in Holland with the works of Jan Steen (1626–79) and Jan Vermeer (1632–75).

*Republic.*[2] The long discussion that ends the chapter functions as perhaps the clearest expression of Ishmael's idealism – his belief that man can know even if the truth he uncovers remains partial and ambiguous – in the work. As well the chapter contains some of the book's finest characteristically Melvillean poetic language.

[. . .] The hatch, removed from the top of the works, now afforded a wide hearth in front of them. Standing on this were the Tartarean[3] shapes of the pagan harpooneers, always the whale-ship's stokers. With huge pronged poles they pitched hissing masses of blubber into the scalding pots, or stirred up the fires beneath, till the snaky flames darted, curling, out of the doors to catch them by the feet. The smoke rolled away in sullen heaps. To every pitch of the ship there was a pitch of the boiling oil, which seemed all eagerness to leap into their faces. Opposite the mouth of the works, on the further side of the wide wooden hearth, was the windlass.[4] This served for a sea-sofa. Here lounged the watch, when not otherwise employed, looking into the red heat of the fire, till their eyes felt scorched in their heads. Their tawny features, now all begrimed with smoke and sweat, their matted beards, and the contrasting barbaric brilliancy of their teeth, all these were strangely revealed in the capricious emblazonings of the works. As they narrated to each other their unholy adventures, their tales of terror told in words of mirth; as their uncivilized laughter forked upwards out of them, like the flames from the furnace; as to and fro, in their front, the harpooneers wildly gesticulated with their huge pronged forks and dippers; as the wind howled on, and the sea leaped, and the ship groaned and dived, and yet steadfastly shot her red hell further and further into the blackness of the sea and the night, and scornfully champed the white bone in her mouth, and viciously spat round her on all sides; then the rushing Pequod, freighted with savages, and laden with fire, and burning a corpse, and plunging into that blackness of darkness, seemed the material counterpart of her monomaniac commander's soul. [. . .]

But that night, in particular, a strange (and ever since inexplicable) thing occurred to me. Starting from a brief standing sleep, I was horribly conscious of

---

2   From Plato's *Republic* (*c.* 370 BCE). In the *Republic* Plato (*c.* 427–347 BCE) sets out his conception of the ideal political state, arguing that the operation of justice within the individual is analogous to the operation of justice within the state. In one section of the *Republic*, Plato depicts humankind as ignorantly trapped in a cave of darkness, unaware even of the limits of their own perceptions. The rare individual is he who can break the chains of ignorance and escape the cave through a long process of intellectual development to become aware of an ideal realm – the true reality of the ideal forms. In Plato's view only such persons are fit to govern, a pretext for his argument that the ideal ruler is a philosopher-king. See the section on Transcendentalism (**pp. 41–4**), Melville's letter to Duyckinck describing his reaction to seeing Emerson lecture (**pp. 48–9**), and the extract by Sealts (**pp. 85–8**) for more on Melville and philosophical idealism.

3   Of or pertaining to Tartarus, in Greek mythology the abysmal regions below Hades reserved for the most wicked sinners.

4   Mechanism used to lift heavy objects on board ship.

something fatally wrong. The jaw-bone tiller smote my side, which leaned against it; in my ears was the low hum of sails, just beginning to shake in the wind;[5] I thought my eyes were open; I was half conscious of putting my fingers to the lids and mechanically stretching them still further apart. But, spite of all this, I could see no compass before me to steer by; though it seemed but a minute since I had been watching the card, by the steady binnacle lamp illuminating it. Nothing seemed before me but a jet gloom, now and then made ghastly by flashes of redness. Uppermost was the impression, that whatever swift, rushing thing I stood on was not so much bound to any haven ahead as rushing from all havens astern. A stark, bewildered feeling, as of death, came over me. Convulsively my hands grasped the tiller, but with the crazy conceit that the tiller was, somehow, in some enchanted way, inverted. My God! what is the matter with me? thought I. Lo! in my brief sleep I had turned myself about, and was fronting the ship's stern, with my back to her prow and the compass. In an instant I faced back, just in time to prevent the vessel from flying up into the wind,[6] and very probably capsizing her. How glad and how grateful the relief from this unnatural hallucination of the night, and the fatal contingency of being brought by the lee!

Look not too long in the face of the fire, O man! Never dream with thy hand on the helm! Turn not thy back to the compass; accept the first hint of the hitching tiller; believe not the artificial fire, when its redness makes all things look ghastly. To-morrow, in the natural sun, the skies will be bright; those who glared like devils in the forking flames, the morn will show in far other, at least gentler, relief; the glorious, golden, glad sun, the only true lamp—all others but liars! [. . .]

But even Solomon, he says, "the man that wandereth out of the way of understanding shall remain" (i.e. even while living) "in the congregation of the dead."[7] Give not thyself up, then, to fire, lest it invert thee, deaden thee; as for the time it did me. There is a wisdom that is woe; but there is a woe that is madness.[8] And there is a Catskill eagle in some souls that can alike dive down into the blackest gorges, and soar out of them again and become invisible in the sunny spaces. And even if he for ever flies within the gorge, that gorge is in the mountains; so that even in his lowest swoop the mountain eagle is still higher than other birds upon the plain, even though they soar.[9]

---

5   Because Ishmael has fallen asleep the ship is no longer aligned in relation to the wind in such a way that the sails can remain full of air. As a result they begin to go limp and shake and rattle like a flag in the wind.
6   In a strong wind, turning directly into the wind would turn the bow of the vessel directly against the prevailing forces acting upon it so the full force of wind strikes the ship and its rigging in a dangerous manner, possibly resulting in damage to masts or the capsizing of the ship itself.
7   Proverbs 21:16: "A man who wanders from the way of understanding will rest in the assembly of the dead."
8   Again an allusion to Ecclesiastes 1:18 (see n. 7, p. 151).
9   Compare this to the final image of Chapter 135, "The Chase—Third Day" on p. 176.

# Chapter 99: The Doubloon

In Chapter 99 several characters approach the doubloon, first nailed to the mast by Ahab in Chapter 36 as a reward for whichever member of the crew first sights Moby Dick on the day he is killed. Up to this point in the novel Ishmael has employed a variety of discourses to exhaustively discuss whales and whaling including, among others, law, philosophy and politics. He has read the whale and read from books on whaling in his attempt both to explain the facts of whales and whaling and to imaginatively infuse his story with a variety of potential meanings. In the chapter from which the excerpt below is taken, reading and interpretation as epistemological modes – ways of discovering truth – are explored dramatically. The reader or audience watches as each character attempts to extract meaning from the signs on the doubloon – frequently invoking popular nineteenth-century school texts in the process and thus parodying conventional modes of acquiring understanding about the world. As Stubb says as he observes each character derive a different meaning from the same single coin, "There's another rendering now; but still one text. All sorts of men in one kind of world, you see." Solipsism, the theory that the self is the only thing that can be known or verified, is thus dramatically portrayed in this scene as another of the many obstacles man confronts in his attempt to know – and perhaps the most difficult to overcome for the chapter ends not with an idealistic exclamation by Ishmael as in Chapter 96, but with foolish-wise Pip's minstrel song: "Jenny! Hey, hey, hey, hey, hey, Jenny, Jenny! And get your hoe-cake done!"

[. . .] It so chanced that the doubloon of the Pequod was a most wealthy example of these things. On its round border it bore the letters, REPUBLICA DEL ECUADOR: QUITO.[1] So this bright coin came from a country planted in the middle of the world, and beneath the great equator, and named after it; and it had been cast midway up the Andes, in the unwaning clime that knows no autumn. Zoned by those letters you saw the likeness of three Andes' summits; from one a flame; a tower on another; on the third a crowing cock; while arching over all was a segment of the partitioned zodiac, the signs all marked with their usual cabalistics,[2] and the keystone sun entering the equinoctial[3] point at Libra.[4]

Before this equatorial coin, Ahab, not unobserved by others, was now pausing.

"There's something ever egotistical in mountain-tops and towers, and all other grand and lofty things; look here,—three peaks as proud as Lucifer. The firm tower, that is Ahab; the volcano, that is Ahab; the courageous, the

1   Quito: the capital of Ecuador.
2   Secret or hidden meaning.
3   Occurring at the equinox (zenith) or top of the coin.
4   Seventh sign of the zodiac represented by two scales.

undaunted, and victorious fowl, that, too, is Ahab; all are Ahab; and this round gold is but the image of the rounder globe, which, like a magician's glass, to each and every man in turn but mirrors back his own mysterious self. Great pains, small gains for those who ask the world to solve them; it cannot solve itself. Methinks now this coined sun wears a ruddy face; but see! aye, he enters the sign of storms, the equinox! and but six months before he wheeled out of a former equinox at Aries! From storm to storm!⁵ So be it, then. Born in throes, 'tis fit that man should live in pains and die in pangs! So be it, then! Here's stout stuff for woe to work on. So be it, then."

"No fairy fingers can have pressed the gold, but devil's claws must have left their mouldings there since yesterday," murmured Starbuck to himself, leaning against the bulwarks. "The old man seems to read Belshazzar's awful writing.⁶ I have never marked the coin inspectingly. He goes below; let me read. A dark valley between three mighty, heaven-abiding peaks, that almost seem the Trinity, in some faint earthly symbol. So in this vale of Death, God girds us round; and over all our gloom, the sun of Righteousness still shines a beacon and a hope. If we bend down our eyes, the dark vale shows her mouldy soil; but if we lift them, the bright sun meets our glance halfway, to cheer. Yet, oh, the great sun is no fixture; and if, at midnight, we would fain snatch some sweet solace from him, we gaze for him in vain! This coin speaks wisely, mildly, truly, but still sadly to me. I will quit it, lest Truth shake me falsely."

"There now's the old Mogul," soliloquized Stubb by the try-works, "he's been twigging it; and there goes Starbuck from the same, and both with faces which I should say might be somewhere within nine fathoms long. And all from looking at a piece of gold, which did I have it now on Negro Hill or in Corlaer's Hook,⁷ I'd not look at it very long ere spending it. Humph! in my poor, insignificant opinion, I regard this as queer. I have seen doubloons before now in my voyagings; your doubloons of old Spain, your doubloons of Peru, your doubloons of Chili, your doubloons of Bolivia, your doubloons of Popayan;⁸ with plenty of gold moidores and pistoles, and joes, and half joes, and quarter joes. What then should there be in this doubloon of the Equator that is so killing wonderful? By Golconda!⁹ let me read it once. Halloa! here's signs and wonders truly!

---

5    The twelve signs of the zodiac are reckoned from the point of intersection of the ecliptic and equator at the vernal equinox, and are named, respectively, Aries, Taurus, Gemini, Cancer, Leo, Virgo, Libra, Scorpio, Sagittarius, Capricorn, Aquarius, and Pisces. Aries is the northernmost of the two equinoxial signs (Aries and Virgo), both associated with storms.

6    Belshazzar was the last of the kings of Babylon. When still young he made a great feast for a thousand of his lords during which he and the revelers drank wine from the sacred vessels Nebuchadnezzar had carried away from the temple in Jerusalem. In the midst of the mad revelry a hand was seen by the king tracing on the wall the announcement of God's judgment. At the insistence of the queen, his mother, Daniel was brought in to interpret the writing. That night the kingdom of the Chaldeans came to an end and the king was slain.

7    Places in New York City.

8    Region in present-day Columbia; Popayan had a famous mint.

9    Golconda, India, famous for its diamond mines and used generically to refer to any source of great riches.

That, now, is what old Bowditch in his Epitome[10] calls the zodiac, and what my almanack below calls ditto. I'll get the almanack; and as I have heard devils can be raised with Daboll's arithmetic,[11] I'll try my hand at raising a meaning out of these queer curvicues here with the Massachusetts calendar. Here's the book. Let's see now. Signs and wonders; and the sun, he's always among 'em. Hem, hem, hem; here they are—here they go—all alive:—Aries, or the Ram; Taurus, or the Bull;—and Jimini! here's Gemini himself, or the Twins. Well; the sun he wheels among 'em. Aye, here on the coin he's just crossing the threshold between two of twelve sitting-rooms all in a ring. Book! you lie there; the fact is, you books must know your places. You'll do to give us the bare words and facts, but we come in to supply the thoughts. That's my small experience, so far as the Massachusetts calendar, and Bowditch's navigator, and Daboll's arithmetic go. Signs and wonders, eh? Pity if there is nothing wonderful in signs, and significant in wonders! There's a clue somewhere; wait a bit; hist—hark! By jove, I have it! Look you, Doubloon, your zodiac here is the life of man in one round chapter; and now I'll read it off, straight out of the book. Come, Almanack! To begin: there's Aries, or the Ram—lecherous dog, he begets us; then, Taurus, or the Bull—he bumps us the first thing; then Gemini, or the Twins—that is, Virtue and Vice; we try to reach Virtue, when lo! comes Cancer the Crab, and drags us back; and here, going from Virtue, Leo, a roaring Lion, lies in the path—he gives a few fierce bites and surly dabs with his paw; we escape, and hail Virgo, the Virgin! that's our first love; we marry and think to be happy for aye, when pop comes Libra, or the Scales—happiness weighed and found wanting; and while we are very sad about that, Lord! how we suddenly jump, as Scorpio, or the Scorpion, stings us in rear; we are curing the wound, when whang come the arrows all round; Sagittarius, or the Archer, is amusing himself. As we pluck out the shafts, stand aside! here's the battering-ram, Capricornus, or the Goat; full tilt, he comes rushing, and headlong we are tossed; when Aquarius, or the Water-bearer, pours out his whole deluge and drowns us; and, to wind up, with Pisces, or the Fishes, we sleep. There's a sermon now, writ in high heaven, and the sun goes through it every year, and yet comes out of it all alive and hearty. Jollily he, aloft there, wheels through toil and trouble; and so, alow here, does jolly Stubb. Oh, jolly's the word for aye! Adieu, Doubloon! But stop; here comes little King-Post;[12] dodge round the try-works, now, and let's hear what he'll have to say. There; he's before it; he'll out with something presently. So, so; he's beginning."

"I see nothing here, but a round thing made of gold, and whoever raises a certain whale, this round thing belongs to him. So, what's all this staring been about? It is worth sixteen dollars, that's true; and at two cents the cigar, that's

---

10 Nathaniel Bowditch (1773–1838) of Salem, Massachusetts, navigator, astronomer and mathematician whose *New American Practical Navigator: An Epitome of Navigation* (1802) was a seminal work in nautical navigation.
11 A popular nineteenth-century elementary-level math primer.
12 Flask.

nine hundred and sixty cigars. I wont smoke dirty pipes like Stubb, but I like cigars, and here's nine hundred and sixty of them; so here goes Flask aloft to spy 'em out." [. . .]

"There's another rendering now; but still one text. All sorts of men in one kind of world, you see. Dodge again! here comes Queequeg—all tattooing—looks like the signs of the Zodiac himself. What says the Cannibal? As I live he's comparing notes; looking at his thigh bone; thinks the sun is in the thigh, or in the calf, or in the bowels, I suppose, as the old women talk Surgeon's Astronomy[13] in the back country. And by Jove, he's found something there in the vicinity of his thigh— I guess it's Sagittarius, or the Archer. No: he don't know what to make of the doubloon; he takes it for an old button off some king's trowsers. But, aside again! here comes that ghost-devil, Fedallah; tail coiled out of sight as usual, oakum in the toes of his pumps as usual. What does he say, with that look of his? Ah, only makes a sign to the sign and bows himself; there is a sun on the coin-fire worshipper, depend upon it. Ho! more and more. This way comes Pip—poor boy! would he had died, or I; he's half horrible to me. He too has been watching all of these interpreters—myself included—and look now, he comes to read, with that unearthly idiot face. Stand away again and hear him. Hark!"

"I look, you look, he looks; we look, ye look, they look."

"Upon my soul, he's been studying Murray's Grammar![14] Improving his mind, poor fellow! But what's that he says now—hist!"

"I look, you look, he looks; we look, ye look, they look."

"Why, he's getting it by heart—hist! again.

"I look, you look, he looks; we look, ye look, they look."

"Well, that's funny."

"And I, you, and he; and we, ye, and they, are all bats; and I'm a crow, especially when I stand a'top of this pine tree here. Caw! caw! caw! caw! caw! caw! Ain't I a crow? And where's the scare-crow? There he stands; two bones stuck into a pair of old trowsers, and two more poked into the sleeves of an old jacket."

"Wonder if he means me?—complimentary!—poor lad!—I could go hang myself. Any way, for the present, I'll quit Pip's vicinity. I can stand the rest, for they have plain wits; but he's too crazy-witty for my sanity. So, so, I leave him muttering."

"Here's the ship's navel, this doubloon here, and they are all on fire to unscrew it. But, unscrew your navel, and what's the consequence?[15] Then again, if it stays here, that is ugly, too, for when aught's nailed to the mast it's a sign that things grow desperate. Ha, ha! old Ahab! the White Whale; he'll nail ye! This is a pine tree. My father, in old Tolland county,[16] cut down a pine tree once, and found

---

13  Popular nineteenth-century book on astronomy.
14  Lindley Murray's *English Grammar*, first published in 1795, was the most popular book of English grammar in the nineteenth century.
15  By tradition, one's rectum falls off. "To contemplate one's navel" is a common expression for solipsism.
16  Possibly Tolland county, Connecticut, but also perhaps fictional, suggesting simply rurality.

a silver ring grown over in it; some old darkey's wedding ring. How did it get there? And so they'll say in the resurrection, when they come to fish up this old mast, and find a doubloon lodged in it, with bedded oysters for the shaggy bark. Oh, the gold! the precious, precious gold!—the green miser'll hoard ye soon! Hish! hish! God goes 'mong the worlds blackberrying. Cook! ho, cook! and cook us! Jenny! hey, hey, hey, hey, hey, Jenny, Jenny! and get your hoe-cake done!"

## Chapter 114: The Gilder

In all editions of *Moby-Dick* prior to 1988 the speech by Ahab excerpted below was thought to belong to Ishmael as there were no quotation marks to indicate that this was Ahab and not the narrator speaking. Restored for the Northwestern–Newberry edition, the quotation marks suggest that the nihilism of Ahab is meant to contrast sharply with the piety of Starbuck and the comic aloofness of Stubb, once again bringing into relief the differences among the various characters in terms of their respective attitudes toward the struggles Ahab outlines in his own speech. If Shakespeare's Lear was "bound on a wheel of fire," an allusion to the medieval wheel of fortune and the belief that man suffers capriciously as the wheel of fortune turns, Ahab portrays himself and all humankind as existing in an even more chaotic state. The periods of storm and calm themselves rise and ebb according to no real order, and whatever postures one assumes in order to face the storm – idealistic youth, skeptical adult, disillusioned nihilist – are themselves in a constant state of flux and in and of themselves signify nothing. We are not in control of which posture we adopt, and we remain in any given position or perspective only temporarily, with death itself as the only final fixed harbor "whence we unmoor no more."

[. . .] "Oh, grassy glades! oh, ever vernal endless landscapes in the soul; in ye,— though long parched by the dead drought of the earthy life,—in ye, men yet may roll, like young horses in new morning clover; and for some few fleeting moments, feel the cool dew of the life immortal on them. Would to God these blessed calms would last. But the mingled, mingling threads of life are woven by warp and woof: calms crossed by storms, a storm for every calm. There is no steady unretracing progress in this life; we do not advance through fixed gradations, and at the last one pause:—through infancy's unconscious spell, boyhood's thoughtless faith, adolescence' doubt (the common doom), then scepticism, then disbelief resting at last in manhood's pondering repose of If. But once gone through, we trace the round again; and are infants, boys, and men, and Ifs eternally. Where lies the final harbor, whence we unmoor no more? In what rapt ether sails the world, of which the weariest will never weary? Where is the foundling's[1] father hidden? Our souls are like those orphans whose unwedded mothers die in bearing them: the secret of our paternity lies in their grave, and we must there to learn it."

And that same day, too, gazing far down from his boat's side into that same golden sea, Starbuck lowly murmured:—

"Loveliness unfathomable, as ever lover saw in his young bride's eye!—Tell me not of thy teeth-tiered sharks, and thy kidnapping cannibal ways. Let faith oust fact; let fancy oust memory; I look deep down and do believe."

And Stubb, fish-like, with sparkling scales, leaped up in that same golden light:—

"I am Stubb and Stubb has his history; but here Stubb takes oaths that he has always been jolly!"

## Chapter 119: The Candles

In one of the most dramatic scenes in the novel, as the ship's masts and rigging glow blue with Saint Elmo's Fire,[1] Ahab seizes the opportunity to rebuke Starbuck once more, taking advantage of the superstitions most seamen associated with the appearance of the rare electrical disturbance, reaffirming his and the rest of the crew's commitment to the quest. Once again reminiscent of Lear, this time the scene on the heath, Ahab defies the first mate, nature and the very gods themselves – the archetype of the tragic hero. See especially the discussion of this scene in the extract from Howard, **pp. 88–90**.

[. . .] "Oh! thou clear spirit of clear fire, whom on these seas I as Persian once did worship, till in the sacramental act so burned by thee, that to this hour I bear the scar; I now know thee, thou clear spirit, and I now know that thy right worship is defiance. To neither love nor reverence wilt thou be kind; and e'en for hate thou canst but kill; and all are killed. No fearless fool now fronts thee. I own thy speechless, placeless power; but to the last gasp of my earthquake life will dispute its unconditional, unintegral mastery in me. In the midst of the personified impersonal, a personality stands here. Though but a point at best; whencesoe'er I came; wheresoe'er I go; yet while I earthly live, the queenly personality lives in me, and feels her royal rights. But war is pain, and hate is woe. Come in thy lowest form of love, and I will kneel and kiss thee; but at thy highest, come as mere supernal power; and though thou launchest navies of full-freighted worlds, there's that in here that still remains indifferent. Oh, thou clear spirit, of thy fire thou madest me, and like a true child of fire, I breathe it back to thee."

---

1   An orphaned child.

---

1   See n. 10, p. 90.

*(Sudden, repeated flashes of lightning; the nine flames leap lengthwise to thrice their previous height; Ahab, with the rest, closes his eyes, his right hand pressed hard upon them.)*

"I own thy speechless, placeless power; said I not so? Nor was it wrung from me; nor do I now drop these links. Thou canst blind; but I can then grope. Thou canst consume; but I can then be ashes. Take the homage of these poor eyes, and shutter-hands. I would not take it. The lightning flashes through my skull; mine eye-balls ache and ache; my whole beaten brain seems as beheaded, and rolling on some stunning ground. Oh, oh! Yet blindfold, yet will I talk to thee. Light though thou be, thou leapest out of darkness; but I am darkness leaping out of light, leaping out of thee! The javelins cease; open eyes; see, or not? There burn the flames! Oh, thou magnanimous![2] now I do glory in my genealogy. But thou art but my fiery father; my sweet mother, I know not. Oh, cruel! what hast thou done with her? There lies my puzzle; but thine is greater. Thou knowest not how came ye, hence callest thyself unbegotten; certainly knowest not thy beginning, hence callest thyself unbegun. I know that of me, which thou knowest not of thyself, oh, thou omnipotent. There is some unsuffusing thing beyond thee, thou clear spirit, to whom all thy eternity is but time, all thy creativeness mechanical. Through thee, thy flaming self, my scorched eyes do dimly see it. Oh, thou foundling fire, thou hermit immemorial, thou too hast thy incommunicable riddle, thy unparticipated grief. Here again with haughty agony, I read my sire. Leap! leap up, and lick the sky! I leap with thee; I burn with thee; would fain be welded with thee; defyingly I worship thee!" [. . .]

## Chapter 132: The Symphony

Chapter 132 culminates with the final attempt by Starbuck to get Ahab to turn the ship from further pursuit of Moby Dick. Fraught with sentimental language and emotion, the scene is one of several where Melville invokes a seemingly out of place sentimentality to expose Ahab's humanities. Schultz's essay in Section 2 (pp. 109–12) is especially relevant, as "The Symphony" not only draws on the conventions associated with sentimental and domestic fiction but seemingly reaffirms that Ahab, like Melville, stands for the heart as Schultz claims. In Ahab's speech in particular the reader is made aware of not only his anguish but, in Schultz's eloquent phrase, "the tenderness that anguish calls up." Yet such tender feelings are fleeting in Ahab, and not enough to dissuade him from his quest, something Starbuck learns to his horror.

---

2  Noble, generous, forgiving.

[. . .] "Oh, my Captain! my Captain! noble soul! grand old heart, after all! Why should any one give chase to that hated fish! Away with me! Let us fly these deadly waters! Let us home! Wife and child, too, are Starbuck's—wife and child of his brotherly, sisterly, play-fellow youth; even as thine, sir, are the wife and child of thy loving, longing, paternal old age! Away! let us away!—this instant let me alter the course! How cheerily, how hilariously, O my Captain, would we bowl on our way to see old Nantucket again! I think, sir, they have some such mild blue days, even as this, in Nantucket."

"They have, they have. I have seen them—some summer days in the morning. About this time—yes, it is his noon nap now—the boy vivaciously wakes; sits up in bed; and his mother tells him of me, of cannibal old me; how I am abroad upon the deep, but will yet come back to dance him again."

"'Tis my Mary, my Mary herself! She promised that my boy, every morning, should be carried to the hill to catch the first glimpse of his father's sail! Yes, yes! no more! it is done! We head for Nantucket! Come, my Captain study out the course, and let us away! See, see! the boy's face from the window! the boy's hand on the hill!"

But Ahab's glance was averted; like a blighted fruit tree he shook, and cast his last, cindered apple to the soil.

"What is it, what nameless, inscrutable, unearthly thing is it; what cozening,[1] hidden lord and master, and cruel, remorseless emperor commands me; that against all natural lovings and longings, I so keep pushing, and crowding, and jamming myself on all the time; recklessly making me ready to do what in my own proper, natural heart, I durst not so much as dare? Is Ahab, Ahab? Is it I, God, or who, that lifts this arm? But if the great sun move not of himself; but is as an errand-boy in heaven; nor one single star can revolve, but by some invisible power; how then can this one small heart beat; this one small brain think thoughts; unless God does that beating, does that thinking, does that living, and not I. By heaven, man, we are turned round and round in this world, like yonder windlass, and Fate is the handspike.[2] And all the time, lo! that smiling sky, and this unsounded sea! Look! see yon Albicore! who put it into him to chase and fang that flying-fish? Where do murderers go, man! Who's to doom, when the judge himself is dragged to the bar?[3] But it is a mild, mild wind, and a mild looking sky; and the air smells now, as if it blew from a far-away meadow; they have been making hay somewhere under the slopes of the Andes, Starbuck, and the mowers are sleeping among the new-mown hay. Sleeping? Aye, toil we how we may, we all sleep at last on the field. Sleep? Aye, and rust amid greenness; as last year's scythes flung down, and left in the half-cut swaths—Starbuck!"

But blanched to a corpse's hue with despair, the Mate had stolen away. [. . .]

---

1    Deceitful.
2    See also Ahab's expression of this idea in Chapter 114, "The Gilder" on pp. 169–70.
3    Possibly alluding to several similar passages from the Bible, including Mark 3:23: "And he called them unto him, and said unto them in parables, How can Satan cast out Satan?"

# Chapter 135: The Chase – Third Day

The catastrophic end of the *Pequod* and her crew builds over the course of three days until on the third and final day Ahab and ship meet their doom. On the first day Starbuck warns Ahab of ill omens portending a fatal end but Ahab brushes him aside, telling the dismayed first mate "Omen? Omen?—the dictionary! If the gods think to speak outright to man, they will honorable speak outright; not shake their heads, and give an old wives' darkling hint." And yet on the final day, the prophecy of the Parsee ostensibly comes true. He appears again, entangled in the broken harpoons and lines that encircle the great white whale. Moby Dick becomes thus the first hearse mentioned in the prediction, and the doomed ship the second. Equally important is Starbuck and Ahab's final farewell, a sentimental moment in which the first mate and captain wash away their grievances with mutually shed tears. Throughout the three-day chase Starbuck has insisted that Ahab has a choice – pursue the whale and surely perish, possibly taking the crew and ship with him; or turn toward land and safe haven, forgetting the quest once and for all. Yet Ahab's obsession prevents him from doing so. As he tells Starbuck on the second day, "Ahab is for ever Ahab, man. This whole act's immutably decreed. 'Twas rehearsed by thee and me a billion years before this ocean rolled. Fool! I am the Fates' lieutenant; I act under orders." As the *Pequod* slips beneath the waves, and the sea rolls over it for the last time, "as it rolled five thousand years ago," the reader is left to his or her own devices to recover whatever meanings are possible from the catastrophe.

[. . .] In due time the boats were lowered; but as standing in his shallop's[1] stern, Ahab just hovered upon the point of the descent, he waved to the mate,—who held one of the tackle-ropes on deck—and bade him pause.

"Starbuck!"

"Sir?"

"For the third time my soul's ship starts upon this voyage, Starbuck."

"Aye, sir, thou wilt have it so."

"Some ships sail from their ports, and ever afterwards are missing, Starbuck!"

"Truth, sir: saddest truth."

"Some men die at ebb tide; some at low water; some at the full of the flood;[2]— and I feel now like a billow that's all one crested comb, Starbuck. I am old;— shake hands with me, man."

Their hands met; their eyes fastened; Starbuck's tears the glue.

"Oh, my captain, my captain!—noble heart—go not—go not!—see, it's a brave man that weeps; how great the agony of the persuasion then!"

---

1   A small open boat; here, the whaleboat of Ahab.
2   High tide.

"Lower away!"—cried Ahab, tossing the mate's arm from him. "Stand by the crew!"

In an instant the boat was pulling round close under the stern.

"The sharks! the sharks!" cried a voice from the low cabin-window there; "O master, my master, come back!"[3]

But Ahab heard nothing; for his own voice was high-lifted then; and the boat leaped on. [. . .]

The boats had not gone very far, when by a signal from the mast-heads—a downward pointed arm, Ahab knew that the whale had sounded; but intending to be near him at the next rising, he held on his way a little sideways from the vessel; the becharmed crew maintaining the profoundest silence, as the head-beat waves hammered and hammered against the opposing bow.

"Drive, drive in your nails, oh ye waves! to their uttermost heads drive them in! ye but strike a thing without a lid; and no coffin and no hearse can be mine:—and hemp[4] only can kill me! Ha! ha!" [. . .]

While Daggoo and Tashtego were stopping the strained planks; and as the whale swimming out from them, turned, and showed one entire flank as he shot by them again; at that moment a quick cry went up. Lashed round and round to the fish's back; pinioned in the turns upon turns in which, during the past night, the whale had reeled the involutions of the lines around him, the half torn body of the Parsee was seen; his sable raiment frayed to shreds; his distended eyes turned full upon old Ahab.

The harpoon dropped from his hand.

"Befooled, befooled!"—drawing in a long lean breath—"Aye, Parsee! I see thee again.—Aye, and thou goest before; and this, *this* then is the hearse that thou didst promise. But I hold thee to the last letter of thy word. Where is the second hearse? Away, mates, to the ship! those boats are useless now; repair them if ye can in time, and return to me; if not, Ahab is enough to die—Down, men! the first thing that but offers to jump from this boat I stand in, that thing I harpoon. Ye are not other men, but my arms and my legs; and so obey me.—Where's the whale? gone down again?" [. . .]

From the ship's bows, nearly all the seamen now hung inactive; hammers, bits of plank, lances, and harpoons, mechanically retained in their hands, just as they had darted from their various employments; all their enchanted eyes intent upon the whale, which from side to side strangely vibrating his predestinating head, sent a broad band of overspreading semi-circular foam before him as he rushed. Retribution, swift vengeance, eternal malice were in his whole aspect, and spite of all that mortal man could do, the solid white buttress of his forehead smote the ship's starboard bow, till men and timbers reeled. Some fell flat upon their faces. Like dislodged trucks, the heads of the harpooners aloft

---

3    This from Pip.
4    Rope was made from hemp.

shook on their bull-like necks. Through the breach, they heard the waters pour, as mountain torrents down a flume.[5]

"The ship! The hearse!—the second hearse!" cried Ahab from the boat; "its wood could only be American!"[6]

Diving beneath the settling ship, the whale ran quivering along its keel; but turning under water, swiftly shot to the surface again, far off the other bow, but within a few yards of Ahab's boat, where, for a time, he lay quiescent.[7]

"I turn my body from the sun. What ho, Tashtego! let me hear thy hammer. Oh! ye three unsurrendered spires of mine; thou uncracked keel; and only god-bullied hull; thou firm deck, and haughty helm, and Pole-pointed prow,—death-glorious ship! must ye then perish, and without me? Am I cut off from the last fond pride of meanest shipwrecked captains? Oh, lonely death on lonely life! Oh, now I feel my topmost greatness lies in my topmost grief. Ho, ho! from all your furthest bounds, pour ye now in, ye bold billows of my whole foregone life, and top this one piled comber of my death! Towards thee I roll, thou all-destroying but unconquering whale; to the last I grapple with thee; from hell's heart I stab at thee; for hate's sake I spit my last breath at thee. Sink all coffins and all hearses to one common pool! and since neither can be mine, let me then tow to pieces, while still chasing thee, though tied to thee, thou damned whale! *Thus*, I give up the spear!"

The harpoon was darted; the stricken whale flew forward; with igniting velocity the line ran through the groove;—ran foul. Ahab stooped to clear it; he did clear it; but the flying turn caught him round the neck, and voicelessly as Turkish mutes bowstring their victim,[8] he was shot out of the boat, ere the crew knew he was gone. Next instant, the heavy eye-splice in the rope's final end flew out of the stark-empty tub, knocked down an oarsman, and smiting the sea, disappeared in its depths.

For an instant, the tranced boat's crew stood still; then turned. "The ship? Great God, where is the ship?" Soon they through dim, bewildering mediums saw her sidelong fading phantom, as in the gaseous Fata Morgana;[9] only the uppermost masts out of water; while fixed by infatuation, or fidelity, or fate, to their once lofty perches, the pagan harpooneers still maintained their sinking lookouts on the sea. And now, concentric circles seized the lone boat itself, and all its crew, and each floating oar, and every lance-pole, and spinning, animate and inanimate, all round and round in one vortex, carried the smallest chip of the Pequod out of sight.

But as the last whelmings intermixingly poured themselves over the sunken head of the Indian at the mainmast, leaving a few inches of the erect spar yet visible, together with long streaming yards of the flag, which calmly undulated,

5   Compare the description here and throughout the chapter to Owen Chase's description in the extract from his *The Wreck of the Whaleship Essex* on pp. 34–7.
6   See extract from Reynolds on pp. 105–7.
7   Inactive or still.
8   A reference to the use by an assassin of a garrote to strangle an unsuspecting victim.
9   A mirage.

with ironical coincidings, over the destroying billows they almost touched;—at that instant, a red arm and a hammer hovered backwardly uplifted in the open air, in the act of nailing the flag faster and yet faster to the subsiding spar. A sky-hawk that tauntingly had followed the main-truck downwards from its natural home among the stars, pecking at the flag, and incommoding Tashtego there;[10] this bird now chanced to intercept its broad fluttering wing between the hammer and the wood; and simultaneously feeling that etherial thrill, the submerged savage beneath, in his death-grasp, kept his hammer frozen there; and so the bird of heaven, with archangelic shrieks, and his imperial beak thrust upwards, and his whole captive form folded in the flag of Ahab, went down with his ship, which, like Satan, would not sink to hell till she had dragged a living part of heaven along with her, and helmeted herself with it.[11]

Now small fowls flew screaming over the yet yawning gulf; a sullen white surf beat against its steep sides; then all collapsed, and the great shroud of the sea rolled on as it rolled five thousand years ago.[12]

## Epilogue

The epilogue was left out from British editions, leaving English readers to wonder just how the tale of the *Pequod* had ever been told in the first place. More than just a plot device explaining how the narrator survived the wreck, the epilogue alludes once more to the book of Job, seemingly offering a last, small shred of hope in the midst of the destruction of the ship and its crew. Job is tested by God but passes the test – his faith remains unshaken in the end. The defiant Ahab who, unlike Job, rages against forces he cannot control and whose blasphemous defiance of conventional piety is sharply contrasted to Starbuck, sees his quest to the very end, never once losing his sense that his rage against that which vexes him is justified. Ishmael meanwhile is content to remain aloof and observe others, causing some critics to see him as a sort of paralyzed voyeur, a cosmopolitan who reposes above the fray adopting the only posture that is sustainable in the face of a malignant but ultimately ambivalent ambiguity. Yet the chance appearance of Queequeg's coffin-life buoy and the chance appearance of the *Rachel*, suggest that even Ishmael's survival is in the end more random occurrence than the result of any deliberate purpose or order which might unambiguously contrast to Ahab's monomania.

10  See Niemeyer's reading of this scene in the extract on **p. 102**.
11  Revelation 12:3–4: "3 And there appeared another wonder in heaven; and behold a great red dragon, having seven heads and ten horns, and seven crowns upon his heads. 4 *And his tail drew the third part of the stars of heaven, and did cast them to the earth*: and the dragon stood before the woman which was ready to be delivered, for to devour her child as soon as it was born."
12  At Noah's flood.

"And I only am escaped alone to tell thee." *Job.*[1]

The drama's done. Why then here does any one step forth?—Because one did survive the wreck.

It so chanced, that after the Parsee's disappearance, I was he whom the Fates ordained to take the place of Ahab's bowsman, when that bowsman assumed the vacant post; the same, who, when on the last day the three men were tossed from out the rocking boat, was dropped astern. So, floating on the margin of the ensuing scene, and in full sight of it, when the half-spent suction of the sunk ship reached me, I was then, but slowly, drawn towards the closing vortex. When I reached it, it had subsided to a creamy pool. Round and round, then, and ever contracting towards the button-like black bubble at the axis of that slowly wheeling circle, like another Ixion[2] I did revolve. Till, gaining that vital centre, the black bubble upward burst; and now, liberated by reason of its cunning spring, and, owing to its great buoyancy, rising with great force, the coffin life-buoy shot lengthwise from the sea, fell over, and floated by my side. Buoyed up by that coffin, for almost one whole day and night, I floated on a soft and dirge-like main. The unharming sharks, they glided by as if with padlocks on their mouths; the savage sea-hawks sailed with sheathed beaks. On the second day, a sail drew near, nearer, and picked me up at last. It was the devious-cruising Rachel,[3] that in her retracing search after her missing children, only found another orphan.[4]

---

1  From Job 1:13–19. Job experiences the first of his several trials by God, as a series of messengers come to him in succession with worse and worse news. "13: Now there was a day when his sons and daughters were eating and drinking wine in their eldest brother's house; 14: and there came a messenger to Job, and said, "The oxen were plowing and the asses feeding beside them; 15: and the Sabe'ans fell upon them and took them, and slew the servants with the edge of the sword; and I alone have escaped to tell you." 16: While he was yet speaking, there came another, and said, "The fire of God fell from heaven and burned up the sheep and the servants, and consumed them; and I alone have escaped to tell you." 17: While he was yet speaking, there came another, and said, "The Chalde'ans formed three companies, and made a raid upon the camels and took them, and slew the servants with the edge of the sword; and I alone have escaped to tell you." 18: While he was yet speaking, there came another, and said, "Your sons and daughters were eating and drinking wine in their eldest brother's house; 19: and behold, a great wind came across the wilderness, and struck the four corners of the house, and it fell upon the young people, and they are dead; and I alone have escaped to tell you." 20: Then Job arose, and rent his robe, and shaved his head, and fell upon the ground, and worshiped.
2  In Greek mythology, Ixion, King of the Lapiths, murdered his father-in-law to avoid paying a price for his bride. When no one on earth would purify him, Zeus took Ixion to Olympus and purified him. While there Ixion attempted to seduce Hera and as punishment was chained eternally to a revolving wheel of fire in Tartarus.
3  Spiritual mother of Israel.
4  See Schultz's discussion of this scene on **p. 112.**

# 4

# Further Reading

# Further Reading

## Introduction

The amount of secondary material on *Moby-Dick* and Melville is staggering. What follows is an extremely selective sampling of books, essays, and editions of Melville's primary works which are available in most academic collections. As with the selected excerpts in the current volume the items below have been chosen for inclusion because they are especially appropriate for undergraduates and first-time readers of Melville's whale. Some seminal works have been included, others have not. Students are directed to the works by Levine and Bryant below for more comprehensive overviews of *Moby-Dick*'s critical history, as well as bibliographies which include more advanced material. The list below favors contextual studies in general over other approaches, as such materials typically function as useful starting points for exploring other issues. Particularly important or noteworthy sources have been annotated.

## Primary Works and Letters

*The Writings of Herman Melville*, eds Harrison Hayford, Hershel Parker, and G. Thomas Tanselle (Evanston and Chicago, Ill.: Northwestern University Press and The Newberry Library, 1968–).

This multivolume series provides standard scholarly versions of Melville's collected works, including his fiction, journals, letters, and poetry. As of 2002 thirteen volumes are in print with two forthcoming in 2003 (*Billy Budd* and *Poems*). *Moby-Dick* is volume 6. Each volume comes with a detailed editorial appendix, including historical notes, textual criticism, and selected related documents. The NN editions are indispensable to serious study of Melville and his work.

*Correspondence*, ed. Lynn Horth (Evanston and Chicago, Ill.: Northwestern University Press and The Newberry Library, 1993).
*Moby-Dick; or, The Whale* (1851; *The Whale*), eds Harrison Hayford, Hershel

Parker, and G. Thomas Tanselle (Evanston and Chicago, Ill.: Northwestern University Press and The Newberry Library, 1988).

*The Piazza Tales and Other Prose Pieces, 1839–1860*, eds Harrison Hayford, Alma A. MacDougall, and G. Thomas Tanselle (Evanston and Chicago, Ill.: Northwestern University Press and The Newberry Library, 1987).

*Moby-Dick: A Norton Critical Edition* (2nd edition), eds Hershel Parker and Harrison Hayford (New York and London: W. W. Norton, 2002). There are countless editions of *Moby-Dick* in print; this edition is heavily annotated by two of the editors of the NN edition of *Moby-Dick*, one of whom is Melville's major modern academic biographer (see Parker below). It is recommended for those looking for a heavily annotated edition of the primary text.

## Biographies

Garner, Stanton B., *The Civil-War World of Herman Melville* (Lawrence, Kans.: University of Kansas Press, 1993). An excellent close study of Melville's activities during the Civil War. Garner offers compelling evidence that Melville was deeply intellectually involved and affected by the power and horror of the conflict.

Parker, Hershel, *Herman Melville: A Biography, Volume I 1819–1851* and *Volume II 1851–1891* (Baltimore, Md. and London: The Johns Hopkins University Press, 1996 and 2002). This two-volume biography is vital to serious study of Melville. Both volumes provide dense, minutely detailed accounts of Melville's life. Although formidable they are excellent reference sources.

Robertson-Lorant, Laurie, *Herman Melville: A Biography* (New York: Clarkson Potter, 1996). An excellent biography for undergraduates, Robertson-Lorant's volume is readable and engaging, and makes no attempt to provide the sort of detail offered in Parker's volumes. This fact, however, does not detract from its usefulness.

## Journals and Electronic Media Devoted to Melville

*Leviathan: A Journal of Melville Studies* (Melville Society and Hofstra University). This is the journal of the Melville Society and is published twice-yearly in March and October.

*Melville Society Extracts* (Melville Society and Hofstra University). This is a scholarly periodical in newsletter format devoted to Melville and published twice a year in February and July.

<http://www.melville.org> – Website dedicated to furthering the study of Melville, his life, and his works.

<http://people.hofstra.edu/faculty/john_L_bryant/Melville/index.swfIshmail> – Homepage of the Melville Society publisher of *Leviathan* and *Melville Society Extracts*

*Ishmail* – Email Listserve devoted to the discussion of Melville, his life, and his works. Subscription information is available at <http://www.melville.org> and the homepage of the Melville Society.

## Recommended General Secondary and References Sources on Melville and *Moby-Dick*

Brodhead, Richard, ed., *New Essays on Moby-Dick* (Cambridge: Cambridge University Press, 1986).

Bryant, John, ed., *A Companion to Melville Studies* (Westport, Conn.: Greenwood Press, 1986). A vital starting point for the study of Melville. This book provides a critical overview and a collection of original articles, several of which are on or related to the study of *Moby-Dick*.

Coffler, Gail H., *Melville's Classical Allusions: A Comprehensive Index and Glossary* (Westport, Conn.: Greenwood Press, 1985).

Higgins, Brian and Hershel Parker, eds, *Herman Melville: The Contemporary Reviews* (New York: Cambridge University Press, 1995).

Jehlen, Myra, ed., *Herman Melville: A Collection of Critical Essays* (Englewood Cliffs, N.J.: Prentice-Hall, 1994). One of the first collections of original articles to focus on more recent critical approaches, including feminism, New Historicism, and multiculturalism.

Kier, Kathleen E., *A Melville Encyclopedia: The Novels* (Troy, N.Y.: Whitson, 1994).

Levine, Robert S., ed., *The Cambridge Companion to Herman Melville* (Cambridge: Cambridge University Press, 1998). A vital secondary reference that includes several excellent original articles, some of which are excerpted in the current volume, as well as a thorough bibliography.

Parker, Hershel and Harrison Hayford, eds, *Moby-Dick as Doubloon: Essays and Extracts 1851–1970* (New York: Norton, 1970). A useful collection of articles representing some of the best work on *Moby-Dick* prior to the 1980s.

Sealts, Merton M., Jr., *Melville's Reading: Revised and Enlarged Edition* (Columbia, S.C.: University of South Carolina Press, 1988). Detailed discussion of books Melville owned, may have owned, may have borrowed, and/or may have read.

Wright, Nathalia, *Melville's Use of the Bible* (Durham, N.C.: Duke University Press, 1949). A still-useful seminal study of Melville's use of the Bible.

## Recommended Essays on Melville and *Moby-Dick*

Barbour, James, "The Composition of *Moby-Dick*," in Louis J. Budd and Edwin Cady, eds, *On Melville: The Best From American Literature* (Durham, N.C.: Duke University Press, 1988), pp. 203–20. Excellent overview of the composition of *Moby-Dick* which in conjunction with the "historical note" in the NN edition (see above) provides a detailed and composite description of the conditions in which Melville wrote the novel, as well as an overview of what led to the textual variants between the English and American editions.

—— "The *Town-Ho's* Story: Melville's Original Whale," *ESQ: A Journal of the American Renaissance* 21 (2nd quarter, 1975). A compelling discussion of the origins and function of Chapter 54 in *Moby-Dick* as a whole.

Baym, Nina, "Melville's Quarrel with Fiction," *PMLA* 94 (1979): 903–23. A major study of Melville's theory of language, how this may have informed *Moby-Dick*, and how *Moby-Dick*'s "failure" affected Melville and his poetics.

Berthold, Michael C., "Moby-Dick and the American Slave Narrative," *Massachusetts Review: A Quarterly of Literature, the Arts and Public Affairs* 36.1 (1994): 135–48.

Bradley, David, "Our Crowd, Their Crowd: Race, Reader, and *Moby-Dick*," in John Bryant and Robert Milder, eds, *Melville's Evermoving Dawn: Centennial Essays* (Kent, Ohio: Kent State University Press, 1997), pp. 119–46.

Cahir, Linda Costanzo, "Routinizing the Charismatic: Melville and Hollywood's Three *Moby-Dicks*," *Melville Society Extracts* 110 (1997): 11–17. A useful overview of the three major film versions of *Moby-Dick*.

Crain, Caleb, "Lovers of Human Flesh: Homosexuality and Cannibalism in Melville's Novels," *American Literature* 66 (1994): 25–53.

Hayford, Harrison, "Unnecessary Duplicates: A Key to the Writing of *Moby-Dick*," in Faith Pullen, ed., *New Perspectives on Melville* (Edinburgh: Edinburgh University Press, 1978). A seminal article that led to much of the information in the historical note in the Northwestern–Newberry edition.

Lauter, Paul, "Melville Climbs the Canon," *American Literature* 66.1 (1994): 1–24. (See **pp. 62–4.**)

Miller, Perry, "Melville and Transcendentalism," *Virginia Quarterly Review* 29 (Autumn 1953): 556–75. Miller's *The Raven and the Whale* (1955) is the fullest account of the literary wars of New York (see **pp. 62–4**). This essay is a highly useful starting point for exploring Melville and Transcendentalism.

Pease, Donald E., "*Moby Dick* and the Cold War," in Walter Benn Michaels and Donald E. Pease, eds, *The American Renaissance Reconsidered* (Baltimore, Md.: Johns Hopkins University Press, 1985, pp. 113–55). A major article on the effects of American cultural nationalism on Melville studies; one of the leading threads in recent reinterpretations of *Moby-Dick* in the last two decades.

Powell, Timothy B., "Herman Melville: Ruthless Democracy," in *Ruthless Democracy: A Multicultural Interpretation of the American Renaissance* (Princeton, N.J.: Princeton University Press, 2000).

Schultz, Elizabeth, "Melville's Environmental Vision in *Moby-Dick*," *Interdisciplinary Studies in Literature and Environment* 7 (2000): 97–113.

Stewart, George R., "The Two *Moby-Dicks*," *American Literature* 25 (January 1954).

Stone, Edward, "The Function of the Gams in *Moby-Dick*," *College Literature* 2 (1975): 171–81.

Wilson, Eric, "Melville, Darwin, and the Great Chain of Being," *Studies in American Fiction* 28 (2000): 131–50.

# Recommended Book-Length Secondary Sources

Bell, Michael Davitt, *The Development of American Romance: The Sacrifice of Relation* (Chicago, Ill. and London: University of Chicago Press, 1980).

Brodhead, Richard H., *Hawthorne, Melville, and the Novel* (Chicago, Ill.: University of Chicago Press, 1976).

Brodtkorb, Paul, Jr., *Ishmael's White World: A Phenomenological Reading of Moby-Dick* (New Haven, Conn.: Yale University Press, 1965). A respected and still excellent discussion of Ishmael's function as a first-person narrator and how this complicates discussions of *Moby-Dick*'s treatment of philosophical issues.

Budick, Emily Miller, *Fiction and Historical Consciousness: The American Romance Tradition* (New Haven, Conn.: Yale University Press, 1989).

Chase, Richard, *The American Novel and its Tradition* (Garden City, N.Y.: Doubleday and Co., 1957).

Dimock, Wai Chee, *Empire for Liberty: Melville and the Poetics of Individualism* (Princeton, N.J.: Princeton University Press, 1989). A much-cited study of Melville, antebellum political discourse, and the discourse of individualism.

Dryden, Edgar A., *Melville's Thematics of Form: The Great Art of Telling the Truth* (Baltimore, Md.: Johns Hopkins University Press, 1968).

Karcher, Carolyn L., *Shadow Over the Promised Land: Slavery, Race, and Violence in Melville's America* (Baton Rouge, La.: Louisiana State University Press, 1980). One of the first full-length treatments of Melville in regard to slavery and US racial ideology. An excellent starting point for discussion of Melville and race.

Levine, Lawrence W., *Highbrow/Lowbrow: The Emergence of Cultural Hierarchy in America* (Boston, Mass.: Harvard Univeristy Press, 1988).

Matthiessen, F. O., *American Renaissance* (New York and London: Oxford University Press, 1941). Matthiessen's book is one of the foundational texts of the study of American literature (see **pp. 21–2**). Although outdated, his readings still cast a long shadow over the study of American literature and of Melville and *Moby-Dick*.

Porte, Joel, The *Romance in America: Studies in Cooper, Poe, Hawthorne, Melville and James* (Middleton, Conn.: Wesleyan University Press, 1969).

Railton, Stephen, *Authorship and Audience: Literary Performance in the American Renaissance* (Princeton, N.J.: Princeton University Press, 1991). An extremely useful study of Melville in relation to nineteenth-century print culture in general.

Reynolds, David, *Beneath the American Renaissance: The Subversive Imagination in the Age of Emerson and Melville* (New York: Knopf, 1988). A major study among the many recent reinterpretations of Matthiessen's work.

Rogin, Michael Paul, *Subversive Genealogy: The Politics and Art of Herman Melville* (New York: Knopf, 1983).

Thompson, Lawrance R., *Melville's Quarrel with God* (Princeton, N.J.: Princeton University Press, 1952).

Vincent, Howard, *The Trying Out of Moby-Dick* (Kent, Ohio: Kent State University Press, 1980). Originally published in 1949, this was one of the first book-length studies of *Moby-Dick*'s thematics and one of the first to try and establish a comprehensive theory of the work as a unified and coherent whole. Vincent's book set the terms for virtually every work of thematic criticism on *Moby-Dick* which followed.

Weisbuch, Robert, *Atlantic Double-Cross: American Literature and British Influence in the Age of Emerson* (Chicago, Ill.: University of Chicago Press, 1986). An excellent and detailed historical account of the mid-nineteenth-century book trade and especially of the competition that existed between British and American writers.

# Index